# *Pieces of My Heart*

Robert J. Wagner has been active in Hollywood for more than five decades and has starred in such films as *A Kiss Before Dying*, *The Longest Day*, *The Pink Panther* and, most recently, the Austin Powers movies. On television, Wagner starred in three long-running series, *It Takes a Thief* (with Fred Astaire), *Switch* (with Eddie Albert and Sharon Gless) and *Hart to Hart* (with Stefanie Powers) and also featured on *Two and a Half Men*. Wagner is married to actress Jill St. John and lives in Los Angeles.

# ROBERT
# WAGNER

with Scott Eyman

## *Pieces of My Heart*

arrow books

Published by Arrow Books 2010

2 4 6 8 10 9 7 5 3 1

Copyright © Robert J. Wagner 2008

Robert J. Wagner has asserted his right under the Copyright, Designs
and Patents Act 1988 to be identified as the author of this work

Published by arrangement with Harper Entertainment, a division of
HarperCollins Publishers, USA

First published in Great Britain in 2009 by
Hutchinson
Random House, 20 Vauxhall Bridge Road,
London SW1V 2SA

www.rbooks.co.uk

Addresses for companies within The Random House Group Limited can be found at:
www.randomhouse.co.uk/offices.htm

The Random House Group Limited Reg. No. 954009

A CIP catalogue record for this book
is available from the British Library

ISBN 9780099538356

The Random House Group Limited supports The Forest Stewardship
Council (FSC), the leading international forest certification organisation.
All our titles that are printed on Greenpeace approved FSC certified paper carry
the FSC logo. Our paper procurement policy can be found at:
www.rbooks.co.uk/environment

Printed and bound in Great Britain by
CPI Bookmarque, Croydon, CR0 4TD

FOR KATIE, NATASHA, COURTNEY

FOR MY MOTHER AND SISTER

AND FOR JILL —

THE WONDERFUL WOMEN WHO HAVE BEEN

THE MEANING OF MY LIFE

# CONTENTS

CONTENTS

*Pieces of My Heart*

Cadet Wagner, 1936, with the world in front of him, pretending to like the uniform a lot more than he did. (COURTESY OF THE AUTHOR)

# PART ONE

# "HE WAS FRED ASTAIRE!"

I was twelve years old when my future passed in front of me.

My father had moved our family from Michigan to California in 1937, when I was seven years old, and I began working at the Bel-Air Stables in 1942. There was no Bel-Air Hotel yet, but housing sites in the neighborhood were selling fast.

One day I took a piece of corrugated tin from some construction scrap, bent the front end up, and fashioned a sled, which I stored by a hill on the eleventh hole at the Bel-Air Country Club. On breaks from the stables, I would get on my sled and slide down the hill, where I would come to rest just under a cluster of trees by the edge of the fairway. And then I would sit on the pine needles at the base of the hill and watch the golfers go by. It was a very boyish thing to do, but that's what I was—a twelve-year-old boy.

On this particular day in 1942, I saw a foursome heading off the eleventh tee. They had just hit their tee shots and were walking toward the fairway. I was sitting there, ten or twenty yards from where their shots had landed. As they got closer, they came into focus, and I could see that the foursome consisted of Cary Grant, Fred Astaire, Clark Gable, and Randolph Scott.

I was . . . transfixed! It was the most amazing experience, not just because I had grown up seeing these men at the movies, at the Fox and the Bruin Theaters in Westwood. It was because they looked . . . freshly minted! They say that some movie stars are disappointing when seen in the flesh—smaller, less prepossessing than they appear on the screen. Not these men. They inhabited life as securely as they inhabited the screen. Put it another way: they filled the room, even if the room was outdoors.

In those days, nobody wore signature brands; each great star was his own signature brand. Fred Astaire didn't wear LaCoste or Brooks Brothers; he had his own style—a tie knotted around his waist instead of a belt. He was Fred Astaire! To see them there, in the flesh, was an amazing experience because these were not men who went out on the town a great deal or hobnobbed in restaurants.

They stopped and hit their second shots—Astaire had the best, most rhythmic swing by far, followed closely by Randolph Scott—and then began walking toward the green. I don't think they saw me. But the important thing was that I saw them.

I realized at that moment that I wanted to be in that club; looking back, I see that this was when I made up my mind to be in the movies—to be an actor.

Within two years, I was walking up and down Hollywood Boulevard, waiting to be discovered. My general theory, insofar as I had a general theory, was that if Lana Turner could be discovered on Sunset Boulevard, I could be discovered on Hollywood Boulevard. I wore a dark brown leather jacket, had my hair slicked back, and would pause in front of plate-glass windows, staring admiringly at my own reflection. The collar was up, and if I say so myself, I had the look.

Someone told me that D. W. Griffith hung around the Hollywood Hotel, so I walked over to the corner of Hollywood and Highland, and it was true—there was Griffith, a dignified, elderly gentleman, sitting quietly in a rocking chair on the veranda, observing the hustle of Hollywood in wartime.

Nobody shared my fascination with my own reflection—that would come later—but that didn't matter. I wanted to be in the movies, and I was going to be in the movies. It was just a question of time.

# ONE

# "IN A SENSE, I WAS A TEENAGE REBEL."

With my parents in front of our house in Bel-Air. (COURTESY OF THE AUTHOR)

There's no bastard like a German bastard, and by all accounts my grandfather Mathias Wagner was a nasty man. He was a stevedore in Mannheim, Germany, where Wagner is a very common name. He came to America in 1876 and found that he needed a wife, so his relatives in Germany sent him some pictures of local German girls who wanted to come to America. Two of the girls in the pictures were sisters; my grandfather picked one sister, and his best friend picked the other. And that's how my father was born: as the result of an arranged marriage.

Robert J. Wagner, my father, was born in Kalamazoo, Michigan, in 1890, but he left home when he was ten years old. I have no doubt he was abused; the Germans of that era would punch their children in the face just to let them know who was boss. My father said that his mother, a glorified mail-order bride, had no say in anything. She was more like a hired child-care worker than a wife.

My dad spent his adolescence selling newspapers on the streets of Kalamazoo, working in railroad stations, in bars, wherever there was a paying job. Because he was so estranged from his parents, I never knew them. My grandfather died early, and by the time I met my grandmother, she had developed dementia, so there was no way to establish a relationship.

My parents met on a blind date in Chicago. My mother's name was Hazel Alvera Boe, which was always a sore spot with her. She hated the name Hazel, so everybody called her "Chat," because she was so talkative. In time, I would call her "C," while her pet name for me became "R." She was a telephone operator when she met my father, and he was selling fishing tackle. Before that, he'd been a traveling salesman who sold corsets, petticoats, and other women's undergarments wholesale throughout the Great Lakes region.

A few years after they met, he was in a hardware store where a guy was mixing a can of paint. My father liked the look of the surface it gave. He found out about the paint company, which was called Arco, and then he found out the name of Arco's president, and he became a salesman for that paint. (Needless to say, my father was a go-getter.) He ended up getting the Ford Motor Company account; he sold most of the lacquer that was applied to the dashboards of Ford cars, and in short order he became very successful. Besides that, both before and after his Ford period, he bought and sold lots around the Palmer Woods area of Detroit. He would build houses, and my mother would decorate them.

My father was the sort of man who was obsessed by his business, and even after his kids arrived—my sister, Mary Lou, in 1926, me on February 10, 1930—that never changed. I was christened Robert John Wagner Jr., but since my father answered to "Bob," and nobody, especially me, wanted me to be known as "Junior," I became known as "RJ," which my friends call me to this day.

Mary Lou was the valedictorian of her class, but she wanted a quiet, domestic life, and she got it. She's a wonderful woman, with a totally different life than mine. She's had five children and numerous grandchildren. She's lived in the same house in Claremont for decades and doesn't venture out that much.

When I was a small child, we all lived in a beautiful house on Fairway Drive, right off the Detroit Golf Club, but the best times with my father were summers in the Upper Peninsula of Michigan, where he had a cabin on a lake. I vividly remember riding through meadows on horseback with my father and uncle. There were no sounds except the whisk of the grass as the horses moved through it, and at night the moon was so bright you could read by it. It seemed like we were the only people alive, and I basked in my father's undivided attention. It was during these times that he taught me how to fish—probably his greatest, longest-lasting gift to me. These were weeks out of Hemingway's Nick Adams stories, and they are my most cherished memories of early childhood.

Also rewarding was the family Christmas, during which my parents went whole hog in spite of the fact that they had an arm's-length relationship with religion. Technically, my father was a Catholic, not to mention a thirty-second-degree Mason, while my mother was a Unitarian, but I don't even know if they bothered to baptize me. They sent me to Episcopal schools, and they sent me to Catholic schools, but we hardly ever attended church as a family, and they simply didn't impose much religion on me. On balance I'm glad—my lack of indoctrination has resulted in a very open attitude toward the different religious factors that motivate people's lives.

Although my father hated my grandfather because of his abusive behavior, my dad was never able to entirely free himself from his upbringing. If I did something mildly wrong, he'd stand me in a corner. For something worse, he'd lock me in a closet. If I did something deemed beyond the pale, I would be hit. When I was little, I stuck something in an electrical socket and blew out every outlet in the house. My father was in the bathroom shaving, and he came roaring out, grabbed me, put me over his knee, spanked me with a hairbrush, then threw me off his lap for this terrible thing I had done.

All this was the custom of that time; there was an attitude that corporal punishment was acceptable, and this was how a lot of the kids who grew up with me in Detroit were raised. I don't think it's any accident that a lot of those rich kids ended up wasting their lives or even killing themselves. The parents had their cars, their houses, a nurse, a chauffeur, white tie and tails, and the children were expected to conform to that model without question.

There was a sense that the children were possessions, and it was no accident that I carried the same name as my dad. From the time I was six, I was sent to camp regularly; a year after that, I was addressed and sent to Hollywood at the age of seven. Literally. My father took me to the train station in Detroit and tipped the porter $10 to make sure the package—his son—arrived safely. On my coat was a tag: "Deliver this boy to Mrs. Pierce, Hollywood Military Academy, Hollywood, California."

As soon as the train pulled out from the station, I ripped the tag off my coat. Now that I look back on it, the entire business with the tag—my father giving orders, me ignoring them as soon as he was out of sight—was a fairly accurate preview of our entire relationship.

My father had opened a checking account for me so that I could pay my expenses on the trip. I remember that in Albuquerque I went into a souvenir shop and bought an antique gun so I could protect myself against the marauding Indians I was sure would attack the train at some point. (Obviously, the movies had already gotten hold of me.)

On the one hand, my father was force-feeding me a very valuable sense of independence. He was also telling me that the world wasn't all that dangerous and that you could survive if you only had a firm destination in mind.

On the other hand, you might ask why a seven-year-old would be sent away from his home in the first place, and the answer would be that my parents had a social life that was very important to them. I always had the vague feeling that I was an encumbrance, something to be brought out on holidays and other occasions marked "Family," and then promptly filed away somewhere else, somewhere out of sight.

I resented this then. I resent it now.

That first year in California was strange. While my parents were building their house in Bel-Air, my sister and I were both in boarding schools—I was at the Hollywood Military Academy, and Mary Lou was at Marymount—and we only saw each other on weekends. Both of us suffered from the loss of Margaret Maleski, a warm, nurturing woman who had done much of the work of raising us back in Michigan. Not having Margaret around, not having anyone to give us unconditional love, was traumatic for both of us.

The result of all this was that more than fifty years later I named a horse Sloan, after the porter on the train I was always taking to one boarding school or another. I loved Sloan the porter because he showed me more affection than my father. And I learned very early that the love of animals never wavers, while the love of people can't always be trusted. As a result, the love of animals has been one of the constants of my life.

My resentment made me a rebellious kid, and I had a way of being a handful at the four boarding schools I attended. Once, when I was twelve or thirteen, I took a BB gun and shot all the lights out in the tunnel of the country club at Bel-Air and generally embarrassed my father by being a smart-ass. The country club incident made him close his fists and go after me—again—but a couple of other men held him back.

My best friend in these difficult years, and for the rest of his life, was Bill Storke. Bill's background was exotic—his mother was the mistress of a very rich man, and there was always the possibility that he was the illegitimate product of that liaison. Bill was six or seven years older than I was and dated my sister for a while. It wasn't long before he became part of our family. My dad got him a page job at NBC, and for the rest of his life Bill served as a sort of unofficial older brother for me.

Shortly after the incident with the BB gun, Bill and I got

loaded, and I got sick all over the floor and the rug, which got my father royally pissed off. "I can't depend on you," he told me and went on to call me a lot of names.

As a result of the way I was raised, I never spanked my own kids, and I'm glad I didn't.

One of the schools I attended was the legendary Black Foxe Military Academy, which had been started by a washed-up silent movie actor named Earl Foxe. Whatever Black Foxe might have done for other kids didn't work for me. I got kicked out and then proceeded to get kicked out of yet another place. I especially hated Black Foxe, hated the regimentation, the way older kids were given ranks like "captain" and used to control the younger kids. I loved the swimming and the athletics, but I simply wasn't cut out for that kind of environment. Black Foxe operated by fear, and that has never worked with me. As far as I was concerned, I was being filed away yet again. More than anything, I just wanted to be riding my horse.

Throughout this period, my mother, who was a little woman, tried to take my side. For that matter, throughout her entire life she took my side. In a few years, she would give me money for gas so I could go to acting tryouts, or she would even drive me there. But she had her hands full with my father because his house and his children were run his way. He ruled. If I came to her with something that was outside her range of authority, she would say, "I can't do that. You'll have to talk to your father."

If the first eighteen years of my life can be reduced to a single sentence, it would be this: I wanted out of my father's life.

In a sense, I was a teenage rebel. Don't get me wrong—I wasn't living in a Dickens novel. I think it's interesting that my father was noticeably easier on my sister, Mary Lou, than he was on me. She was a girl, and as his son, I not only had to succeed—I had to succeed on his terms.

That said, I remain in awe of his business acumen. My father

13

was a singular man in most respects, but like everybody else, he took a bath in the Depression. Until then, the auto business had been on fire, and he'd been very successful. My mother had a very bad asthmatic condition, so they were going to leave Michigan and move to Arizona, but then they fell in love with California.

He bought a lot in Bel-Air, overlooking the Bel-Air Country Club, which was an example of his innate investment savvy— Bel-Air was nothing at that point. From there, he bought a lot at Rancho Santa Fe, in the desert, and more lots in Bel-Air. He'd buy a lot, build a house on it, then sell it and make a lot of money. And then he got into the aviation business. Along comes World War II, and once again he's—you should pardon the expression— flying high. And that time he held on to his money.

It's clear to me now that my father had a depression mentality before the Depression, and the result was that he lived his entire life on the short side—always a room, never a suite. He was the sort of rich man who never wanted people to think he had any money. He'd want us to wear clothes after they'd begun to wear out. Yes, he gave me a horse, and I had to take very good care of the horse—fair enough. But if the horse needed something, I had to go through hell to get it.

Years later we'd be in Europe and he'd look at the bill and begin bitching about how much things were costing. "Why are we here?" he would say. "I know they're charging us more than they're charging other people!"

After I was in the movie business, I went to Hong Kong to shoot a picture, and he came with me. By that time he was watching my expenses the same way he watched his own. He kept a log of what I spent on food or at the dentist. It kept him occupied, which was fine with me. We took a rickshaw together, and he gave the driver some money. The rickshaw man gave him his change in yens, which neither of us could compute. My father began obsessing over whether or not he had been shortchanged. I finally had to tell him, "Dad, forget about the money! Look around, notice where you are. Let it be."

Apropos of this mind-set, I went to school with Sydney Chaplin, Charlie's son. Sydney told me how his dad once accidentally gave a cab driver a $100 bill when he'd meant to give him a $10 bill. Charlie was miserable for three days after that. He wanted to find the cab and get the driver to give him back his change. Both Chaplin and my father had been truly poor, and it deformed them emotionally. It's impossible to relax, or even have much happiness, with that point of view.

Although I wouldn't have wanted a marriage like my parents had, they seemed happy. I never knew my father to be a philanderer, even though he spent a lot of years as a traveling salesman. He certainly had his secrets, but they wouldn't come out until after he died.

The end result of my childhood and my relationship with my father was that I consciously went 180 degrees in the opposite direction. My father would take me to movies on Thursday nights, but he wasn't a movie fan the same way I was. The arts didn't really interest him—he was a bricks-and-mortar man. Bill Storke once told me something that's stuck with me: "Your father never gambled on you," he said, and I think he was right. But then, my father never gambled. For him, money was strictly for security, and there was no such thing as enough security. For me, money has always been for sheltering the people I love, and for pleasure. My father was only interested in investments that had a guaranteed return, and I suspect he saw his son as an investment that showed no signs of paying off.

# TWO

# "I WAS THE FOCUS OF A CIRCLE OF LIGHT."

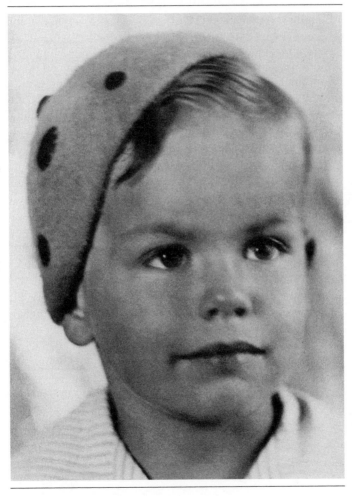

The beret indicates a certain theatrical bent, *n'est-ce pas?*

ecause my father had money and belonged to the Bel-Air Country Club, I had entrée to a life most people couldn't dream of, and I never took it for granted. One fortunate by-product of the private schools I was attending was that I was cheek by jowl with a lot of kids with famous parents.

The first movie star I met was Norma Shearer. I was eight years old at the time and going to school with Irving Thalberg Jr. His father, the longtime production chief at Metro-Goldwyn-Mayer, devoted a large part of his creative life to making Norma a star, and he succeeded splendidly. Unfortunately, Thalberg had died suddenly in 1936, and his wife's career had begun to slowly deflate.

Just like kids everywhere else, Hollywood kids had playdates at each other's houses, and one day I went to the Thalberg house in Santa Monica, where Irving Sr. had died eighteen months before.

Norma was in bed, where, I was given to understand, she spent quite a bit of time so that on those occasions when she worked or went out in public she would look as rested as possible. She was making *Marie Antoinette* at the time, and to see her in the flesh was overwhelming. She very kindly autographed a picture for me, which I still have: "To Cadet Wagner, with my very best wishes. Norma Shearer."

Years later I would be with her and Martin Arrouge, her second husband, at Sun Valley. No matter who the nominal hostess was, Norma was always the queen, and no matter what time the party was to begin, Norma was always late, because she would sit for hours—hours!—to do her makeup, then make the grand entrance. She was always and forever the star. She had to be that way, really, because she became a star by force of will—hers and Thalberg's. Better-looking on the screen than in life, Norma Shearer was certainly not a beauty on the level of Paulette Goddard, who didn't need makeup, didn't need anything. Paulette could simply toss her hair and walk out the front door, and strong men grew weak in the knees.

Norma found the perfect husband in Martin. He was a lovely man, a really fine athlete—Martin was a superb skier—and totally devoted to her. In the circles they moved in, there were always backbiting comments when a woman married a younger man—"the stud ski instructor," that sort of thing. But Martin, who was twelve years younger than Norma and was indeed a ski instructor, never acknowledged any of that and was a thorough gentleman all his life. He had a superficial facial resemblance to Irving Thalberg, but Thalberg had a rheumatic heart and was a thin, nonathletic kind of man—intellectually vital, but physically weak. Martin was just the opposite—strong and virile, with a high energy level. Coming after years of being married to Thalberg and having to worry about his health, Martin must have been a delicious change for Norma.

Another classmate was Peter Potter, Fred Astaire's stepson. Peter and I were both at the Hollywood Military Academy, which was located on the corner of San Vicente and Bristol. Peter and I would have playdates at his house, and Fred would pick me up from the school in a cream-colored convertible—a Packard, I think. Even though I was just a small kid, Fred was always very kind to me. It's one of those strange twists of fate that thirty years later he'd be playing my father on *It Takes a Thief*.

When I was eight years old, there was a preview of a Paramount picture called *The Biscuit Eater* at the Village Theater in Westwood. It was about a white kid and a black kid who take the runt of a litter and try to turn him into a champion bird dog—a sweet, lovely little picture that, because of my passion for dogs, moved me terribly.

At the end of the movie I was crying, and when I came out of the Village Theater still sniffling, there was the dog from the movie! The trainer had brought him to the screening for some publicity, and I was so thrilled to see the dog that I ran right up to him and threw my arms around him. Luckily, he was a well-trained dog and didn't bite me or shy away. Well, the photographers who were there were just delighted—a picture of a sobbing child with a dog is guaranteed to get good placement in any newspaper at any time.

As the photographers were shooting and the flashbulbs were going off all around me, I distinctly remember thinking, *Gee, this is pretty good!* I was the focus of a circle of light, the center of everybody's attention, and I liked it. It was one of the key moments of my life.

The years of my early adolescence were tough for me. I was something of a jock, excelling in baseball, swimming, and tennis, and I was also good on a horse. Academics were another thing entirely. It wasn't that I didn't have the aptitude, although I'm sure some of my teachers would have insisted otherwise. It was that I was bored and rebellious and didn't try to conceal it.

In retrospect, my parents had a lot of trouble with me. I was always with tutors; one time, at Harvard Military School, I got caught with a girl, and there was a point when I went from being kicked out of Black Foxe to getting kicked out of Harvard to being at Cal Prep—which I liked—and then it was St. Monica's and living at home.

These years were lightened only by my increasing addiction to the movies. When I was at Black Foxe, RKO came to the campus to shoot some scenes for *Best Foot Forward*. Our company of cadets marched by, and the Hollywood crew photographed us. I was fascinated by the trucks, the crew, the way the shoot and the extras and all the paraphernalia of moviemaking were organized.

Everything seemed to contribute to my passion for the movies. One of the kids I went to school with was the son of Edgar Rice Burroughs, whose ranch, dubbed Tarzana, was later developed into an entire town. Mr. Burroughs would invite a bunch of the kids out to his ranch, and believe me, in the days before freeways Tarzana was a trek. Of course, we were all nuts about Tarzan, so we knew who Edgar Rice Burroughs was. It wasn't just another trip to a parent's house.

It turned out that Burroughs had wired his gardens for sound, and there was a profusion of jungle noises coming from the trees. We'd hear monkeys gibbering and ask "Who's that?" and Mr. Burroughs would say, "That's Cheetah." And then we would hear Tarzan's yell, and he would nod and say, "That's Tarzan." We'd all stare wide-eyed at the vegetation waiting for Johnny Weissmuller to show up. Burroughs was a gracious, wonderful gentleman, and we all loved to visit him.

As momentous as my commitment to the world of the movies was my discovery of sex, which happened just around the time I saw Astaire, Gable, Scott, and Grant at the Bel-Air Country Club. I was about twelve and a half, in junior high at Emerson. This wonderful, sweet girl sent me a note: "I would like to make love to you." She didn't have to ask twice. I folded up the note and went right over to her desk and made a date.

Afterward, I thought I had discovered the greatest thing on earth. Certainly, it was a lot better than masturbation. Someone must have broken the girl in awfully early, because she wasn't a virgin. She told her friends about me and it gave me easy access to some of the other girls who, unlike official dates, were not shy.

Meanwhile my first official dates were with Alan Ladd's daughter Carol, Harold Lloyd's daughter Gloria, and Joan Bennett's daughter Melinda. It was around this same time that I went to a pool party and met Roddy McDowall, who was already part of Elizabeth Taylor's group of teenagers. Roddy was then as he always was—immensely kind and decent, with a caring, empathetic quality that made him one of the most beloved members of the Hollywood community. Roddy and Elizabeth would be the most intimate of friends for the rest of his life, but then one of Roddy's great gifts was that all of his friends felt that they were on the most intimate of levels with him.

The proximity of the movie business to my life only increased my hunger. One day I was hitchhiking on Sunset Boulevard when it started to rain. A car stopped for me, I hopped in, and when I turned to thank the driver my mouth stopped working. He looked just like Errol Flynn. Dear God, it *was* Errol Flynn, and I had just seen *Objective, Burma!*

I gulped and said, "You're Errol Flynn!"

"Yes, I am," he said, and the nearness of Errol Flynn was so staggering that that perfectly innocuous exchange is all I can remember of the entire ride.

Another time Alan Ladd was shooting some scenes on an estate in Bel-Air, and I snuck onto the set to watch. He was standing behind some bushes waiting to make an entrance, and I got a chance to watch him work. He was a powerful screen actor—that great voice, that blond hair, that sense of stillness. And yes, he was small, but not that small—about five-foot-six, with a terrific swimmer's body. The problem was that his image was not that of a guy who was five-six. On screen, he was six-three, so when people saw him they were always surprised, which made him insecure.

Years later I did a magazine layout with Alan at his ranch in Hidden Valley and got to know him. Alan Ladd was an extremely kind man, and a good horseman who knew how to handle an animal. Unfortunately, he had a complicated series of disappointments involving his marriage to Sue Carol, smoked a lot of cigarettes, and got hooked on booze, which greatly affected his looks and his career choices. At the end, his family was watching him closely, but not closely enough.

Throughout these years I never had any career goal other than acting, and I see no need to apologize for it. I thought then and I think now that making people smile and taking them out of their problems for an hour or two is a wonderful way to spend a life. I know that because that's what the movies did for me. When I would come home from an afternoon at the movies, I would go to my bedroom and act out the best scenes from whatever I'd seen that day, and my problems with my father were forgotten. That era provided a profusion of wonderful actors and actresses to admire—and not always the ones remembered by posterity. Take Joel McCrea, for instance, a real cowboy and a good actor who could excel in westerns like *Union Pacific* or *The Virginian*, but who was also wonderful in comedies like *The Palm Beach Story* for Preston Sturges—and comedy is the hardest thing an actor can do.

I was always trying to turn my passion from the theoretical into the practical. When I attended the Hollywood Military Academy, we did a production of *The Courtship of Miles Standish*, and I played a female character—Priscilla Alden! I also played Tiny Tim in a production of *The Christmas Carol* and kept up with the amateur theatricals, thankfully in male parts. I was coming up in the world!

One of my close friends in school was named Noel Clarabitt. Helena, his mother, had a little tearoom, and I would work for her, polishing the antiques and crystal and busing the tables. I would be over at their house a great deal, and she became a big influence; she was Russian, and they drank wine and played classical music, which was a different environment than I was used to.

Southern California was paradise in this period. For one thing, there weren't that many people, which meant there weren't that many cars, which meant there was no smog at all. The air was so clear that when the smudge pots were lit in preparation for a freeze in the orange groves, you could smell them all over town. There was a superb transit system in the Red Line, which went from downtown L.A. all the way to the ocean. One of the main routes was down San Vicente Boulevard; what's now the large grassy divider in the middle of the road was the trolley track. In more congested areas, the Red Line took back routes, but when the cars got to Hollywood, there would still be stops at Highland and La Brea. People would take the Red Line all the way to the beach, where the car was turned around on a large turntable before it headed back downtown.

You could stand on a mountaintop in Malibu or Santa Monica and see all the way to Catalina. Literally. On top of Sepulveda, you could look out into the San Fernando Valley and see nothing but chicken and avocado ranches. The primary industries were movies and aircraft, which had boomed during the war.

The old Los Angeles I grew up with is all gone now, except for a couple of places that are entirely commercial. If you want, you can go to the Huntington or to Olvera Street, but those are museums, each in its own way. The Red Line disappeared because the rubber and fuel companies wanted the trolley cars out so they could make more money. But that's the way of the world; when I was at Cal Prep, I used to fish for steelhead in the Ventura River up near Ojai, and now the Ventura River doesn't even run there anymore.

I finally began to get some serious traction when I began

caddying at the Bel-Air Country Club. One of the admirable by-products of my father's value system was a belief in hard work. He always wanted me to be earning my keep, and since it got me out of the house, I was all for it.

Under ordinary circumstances, there would have been a lot of competition for those caddy jobs at Bel-Air and I would have gotten shut out because I was too young. But after Pearl Harbor, all the older caddies went to war or got more lucrative jobs in the aircraft factories as they ramped up production, so I was able to nab a spot I wouldn't have gotten for at least a couple of more years.

The Bel-Air Country Club gave me a matchless opportunity to meet and watch people, but it also gave me a primer in some of the less palatable personalities in the business. Most of the extremely right-wing members of the Motion Picture Alliance frequented the Bel-Air. Adolphe Menjou was often there, prissy and slightly effete, the sort of man who never read a novel, only the *Wall Street Journal*. When Lew Ayres claimed conscientious objector status during World War II, the right-wingers at Bel-Air thought he was a coward and ostracized him. Lew was a strong man, a good man, and went his own way, eventually serving with distinction as a medic, which is more than the people who felt entitled to condemn him ever did.

If you caddied the full loop at Bel-Air, eighteen holes, you'd get paid two or three dollars. All the players tipped about the same—a dollar or so. Clark Gable always gave you a little extra, but it wasn't a tipping society. In any case, I have a lingering feeling that my passion for show business got in the way of what should have been my passion for caddying.

Once, I stole a script out of Robert Sterling's golf bag and took it to a friend of mine named Flo Allen, who later became an agent. We read it over and tried to figure out how it should be acted. There was one scene in the script we worked on particularly hard.

It began: "Want a cup of coffee?"

"Sure."

"Cream and sugar?" And so forth, with lots of byplay with props. To this day, whenever I call Flo, I open by saying, "Want a cup of coffee?" Considering the level of effort I was putting into trying to learn how to act versus the level of effort I was putting into caddying, it was a miracle nobody complained. It was a bigger miracle that I didn't get fired.

The fact that I was working at Bel-Air didn't make my dad any more kindly disposed toward me. Things got so bad at home that when I was fourteen or fifteen I seriously considered joining the merchant marine. Bill Storke had joined up, and that gave me the same idea. World War II was still on, and they needed men, but the cutoff age was sixteen. No dice.

Right after the war, in 1945 and '46, I began spending a lot of time on Catalina, and I started hanging around John Ford's crew of reprobates, who all docked their boats at Avalon. Ward Bond was always there, and Robert Walker—he would court and later marry Ford's daughter, Barbara—as well as John Wayne of course, and Paul Fix.

Ford's group, as well as other people who had boats, began a series of softball games. I never pitched but could play anywhere in the infield or outfield; first base was an especially good position for me. All of these men had been athletes—"Duke" Wayne and Ward Bond had been teammates on the USC football team—and they knew how to play baseball. They were good athletes, and good athletes have a certain native proficiency at any sport, but what I found surprising was that they were also extremely competitive; it might have been only a pickup game of softball, but they played hard and they played to win. John Ford was around but didn't play much, which, now that I think of it, was odd because he had been a jock when he was a kid.

It was while I was spending a lot of time around Catalina that I met a sailing man named J. Stanley Anderson. His daughter had been hurt in an accident, and I used to cheer her up by doing imitations of famous actors. Anderson had connections in the movie industry and, in due time, would lend me some of those connections.

On those rare occasions when I wasn't thinking about acting, I discovered that you can learn a lot about a man's nature by observing how he plays sports. Bing Crosby, for instance, was a very fine golfer, but beyond that, he was a smart golfer. He knew the game, had a great swing, and was very consistent. He worked a course the same way he worked his career: he made it look easy, but he was thinking all the time, and he had good instincts. Fred Astaire was a good golfer because he had superb timing and rhythm, which is the essence of sport as well as of dance.

By comparison to today, golf was in its infancy. There wasn't a profusion of courses, and those courses that did exist weren't all that crowded. It was a more leisurely sport and a more casual time, so it was easy to strike up a conversation with the players if they were so inclined—or even if they weren't. Randy Scott said he could be right in the middle of a back swing when I would interrupt with some question about the movie business.

Clark Gable was charming, engaging, very unpretentious, the sort of person you felt comfortable talking to about almost anything. One day I told him I wanted to be in pictures. He liked the way I looked, and oddly, he liked the way I caddied, so he took me over to MGM to meet Billy Grady, the head of talent. Grady told me I needed to go to New York, go on the stage, and get some seasoning. "You need help," he said. "You need an edge." MGM and the other studios covered the stage, and they'd watch my progress. "Read a lot of books," he said. "Read them aloud in the backyard, to roughen and lower your voice."

I realize now that this was his Acting 101 speech to anyone who came to his office, but at the time it was a very important conversation. I also went to see Lillian Burns Sidney, who was the drama coach at MGM and who sang my praises to her class later on.

And then Stan Anderson, whose daughter I had entertained with imitations, sent me to see Solly Baiano at Warner's. I did my impersonations of Cagney, Bogart, and the rest for Solly, and all he said was, "Well, that's all very well, but we've already got Cagney, and we've already got Bogart. What about doing you?"

That rocked me back. I thought about it and sensibly pointed out that "I can't do me. I don't know who me is."

In spite of my unformed state, Solly liked me and was going to put me into a movie. But fate intervened when the studio was closed down by a strike, and I had to go back to St. Monica's, where I was going to high school. After that, I tried Paramount, where a lovely woman named Charlotte Cleary treated me with great kindness and enthusiasm. I auditioned in what they called "the fishbowl." The fishbowl looked like a projection room with a small stage area in front of the screen. At the back of the room was a glass window, and you couldn't see through it to find out who was watching you. It was like being in a police lineup, and it was unnerving. When the scene was over, they'd talk to you through a PA system. You couldn't see who you were playing to, and it didn't work for me at all.

My father's response to all this unvarying: "What the hell are you doing? What makes you think you can act?"

"I want to try it."

"Well, you're not going to try it. Go work in a steel mill this summer and learn about alloys."

This exchange, with minor variations, went on for years. For a while I was out there with a briefcase, fronting "Robert J. Wagner and Son." I didn't know much, but I knew I didn't want to be the back half of "Robert J. Wagner and Son."

Another dead-end job was selling cars, although one day I got in to see Minna Wallis under the pretext of selling her a Buick. Minna Wallis was Hal Wallis's sister and a well-regarded agent. Years earlier, she'd had an affair with Clark Gable and gave him a considerable career boost with her advice. I was a lot more interested in impressing her with the sleek beauty of Robert Wagner than I was in impressing her with the sleek beauty of a Buick. She was very encouraging, and years later I gave her an autographed picture on which I wrote, "Any time you want to buy a Buick, let me know."

Finally, my father capitulated slightly. My mother had been working relentlessly on him, and it had become increasingly obvious that I wasn't going to college. I was offered scholarships to USC and Pomona, for diving and swimming, but I don't think I could have made all-state. I was ranked about thirty-second in the state in tennis, which wasn't bad, but I wasn't really good enough to be a professional.

There were really only two paths: my father's way into business, or my way into show business. I remained adamant. Finally, my mother threw herself into the fray. She insisted that they had to let me at least try my way, so my father and I came to an agreement. When I graduated from St. Monica's, he gave me a convertible and $200 a month for a year. If I couldn't get into the movies in a year, on that money, I had to go into business with him. It wasn't a great deal, but it was a better deal than anything he'd offered me up till then. We shook on it.

I had met William Wellman on the golf course at Bel-Air. He was a friend of my dad's and a very fine, successful director who had given a lot of people their start, including Gary Cooper in *Wings,* Wellman's great World War I epic that won the first Oscar for "Best Picture" in 1927. My father swallowed hard, went to Wellman, and said, "I've got this kid who wants to be in the movies. Can you do anything?" Wellman probably heard this same line two or three times a week, but he gave me a small part in a good film he was making at MGM: *The Happy Years.* You never saw me—I was behind a catcher's mask, and you would have had to have been my mother to recognize me—but I was in a movie. Needless to say, I was over the moon.

Wellman had the reputation of being a wildly enthusiastic but temperamental taskmaster, but he was great to me; he even put me in another scene I wasn't supposed to be in. It was my first movie, but I didn't have a sense of how movies worked overall. I earned precisely $37.50 on *The Happy Years,* which I'm sure didn't make my father feel any better about my choice of a career. Far more important than the money was the fact that I was now entitled to membership in the Screen Actors Guild—not bad for eighteen years old!

With an appearance in a major studio film behind me, I went to Phil Kellogg, a well-regarded agent about town. Kellogg was with Berg-Allenberg, and he was Bill Wellman's agent. With the bravado of youth, I asked him if he would handle me. I was really just grasping at straws, and Kellogg responded by giving me a talk about how difficult the business was, how many kids there were like me, and so forth. In a very nice way, he was trying to discourage me. After half an hour, he suddenly stopped, and I went away without an agent. But I've always been a positive, basically optimistic person, and I had a bumptious self-confidence—you couldn't dissuade me. I just figured that if Kellogg didn't want to handle me, someone else would.

Fully forty years later, I was having a talk with Kellogg and thanked him for taking so much time with a green kid. And he told me that he'd actually been told to talk me out of being in the movies, but my enthusiasm got the best of him, and after a while he had to stop.

"Who told you to talk me out of it?" I asked, although I already knew the answer.

"Your father and Bill Wellman," he said.

Well, at least my father was consistent. For the year that he financed me, I worked as an extra and did everything there was to do so long as it was on a movie lot. I was always trying to get meetings with a producer, and if I was working in a crowd scene, I'd try to get placed in the front. For a time I was going out with Gloria Swanson's daughter Michelle. Gloria was preparing *Sunset Boulevard,* and she listened as Michelle and I told her how much we wanted to be actors. Gloria gave us a copy of the script of *Sunset Boulevard,* and Michelle and I worked up a scene. Then Gloria had her friend Chuck Walters, a good director at MGM, come and watch us do the scene, then give us notes.

All my scrounging and determination got me a lot of one-day jobs, and one thing led to another, as it usually does. One night I was at a club called the Beverly Hills Gourmet, where a songwriter named Lou Spence was playing the piano. I was up there by the piano singing some comedy lyrics that Spence had written to the tune of "Tea for Two" when a well-known agent named Henry Willson came in with his secretary. He sent a card over to the piano with a note that said if I was interested in being in pictures, I should come and see him. Well, I knew who Henry Willson was; everybody knew who Henry Willson was—a very important man at Charles Feldman's Famous Artists Agency. I also knew he was gay, although he wasn't mincy.

Famous Artists had strong connections at Fox, and that's where he sent me over to test. Years later, after I made it, a reporter asked Willson what he had seen in me. God knows, I was curious about that myself, because as Natalie Wood would say about me, "He was a star before he was an actor."

Willson replied that what had impressed him was "the changing expressions on his face. I watched his face mirror every thought and word—that, together with his looks and bright, clean-cut personality. I saw a sincerity and relaxed quality that would come right across the screen. Given the opportunity, I was sure he couldn't miss."

During the time that he represented me, Willson never made a pass, although if I had put myself out there, he would have been on me in a second. He always treated me professionally, but there's no question that Henry was sexually acquisitive. Once, he hitched a ride with me to the Racquet Club in Palm Springs. I was going there because there was a girl there I wanted to see, but Henry picked up a guy at the club using me as bait, which pissed me off royally.

Years later Mike Connors and I counted up the number of straight clients Henry had at that time. We were able to come up with three: the two of us and Rory Calhoun. It was really another time. In those days most gay men were in the background. To get together, they'd rent houses or go on beach parties, because there weren't that many gay bars around. Now there's a book for every town telling gays where to go, and gays are in the foreground.

Henry was a very tricky guy, and I don't think he was an admirable person. He pulled a particularly horrible stunt on Rory Calhoun, when he leaked Rory's juvenile record of grand theft auto to *Confidential* magazine in order to get them to sit on a story about Rock Hudson being gay. He gave up one client—Rory—to save a more important client—Rock. Years later, after Natalie Wood and I had remarried, Henry called and wanted us to pick up the mortgage on his house. He'd blown all his money, among other things, and he couched his request for help in the sinister overtones of a threat. He wouldn't want anything derogatory about us to come out, and so forth. We ignored him.

Just before I tested at Fox, I heard about a script at MGM that Stewart Stern had written. It was called *Teresa*, and it was about a young American soldier and his Italian war bride. The director was Fred Zinnemann, not yet the major figure who would make *High Noon* and *From Here to Eternity*, but clearly a rising star, one who already had the reputation of being a wonderful director. I got an interview, and Stewart and Fred both were very encouraging, even though I was painfully inexperienced. Stewart very kindly worked with me for about a week, taking me through the scene moment by moment. After a week, I went to MGM and made the test, which Fred directed himself.

MGM took one look at my test and gave the part to John Erickson. I don't blame them; I was just too green. A little while later I received a wonderful letter from Zinnemann, telling me that although I wasn't right for this particular part, I was a genuine talent and I had a wonderful career ahead of me. In the sixty years since, I have never been turned down with more class. It was completely misleading in that I thought Zinnemann's graciousness and style were a nominal part of the movie business. It took me a couple of years to figure out that Zinnemann was one of the few people of that era who would show such kindness to a young actor. It was Fred Zinnemann who taught me that the mark of a gentleman is how he treats people he doesn't have to be nice to.

Fade-out.

Fade-in.

Forty years later, Jill St. John and I were in London, and Fred Zinnemann was getting an award at the National Film Theater. We went over for the evening, and not only did he remember my test, but he remembered the letter! Fred Zinnemann was a great director, of course, but what is more important is that he was also a great man.

It was around the time I was testing for *Teresa* that I met Albert "Cubby" Broccoli, who was an agent at Charles Feldman's Famous Artists before he became a producer and achieved deserved fame and fortune with the James Bond films. Cubby came up through the trenches. Before he was an agent and producer, he sold jewelry, he sold Christmas trees, he worked in a studio mailroom, and he was an assistant director at Fox.

To know Cubby was to be his friend, and it was Cubby who took me around to some of the studios. I was with Cubby when we were both thrown off the MGM lot. It seemed that Charlie Feldman had begun an affair with an actress in whom a certain MGM executive had a deep and sustaining personal interest, so Feldman and everybody who worked with him were deemed persona non grata.

Despite that faux pas, Cubby and I hit it off, and for years I was invited to his house for Christmas and New Year's. He and his wife opened their arms to me, and when Cubby's health began to fail, I made sure to return the favor. I visited him regularly, as a great many people did. When he died, I gave the eulogy at his funeral—a small favor for a man who had done so much for me—and many others.

After testing for *Teresa*, I went over to Fox. I had known the Zanuck kids—Susan, Richard, and Darrylin—socially, not that that would cut me any slack when it came to business. I made my test, and Darryl Zanuck looked at it the next night—Darryl always worked a late day. He ran the footage and said, "I don't think so. Too inexperienced."

34

But Helena Sorrell, the studio's drama coach, asked him to run the test one more time. "Look at his smile," she said. "I think I can do something with that smile."

So Darryl ran the test again, sighed, and said, "Okay, Helena, if you say so. We'll give him six months." I signed a standard studio contract that started at $75 a week. I was eighteen years old, and since I was still a minor, part of my salary was withheld under the Coogan law. There were options—all on the studio's side—every six months, with a slight salary boost with each option that was picked up. My $75 a week would become $125 a week, for instance. If you were picked up for an entire year, you were guaranteed forty weeks of salary out of fifty-two, but the studio could put you on furlough anytime it wanted, during which time you weren't paid.

During the forty weeks you were being paid, you could be making movies, of course, but the studio could basically tell you to do anything else it wanted as well—publicity tours, testing with other actors, whatever the studio chose. Since we were being paid, nobody much minded.

The fact that I could make $75 a week caddying at Bel-Air, or selling cars, or working for my father didn't bother me at all. Far more important than the money was the fact that the contract got me inside a movie studio. The contract didn't arrive quite within the year my father had given me, but it was close enough so that I didn't have to go back to being the back half of "Robert J. Wagner and Son," which was all I cared about.

Twelve years later, Fox was paying me $5,000 a week.

# THREE

# "BABY, I WAS IN THE MOVIES!"

Susan Hayward helping a very eager and very inexperienced actor through his paces in *With a Song in My Heart*. (*WITH A SONG IN MY HEART* © 1952 TWENTIETH CENTURY FOX)

wentieth Century Fox was a studio by, for, and about Darryl Francis Zanuck. It had been formed in 1935 when Zanuck and his friend and business associate Joseph Schenck merged their Twentieth Century productions with the moribund Fox organization. Before that, Darryl had been head of production at Warner Bros. until he realized it was primarily a family business and somebody named Zanuck could never be a member of the family.

In 1933 Darryl went independent with Twentieth Century, which released through United Artists and had a great success. But Twentieth Century had to rent studio facilities, which cost a lot of money, so when the Fox organization became available, acquiring it solved both companies' problems: Darryl got a first-rate studio complex, and Fox got a production head who understood how to make movies people wanted to see.

Physically, Darryl was a small man, and like many small men, he was commanding and very competitive. He had to be good at everything he did, so when Darryl played polo or croquet, it was always at a very high level. Luckily, he also had a very good sense of humor and was fond of practical jokes, a trait I understand he picked up from Douglas Fairbanks Sr., who had mentored him when he was a young man.

Zanuck staffed his studio with top-notch people throughout the departments. The head of publicity was a wonderful man named Harry Brand, who looked just like what you'd imagine a studio publicity chief would look like. Harry usually wore a fedora and was, as they say, heavily connected. He had an in with every police department in California, knew everything that was going on, and could fix anything that needed to be fixed.

In due time, Harry would fix a couple of things for me. Once, I was going into an electrical supply store in Westwood when a guy picked a fight with me. He pushed me, and I foolishly responded by ramming his head into the grille of my car. Technically, this was a felony assault.

Harry took care of it.

Then there were a couple of incidents involving women playing the old badger game. One go-round in a hotel room and they promptly screamed, "I'm pregnant!" even though it was never true.

Harry took care of it.

Zanuck was an incredibly dynamic man who could be seen going up the studio street to the studio café every day for lunch. He would be swinging his polo mallet and behind him would be a retinue of producers, editors, and his French teacher. A few years before I got there, his right-hand man had been William Goetz, Louis B. Mayer's son-in-law, who brought with him an investment in the studio from Mayer. Darryl took the money, but he never respected Goetz.

When Darryl went into the service during World War II, he handed management of the studio over to Goetz. While Darryl was gone, Goetz never missed a chance to run him down verbally. Darryl heard about this, of course, and when Darryl returned, he and Goetz got into an argument—all the moguls were tremendously competitive and regularly engaged in knockdown, drag-out fights with each other. Darryl finally told Goetz he could hire a valet to do his job. Goetz was offended and left the studio to found International Pictures, which later merged with Universal.

For a replacement, Darryl hired Lou Schreiber, who had

been Al Jolson's valet. He hadn't been kidding: he literally hired a valet, and nothing much changed around the Fox lot.

I soon heard about Darryl's idiosyncrasies. Every day at four o'clock the atmosphere around the front office became noticeably hushed as Darryl was serviced by one of the contract girls. Darryl was notorious for his proclivities with women, and he had a bad habit of becoming obsessed by his mistresses; he couldn't take sex lightly and always had to try to elevate his girls to a level where they would be more than glorified call girls, worthy of Darryl F. Zanuck. Not all of them were anywhere near as interested in a starring career as Darryl was—his ego was more involved than theirs was.

I knew Darryl's children, and they always seemed to adore him. But Darryl was not the sort of man to play catch with his kids—none of those men were. Their identity consisted of their careers and their responsibilities. Think about those responsibilities for a moment: matching up stories—thirty a year!—with the right writers, the right actors, and the right directors; placating stockholders; and wondering if television was going to obliterate the movie business and trying to make pictures accordingly. Darryl really only saw the kids on the weekends, and there wasn't a lot of weekend—Darryl worked a six-day week.

When I drove onto the Fox lot as a contract player, I made sure not to have any airs about me. I wasn't trying to be something I wasn't. I was very anxious to find out why some people became stars and other people didn't; I wanted to learn what to wear, how to act, what kind of image to project. I was very analytical about it. I was there every morning whether I was working or not, eager and ready to learn. My life was finally opening before me, and I was smart enough to know it.

I now had my own apartment, at 1298 Devon, off Beverly Glen between Wilshire and Santa Monica. It was a terrific little one-bedroom apartment that I decorated myself and, even better, was paying for myself: $125 a month.

Helena Sorrell began working with me. She would choose scenes, mostly from movies, not plays, because the scenes were shorter, thus easier. After a while we'd get the scene on its feet with an actress and rehearse the material, and we'd end up using it for a test. I was always testing with somebody or another, for some part or another. I tested with everybody and for anything. With actresses, with actors, for westerns, for gangster pictures, you name it. Sometimes I was in a test with another young actor the studio was interested in, so all you could see was the back of my head, but I didn't care. I was in the movies.

I had motivation in front of me and in back of me. It wasn't just that I wanted to be a movie star; I didn't want to have to go back to my father with my tail between my legs. Because I wanted it so badly, I was pretty nervous and carried a lot of anxiety. I got to know the writers, I got to know the directors, and I made it my business to know which scripts were moving toward production and which were moving toward the shelf. Aside from all this, I could fit into the old wardrobes of Tyrone Power and Mark Stevens, which helped.

Helena regarded me as her personal project, and she used every trick in her book to get me up to speed. For a long time my voice was a problem—it was too high-pitched and I knew it, so I would throw lines away or mumble. Helena had to pretend to be hard of hearing to get me to speak up. For extra voice coaching, I went to see Gertrude Fogler at MGM. Gertrude had been at MGM for the twenty years since talkies arrived and, beginning with John Gilbert, had worked with practically every actor on the lot. She was an excellent voice teacher, which was good—I was paying for her lessons myself.

When I wasn't working with Helena or Gertrude, I was in the wardrobe department, the sound department, the camera department, the set department. I was on the stages, watching people act. Hell, I even watched the studio cops. My basic attitude was that anything they asked me to do wasn't a job but an opportunity. I was working in a movie studio, and I was determined to find out how all those gears meshed.

I had enthusiasm and a lot of admiration for the people at Fox, and I made sure that everybody knew it. I was amazed at how a movie came together, and to be completely honest, that amazement has never left me. I've made eighty movies and hundreds of hours of television, and I sit in a theater to watch a movie and I'm still thrilled.

Shortly after I was signed at Fox, the process of casting the two leads for *Teresa* became a story. Edwin Schallert had been the lead movie critic for the *Los Angeles Times* since the silent days, and MGM showed him a batch of the tests for *Teresa*. He came out with a story headlined "Robert Wagner a Dark Horse for 'Teresa' Part." Evidently, Schallert thought I was a lot better than MGM did.

Of course, the people at Fox found this very disturbing, as I had just been signed by them, and here I was almost getting a part at MGM. But it had a very positive effect, because the news that Fred Zinnemann had thought enough of me to direct my test got me in to see Lewis Milestone, another very fine director, who was putting a picture together called *Halls of Montezuma*—the first time I got billing in a movie.

I played a private, which was appropriate. When I met Milly—Milestone's nickname—I was very wide-eyed. "You made *All Quiet on the Western Front*!" I said. "That was a long time ago!" He wasn't too thrilled and said, "It wasn't that long ago." Actually, the movie had been made only twenty years before, but I was only twenty myself, so I pled ignorance.

The script was about the Marines in the Pacific campaign of World War II, and it wasn't much, but the cast was truly excellent: Richard Widmark, Jack Palance, Karl Malden, Marty Milner, Neville Brand, Richard Boone, and Jack Webb. Widmark was a terrific guy—years later I bought some land from him, so we had adjacent ranches where we raised horses—while Karl and I began a friendship that has lasted for nearly sixty years. Years later, Marty Milner and I went to see Milly on one of his birthdays, and he told us he should have been smarter about his contract and gotten 10 percent of the cast's future income—he would never have had to worry about money again.

After that, I was a Navy underwater demolition swimmer in *The Frogmen*, Claudette Colbert's junior executive son-in-law in *Let's Make It Legal*, a doomed Marine in John Ford's *What Price Glory?* and the inventor of the Sousaphone in *Stars and Stripes Forever*. These were all small supporting parts, but they were all well-chosen supporting parts—showy, with highly dramatic or emotional moments attached to each character.

*Let's Make It Legal* was one of the early films of Marilyn Monroe, but she wasn't the problem. I was. I was so green that I had to do forty-nine takes of one shot—a number I've never forgotten. Not all of it was my fault—Claudette Colbert went up a couple of times, the camera broke down, and the dialogue got changed—but most of it was my fault. Forty-nine takes. Jesus!

Claudette Colbert could have blown me right out of the water for being such an amateur, or she could have insisted that I be replaced, but she didn't. I found her a very caring, giving woman, with a lot of guts and a very special aura around her—a great star. Over forty years later she came to see me when I did *Love Letters* in the theater, and I felt honored by her presence.

It would be fair to say that I wasn't very good in this period, but I was diligent. I was also cooperative and I had enthusiasm, which is probably all that made me bearable to some of the pros I was working with. Now, when I look back at some of those early performances, I cringe a little and silently thank the public and the other actors for their patience.

Technically, *Let's Make It Legal* wasn't the only time I worked with Marilyn. She had tested with me for several parts that she got, and I think I was in the test that got her a contract at Fox. I adored her. At this point in her career she wasn't troublesome at all. She knew her lines cold, was terribly sweet and eager to please, and I loved her. My God, we were so young! I took her out a couple of times, but nothing happened. There were a lot of people in line before me, if you get my drift. It was a tricky situation, but she was a darling, and I thought the world of her.

Then Darryl sent me the script for a movie called *With a Song in My Heart*, a Susan Hayward picture about the singer Jane Froman, who had been terribly hurt in a plane crash but revived her career anyway. I had precisely two scenes and a couple of lines of dialogue. In the first scene, I meet Froman in a nightclub, and she brings me up on the little mobile stage she used after her accident and sings two songs to me: "Embraceable You" and "Tea for Two." My response, as indicated by the script, was to smile and look bashful. Well, that was certainly in my skill set.

The second scene took place after I'd gone off to war and become a victim of shell shock. Although my character hasn't said ten words since he got hurt, I manage to tell Hayward/Froman I'd like to hear her sing "I'll Walk Alone." Bingo! I'm cured.

I'm embarrassed to say that I read the script and didn't see it. "This isn't very much," I told Darryl. And with great patience, he told me, "This will be the biggest break you will have had in your career. You will be on the screen for three minutes. When people come out of the theater, they will want to know who you are."

That was the last time I questioned Darryl Zanuck's judgment about the movies. I was too young to realize that Darryl was placing me, sculpting moments for me that would compel the audience's attention. He was taking very good care of me.

When we shot my scenes for *With a Song in My Heart*, Walter Lang directed me almost exactly as he would have directed Rin-Tin-Tin. Let me explain: Dogs have only a couple of expressions—if you're making a movie and you want a dog to look intense and his ears to spring up, you show him a cat. Well, Walter wanted me to cry, and he didn't want me to fake it, so when he directed the scene, he was crying. And even if the dramatic construction of the movie was slightly corny, that moment—what passed between Susan and Walter and myself—was absolutely true.

When Susan was playing to me, I responded automatically. I didn't have the craft to produce tears on my own, and Susan realized it. She was completely focused on me, giving me what I needed to give her back an emotional reaction. And when she sang "I'll Walk Alone," I cried. It was as if I were a child actor, which, in a very real sense, I was. And after the scene was over, it was Susan who fell apart. She was sensational in the picture, and Watson Webb, who would become a good friend, edited my scenes beautifully.

In my callowness, I thought the power of a part was judged by the amount of time the character is on screen; I hadn't seen Bill Wellman's *Wings*, which featured Gary Cooper in a scene that lasted about two minutes. Before that, Coop was just another young actor; after that, he was a star. After *With a Song in My Heart* opened, Susan was nominated for an Oscar for best actress, the film was a big hit, and I wasn't exactly a star but for the first time people knew who I was. The Korean War was on, and to the women in the audience that boy I played represented the men in their lives—mothers thought of their sons, wives thought of their husbands, and girls thought of their sweethearts.

I was good enough in these pictures, but I was so terribly young. The energy and innocence you can see in *With a Song in My Heart* and *Stars and Stripes Forever* isn't acting—that was me. Walter Lang and his wife Fieldsie liked me, and Walter often took me fishing. Walter was a very solid human being, and Fieldsie was a ballsy, lovable woman. She had been a bathing beauty for Mack Sennett, and after that she had been Carole Lombard's secretary. Clark Gable remained close to them after Carole's death; he would often come to their house to play poker. The result was that Gable and I became closer than we had been as golfer and caddy.

My first real trial by fire was John Ford. Believe me, if you can survive John Ford in a bad mood, you can survive anything. Jimmy Cagney and Dan Dailey were the stars of *What Price Glory?*, which was originally a very strong antiwar statement in its theatrical version and in Raoul Walsh's 1926 silent version. In Ford's version, it became mostly about male camaraderie. Besides Cagney and Dailey, the cast was dotted with wonderful character actors—Bill Demarest, James Gleason, Wallace Ford—and then there was me, the green kid, which in Ford's world was a euphemism for "designated patsy."

Ford was a tall, lean man who had had a distinguished career in the Navy during World War II (he would eventually rise to the rank of admiral) as a break from his distinguished career in Hollywood (he won five Oscars). He wore a slouch hat and dark glasses and had a sharp, pointed command personality, although he never raised his voice. Ford didn't call me RJ and didn't even call me Bob. Throughout the picture, he called me

Boob. One day we were shooting on the French street that had been built for *The Song of Bernadette*. I was to come out of a house with Bill Demarest, Wally Ford, and Dan Dailey. We did a take, Ford said, "Cut," and then he walked the length of the street and came up to me.

"You know, Boob, if you can't see the camera, the camera can't see you. You be clear to the camera." And then he pushed me, hard. I wasn't expecting it, and I fell flat on my ass. By the time I hit the ground, he'd turned and was walking back up the street. I was too stunned to be angry. I struggled to my feet and said, "My God!"

Jim Cagney was standing next to me and said, "Don't worry, kid. He does that. You'll be all right. Just remember your lines, that's all you have to do."

If Ford had had the camera running when he knocked me down, I would have gotten the Academy Award. Another time he picked up a rock and started to throw it at me. He was basically interested in destabilizing me, and he succeeded. He scared the living hell out of me. The fact that he had scared the living hell out of John Wayne, Harry Carey Jr., Ward Bond, and practically every other person who had ever worked with him was very small consolation.

One day on the set Ford was sitting in his director's chair when he turned to me. "Boob?" he said.

"Yes, sir, Mr. Ford!"

"Don't look now. Over there? That man? That's Barry Norton. He played your part in the original picture. He's the king of the queens. He's an extra now. That can happen to you."

"Yes, sir, Mr. Ford." I turned around and bumped into another man. "That's King Baggott," Ford said. "He used to make $27,500 a week. See where he is now, Boob?"

What a tough son of a bitch. I didn't find out until years later that the second guy wasn't King Baggott; King Baggott had been a high-priced actor and director who drank himself out of the business and ended up as a security guard at MGM. He died in 1948, the year I signed with Fox and a couple of years before I worked with Ford on *What Price Glory?* But it might as well have been King Baggott, because whoever that man was, Ford used him to scare the hell out of me, and I've never forgotten the lesson. He was telling me that making movies was a brutal business, that things end, and I needed to hold on to my money. He was telling me something I needed to learn, and for that I thank him, if not for the way he told me.

My primary consolation during *What Price Glory?* was Corinne Calvet, a gorgeous woman but one who didn't have the clarity needed for a major career. As for Jimmy Cagney, he was as wonderful to me as Ford was harsh. I had known Cagney when I was a kid, when I had jogged his horses for him. Jimmy kept Morgans and trotters, and he was a very giving, generous man whom I had admired for years. Here I was, only a couple of years into my career, and I ended up dying in his arms in a John Ford movie!

As an actor, Cagney was very free and open. The emotional coloring of his work could vary quite a bit from take to take, although he was always very concerned about matching his action. Among that generation of actors, the only one with whom I worked who I found to be uninterested in much variation was Henry Fonda. He didn't vary much, and he didn't use much. He didn't even use other actors much.

Throughout this period I trusted in Darryl to do right by me, and I must say that he never failed me, not once. The studio system could be emotionally difficult, because I wasn't the only hopeful juvenile leading man being groomed for a career. There were a dozen or so at each studio, all starting out at $75 a week, all more or less good-looking, all more or less types who could conceivably replace an older leading man who was already at the studio. I was tagged as a possible replacement for Tyrone Power, as was Jeffrey Hunter—a fine man, a good actor, and a valued friend. One of the small tortures of the way the studios operated was that there were plenty of other people who were something like you. Every time you looked around, you saw someone who was a living, breathing implication that you were replaceable. And the sad fact was that you were.

On the other hand, the studio system gave you opportunities to fail, to learn, to fail less miserably, to gradually master your craft. And the studio did have a way of taking care of you if it thought you had something. For the publicity tour for *Let's Make It Legal,* MacDonald Carey, Joyce McKenzie, Larry Carr, and I were sent on the road. We went through Philadelphia and then on to a lot of Midwest towns, dancing and singing on the stage, then signing autographs as a live attraction before the film. We all lived together, and it was fun.

Mac Carey had been around for years, making a hit on Broadway in *Lady in the Dark* with Gertrude Lawrence and working with Hitchcock in *Shadow of a Doubt* and a lot of other movies. Mac was kind enough to take me under his wing and tell me how the studio game was played—what things were important and what things weren't.

For most of the tour Mac and I roomed together, but just after we got to New York the studio put us up at the Warwick Hotel, right across the street from the Stage Delicatessen. At that point his wife came to town, so I was thrown out of the room. His wife promptly got pregnant, and I've always thought I deserved at least some of the credit.

I had been to New York only once before—my dad had taken us there—but I had never been there professionally, and on an expense account to boot, and that made all the difference in the world. I've been passionate about the city ever since, at the studio's expense or my own.

For the most part, I wasn't disappointed by the people I was meeting around the studio, although Paul Douglas was certainly an exception. He was a brusque, unpleasant man, always carrying around a sour edge about something or another. I've never understood why someone would want to live like that; whenever I've had a problem with somebody, I confront it head-on. And then I step back and wait. I usually find that the direct approach works.

The perquisites of a rising young actor in Hollywood were and are obvious, and I did my best to get my share.

I met Joan Crawford at a cocktail party and sensed that she was interested in me. She suggested I follow her back to her house in Brentwood. After I got there, she asked me if I would like a swim. Sure, I said. She told me that there were some trunks down by the pool and I could help myself. I went down to the pool, took my clothes off, put on a pair of trunks, and got in the pool.

After a few minutes, Joan came out of the house with absolutely nothing on, did a very graceful dive off the board, swam the length of the pool underwater, and came up right between my legs.

"Hi there!" she said in her brightest, most vivacious voice. It was a lovely, creative invitation, and I responded accordingly. She was a dynamic lover, both domineering—which you might expect—and yielding—which you might not. All in all, a memorable one-night stand.

Around this same time I drove my 1950 Ford convertible into a drive-in restaurant called Jack's at the Beach. The top was down, the day was lovely, and I was a young actor about town. I looked over, and there was Yvonne De Carlo next to me in her car. She was at the height of her career as well as of the physical splendor that was on display in tits-and-sand Universal pictures like *Song of Scheherazade* and *Slave Girl,* as well as noirs like *Brute Force* and *Criss Cross.* We looked each other over, and she nodded her head for me to come over. I backed my car up, parked it in the rear of the restaurant, and got into Yvonne's car.

"I'm Robert Wagner."

"I know. I'm Yvonne De Carlo."

"I know. I'm such a fan of yours."

One thing led to another, and we went back to her house. Three days later, I staggered out, depleted and disheveled. I wasn't sure what month it was, but I dimly remembered leaving my car at the drive-in. Luckily, it was still parked where I'd left it.

A week later, I ran into Tony Curtis. "You can't imagine what just happened to me," he says. "I pull into Jack's at the Beach. Yvonne De Carlo pulls up next to me! She looks at me, I look at her. Well, to make a long story short. . . ."

I just stared at him, then I began laughing hysterically. Baby, I was in the movies!

It's interesting how friendships form and either strengthen or recede with time. Tony Curtis and I were friends for years, had a bad falling-out, then patched things up. But Robert Stack and I were pals for more than forty years with never a cross word. Initially, it was based on the fact that each of us possessed an athletic skill the other one was interested in. Bob was a world-class skeet shooter, and he taught me how to shoot; I was a good golfer, and I taught him how to play. Beyond that, we shared a similar background and a positive outlook on life, and we both genuinely enjoyed being in show business.

Bob died in 2003, and I was so moved when he left me a beautiful pair of pearl and diamond studs, accompanied by a note he'd written thanking me for my friendship. Believe me, the honor was all mine.

There weren't really issues with drugs in those days—the most you'd ever see was some marijuana if you were hanging around musicians. But one way or another, there has always been a need for people to blow off the steam that builds up in the pressure-cooker atmosphere of show business. Take, for instance, OK Freddy.

By common consent, OK Freddy had the biggest cock in Hollywood. It was twelve inches long, with the thickness of a baby's arm. I never knew his real name—I don't know that anyone did, as he seemed to be universally known as OK Freddy. Freddy was an extra, and he was always around and always working, mostly because if anybody, at any time, asked him, "Freddy, show us your cock," Freddy would say, "Okay," and bring it out—depending on the circumstances and the company, a formula for either enduring popularity or serious jail time. He was a very pleasant, amiable man, but then, most men would be pleasant and amiable if they were carrying what OK Freddy had.

My favorite experience with OK Freddy involved Gary Cooper, who loved practical jokes. Coop was throwing a party at his house, and among those attending was Henry Ford II and his wife. Coop had hired both OK Freddy and Vince Barnett for the evening. Barnett was a character actor who often played the part of a waiter at parties, where he would proceed to insult out-of-town guests or anybody else who didn't know it was a setup. One of Vince's set-pieces involved accusing people of stealing silver, but he would also customize his attacks. Once he told Jack Warner he didn't know how to make pictures, and he also accused Charlie Chaplin of monopolizing the conversation. OK Freddy, also working the party as a waiter, carried a tray of hors d'oeuvres, among which was his massive unit, jostling the garnish and pâté.

For this particular party, Vince Barnett was playing the part of a doctor, and he got into a loud argument with Henry Ford II. Coop came over, pretended to be angry at his guest being insulted, and decked Barnett. When he hit the ground, Barnett bit down on a blood capsule he had in his mouth, and the fake blood cascaded down his chin and onto his white shirt. Mrs. Henry Ford II proceeded to faint dead away! Clearly, they didn't have people like Vince Barnett and OK Freddy around the country clubs of Detroit.

After *With a Song in My Heart* was released, the fan mail began to pour in. In those days the studio looked at fan mail the same way that modern TV networks do ratings—as a leading indicator that someone was provoking a reaction. Suddenly, there were thousands of letters every week asking for autographed photos, biographies, fan club information. I was becoming a bobby-sox idol, along with Tony Curtis and Rock Hudson. In very short order, the studio started up a monthly newsletter called *Wagner's World,* and my fan club signed up 250,000 members.

By 1952 I was regarded as a rising young star. Darryl Zanuck's daughter Susan liked me—she liked me a lot. She was just getting out of high school, and I began to take her out. I really enjoyed her company, but I wasn't in love with her, and the problem was that she was obviously enthralled—when she went to Paris, she brought me back a beautiful gold watch.

I sensed that this could be a very dark part of the woods, with obvious potential for disaster, at least in relation to my career. My father, on the other hand, thought marrying Susan Zanuck was a great idea. He liked the dynastic implications and thought the marriage would mean job security for me. Darryl knew what was going on, and since he liked me a lot, he was perfectly happy with my being involved with Susan. I wrote Darryl a letter, explaining the awkwardness I felt, and I told him I certainly didn't want to hurt Susan, or myself.

Darryl was a class act. "I will always be in your corner," he wrote in his reply, and he assured me that "this has nothing to do with your career." He continued to invite me down to the Zanuck house in Palm Springs, where I got to know his wife, Virginia, and the rest of the family. Virginia was a lovely, tenacious woman who took great pride in being Mrs. Darryl Zanuck. Despite all of Darryl's wanderings—and they were legion—she never gave up. In the end, she got him back.

For a time I went out with Debbie Reynolds, just before she went over to MGM and made *Singin' in the Rain*. She was a contract player at Warner's, and I was a contract player at Fox. We never had an affair, although I think it's fair to say that she liked me very much. Basically, we were kids together.

As if Susan Zanuck wasn't enough potential trouble, along came Bella Darvi. Her real name was Bayla Wegier, and she had spent time in a concentration camp during the war. Darryl met her in 1951, placed her under contract, then placed her in his bed. Now that I think of it, it might have been the other way around. Anyway, he paid off her gambling debts, decided he would make her a star, and changed her name. Darvi came from the first letters of his name and Virginia's. I understand that for a time she even lived in their house.

Bella made three movies for Darryl, none of which was very good. I met her on the lot, and she made it very clear that she would like us to have some private sessions that would have nothing to do with acting. I never thought she was particularly beautiful, but she did have great personal presence that didn't quite come across on camera.

Did I consider going to bed with her? God Almighty, no! Aside from my affection for Darryl as a man, I also respected him as my boss, and I would never have poached on his territory. Plus, Bella was obviously unstable—she gambled away vast amounts of Darryl's money. Mrs. Wagner didn't raise a fool; I went on my way.

With my career gathering momentum and my contracted raises clicking in, it was easier for me to indulge in my passion for music, specifically jazz. I had been brought up on American music because my mother played the piano and we always had plenty of 78-rpm records of the big bands of the thirties—Benny Goodman and so forth.

But my introduction to jazz came courtesy of Herbert Stothart Jr., who had been with me in one of the many military academies where I was interned. His father was a former professor, head of the music department at MGM, and had composed some famous operettas in the 1920s before he came to Hollywood. Stothart was a serious musician, and he had passed his passion on to his son, who exposed me to people like Chick Webb, who had a young girl named Ella Fitzgerald working as his vocalist.

In the early fifties in Los Angeles, there was a lot of jazz being played at clubs like the Crescendo and the Interlude. Chet Baker was always around, as were Jeri Southern and Frances Faye. I became a fan of Stan Kenton and all the people Norman Granz was recording. Supremely, I became a fan of Billie Holiday. Basically, I followed her from gig to gig. And if I was in New York, I always made it a point to go to a place called the Embers, where Peggy Lee liked to work.

I got to know Holiday, who was a tiny little thing; it was like meeting a doll. I thought she had the most fantastic talent of any singer of her time—or ours. Sometimes she was on drugs, and you weren't sure she was going to be able to make it to the end of the song, let alone finish the set, but she always did. And even if she hadn't made it, it wouldn't have mattered, because she sang every note from her soul, and the emotion trumped the notes. (In a sense, Judy Garland was the same way.) I was in New York when it was announced that Holiday was dying, and I tried to get into Bellevue to see her, but I was too late.

I sat there for hundreds of nights listening to these men and women, amazed at how they got to those notes, got to that emotion. Jazz became very beneficial for me. I came from a background where if something was set, it was set in stone. And here were artists, people who were communicating emotion—the same thing I wanted to do—who worked with freedom, who were open, who joined together in an attitude of community and made things happen with great musicality, and who did it while maintaining their personalities. You can listen to three or four notes on the trumpet and know it's Louis Armstrong—there are thousands of trumpet players, but nobody else has that unique Armstrong sound. It's the same thing every actor strives for—a tone that's all their own.

# FOUR

# "BARBARA WAS THE FIRST WOMAN I EVER LOVED."

Barbara and me in our only scene alone in *Titanic*. It wasn't much of a scene, but it sparked one of the most intense and rewarding relationships of my life. (© TWENTIETH CENTURY FOX/EVERETT COLLECTION)

arbara Stanwyck and I began our relationship on *Titanic,* although we had actually met years before. For a time, my father had an eight-acre ranch in Chatsworth, across from the racetrack. Martha Scott also lived there, and I used to take care of her horse. We'd go riding, and I would see Barbara and her husband, Robert Taylor, riding. I would go trotting along with them, never thinking I'd be involved with her some-day.

Later, Barbara had a beautiful ranch at the corner of Devonshire and Reseda, with her agent, Zeppo Marx. It's now a shopping center, but when Barbara owned the ranch, it had paddocks that were impeccably maintained and run, like everything Barbara touched.

As *Titanic* began production, there was an immediate chemistry between Barbara and myself—a lot of looks across the room. At this point Barbara Stanwyck was a legendary actress, universally respected for her level of craft and integrity. She also had the most valuable thing a performer can have: good taste. Besides a long list of successful bread-and-butter pictures, Barbara had made genuine classics for great directors: *The Bitter Tea of General Yen* and *Meet John Doe* for Frank Capra, *Stella Dallas* for King Vidor, *The Lady Eve* for Preston Sturges, *Ball of Fire* for Howard Hawks, and *Double Indemnity* for Billy Wilder. Barbara carried her success lightly; her attitude was one of utter professionalism and no noticeable temperament. As far as she was concerned, she was simply one of a hundred or so people gathered to make a movie—no more, no less.

*Titanic* was a heavy production logistically, but a pleasant shoot because of the director, Jean Negulesco. Jean had a light, very pleasant personality—whenever I think of him, I think of champagne—and was very helpful to a young actor. He was also a talented artist and asked me to sit for a portrait, which I still have on my wall.

After the picture had been shooting for a couple of weeks, Jean had a party at his house on a Saturday night. I escorted Barbara and stayed close to her throughout the evening. I was enthralled by her and terribly attracted to her, but I couldn't tell if she returned the favor. She was friendly, but not overly so.

When the party was over, I drove Barbara back to her house on Beverly Glen and took her house key to open her front door. I had to bend over to find the lock, and I only opened the door a crack. I wasn't sure how to proceed. Would she invite me in, or would she just take her key, pat me on the cheek, and thank me for a lovely evening? And then I straightened up to look at her with what I'm sure was a hopeful expression, and I saw something I hadn't seen in her eyes before. It was a magical look of interest . . . and appreciation . . . and desire.

I immediately took her in my arms and kissed her. I had never had a reaction from a woman like I had from Barbara. A different kiss, with a different feeling.

We went into the house; we opened a bottle of champagne; we danced. I left at dawn.

After that, things happened very quickly. She gave me a key to her house, and I gave her a key to my apartment. If we were in town, we spent every weekend together. She cooked for me—she was good in the kitchen, but then she was good everywhere. We watched the Friday night fights on TV, and on Saturday or Sunday afternoons we'd go for long walks in the mountains above Malibu. Occasionally we would go to a movie, slipping in after the lights went down. Whenever we went out, Barbara would wear a scarf over her head, or a kind of hat, so it would be hard to tell who she was.

For the next four years, we became part of each other's lives. In a very real way, I think we still are.

Barbara proved to be one of the most marvelous relationships of my life. I was twenty-two, she was forty-five, but our ages were beside the point. She was everything to me—a beautiful woman with a great sense of humor and enormous accomplishments to her name.

As a person, she was a great deal like the character she played in *Ball of Fire*, a stripper called Sugarpuss O'Shea. She had a wonderful, free, open quality in that picture, and that's what she was like as a woman. Reclusive by nature, she was happy to just stay home, but she read everything. She got me reading books as a way of life and, if I asked her, would help me out with my acting. We only had one scene together in *Titanic*—I played her daughter's boyfriend!—so there was a limit to what I could learn by working with her. She taught me what to do with my hands, how to get over my self-consciousness, and how to lower my voice, which I thought was still too high. And she taught me to be decisive with things like entrances.

"When you walk in," she told me, "be sure you're standing up straight. Walk in with confidence." She didn't want me to sidle into a scene as if I were ashamed to be in the movie. Make the entrance! Take the scene!

But I wasn't going there for acting tutorials. I was in love with her. She was very loving, very caring, very involved with me, and highly sexed. Making love with her was an entirely different thing than I had ever experienced. I had been with girls, and I had been with women, but I had never been with a woman with her level of knowledge, her level of taste. I was so incredibly taken with her, taken by her.

We were both at turning points in our lives. She had been married to Robert Taylor for over ten years when he went to Italy to make *Quo Vadis* and had an affair, at which point Barbara threw him out. She was bitter about Taylor; she acted very quickly, almost reflexively, although I don't know that she thought it was too quick. I don't know precisely what went on between them; we never got into it. In fact, I went hunting with Bob Taylor a few times, and I think he might have known about us.

At any rate, she had just gotten her divorce when we met. She was at a very vulnerable moment in her life and career. The forties are a dangerous time for any woman, and especially so for an actress whose work is her identity—definitely Barbara's way of life. The transition to playing middle-aged women has unnerved a lot of actresses—some of Barbara's contemporaries, such as Norma Shearer and Kay Francis, quit the business rather than confront it—but she faced it straight on because that's the kind of woman she was. The continuity of her career was more important to her than any individual part. Like so many people in show business, she was a prisoner of her career. Because of my youth, I suppose in one sense I was a validation of her sexuality.

She had an old friend from the vaudeville days named Buck Mack who lived with her. Buck had been part of a vaudeville team called Miller & Mack and had been an extra in *Citizen Kane*. In modern terms, he was a personal assistant: he ran the house, kept everything running smoothly, and watched over her. At first, Buck regarded me as an interloper, but it wasn't long before he saw that Barbara and I genuinely loved each other, and he and I became good friends.

Because of the age difference, neither of us wanted to have our relationship in the papers, and with the help of Helen Ferguson, her publicist and one of her best friends, we kept it quiet. There were only a few people who knew about us. Nancy Sinatra Sr. was one of them, because she and Barbara were close friends. I didn't tell anybody at Fox about our affair, although

Harry Brand might have known, if only because Harry knew everything.

Likewise, I always assumed that Darryl Zanuck knew, although he never said a word about it to me. That might have been because Darryl and Barbara had something of a history, a bad one: Barbara told me that Darryl had chased her around his office years earlier, and I got the distinct impression that she hadn't appreciated the exercise.

And my parents knew, because Barbara called their house a few times looking for me. I finally told them we were seeing each other, although I didn't give them all the details. They met her once, at a party at Clifton Webb's house, and my mother was upset that I was in love with an older woman. As for my father, as with most other events in my life, he was not in my corner.

And I eventually told Spencer Tracy about it. All he said was, "Wonderful! Are you happy? If you're happy, that's all that matters."

Because I was so involved with Barbara, I was off-limits for other women, which was something of a problem for the studio. They wanted to promote the image of a carefree young stud—never my style—so I had publicity dates with young actresses around town like Lori Nelson or Debra Paget. This was a relic of the days when the studio system was in its prime. The studio would arrange for two young stars-in-waiting to go out to dinner and a dance and assign a photographer to accompany them. The result would be placed in a fan magazine. It was a totally artificial story documenting a nonexistent relationship, but it served to keep the names of young talents in front of the public. As far as I was concerned, it was part of the job, and usually pleasant enough.

When reporters would ask me about my romantic life, which they did incessantly, I had to say things like, "If I go out with one woman a few times, it's considered a romance. If I date a lot of girls, I'm a Casanova. It's one of those 'heads-you-win-tails-I-lose' deals. I don't think it's anybody's business what I do." The last sentence contained my true feelings.

In most respects, Barbara was a man's woman, although her home was lovely. Like me, she was an animal lover—she kept poodles. Her son, Dion, was in the service at this point—I never actually met him—and she was hopeful that the Army might help him. She had adopted Dion when she was married to Frank Fay, one of the most dreadful men in the history of show business. Fay was a drunk, an anti-Semite, and a wife-beater, and Barbara had had to endure all of that.

I don't think she was going to an analyst at this point, but she did make regular visits to a man who gave her sodium pen-tothal. It wasn't like the LSD therapy that came later, which Cary Grant tried and got so much out of. Barbara had a lot of things going on in her head, but she didn't put it out there for conversation, let alone public consumption.

When I was with her, it was all about us. There wasn't a lot about anybody else, not Frank Fay, or even Bob Taylor. She had a small scar on her chest, where someone had once put out a cigarette on her. I think it was Al Jolson, speaking of sons of bitches. Jolson had been crazy about her back in the New York days, when she was a young actress on Broadway. She would talk about him once in a while, mainly about what an asshole he had been.

Spending time around her house, I came across a cache of 16mm movies in her basement. It turned out that Barbara had a lot of her own movies, and I convinced her to spend some time watching them with me. I ran the projector. She had prints of *Union Pacific, Ball of Fire,* and *Baby Face,* among others. She didn't particularly like watching them, but she did enjoy remi-niscing about their production: how she got the part, what the location was like, that sort of thing. She liked people with humor and always spoke highly of Gary Cooper, Joel McCrea, and Frank Capra. Oddly enough, she wasn't crazy about Preston Sturges; she seemed to feel that he expended all his charm and humor for his movies and that there wasn't anything left for his actors.

In broad outline, all this sounds a little bit like the scene in *Sunset Boulevard* where Gloria Swanson sits with William Holden and watches a scene from *Queen Kelly,* rhapsodizing about her own face. But Barbara couldn't have cared less about how she looked; as I watched her films with her, it was clear that, for her, the movies were a job she loved, as well as a social occasion for a woman who was otherwise something of a loner.

Barbara and I were together for four years. What ultimately broke it up was the fact that it couldn't go anywhere—it was a classic backstreet romance. I was going on location to make movies, she was going on location to make movies, and there was no chance of a marriage in that place and time, so it was bound to run out of steam. She finally sat me down and told me that it was too difficult for her. She loved me, but. . . .

I couldn't argue with her reasoning. There was simply no way we could have been married at that time. I would have always been Mr. Stanwyck, and we both knew it.

And that's how it came to an end.

She was an enormous influence in my life, and still is. I remain immensely grateful. I gave her things, nice things, such as a four-leaf clover necklace made out of platinum and diamonds, a piece of jewelry she always set special store by. But the things I gave her were dwarfed by the things she gave me. If I had to limit it to just one thing, I would say she gave me self-esteem. To have a woman of her beauty and accomplishment see value in me and give herself totally to me couldn't help but have a powerful impact on my psyche. Barbara was the first savior in my life.

More concretely, she gave me values I never had before. I've mentioned that she gave me a love of reading, but she also taught me to appreciate art. I still have two landscapes she gave me, one of San Francisco, the other of Paris. Without her, there's no doubt in my mind I would have gone in a different direction, and not a better one. For one thing, I would have spent more time with my contemporaries, and frankly, none of my contemporaries were in Barbara's league.

I always kept in touch with Barbara. I don't know who the men in her life were, although I'm sure they existed. I know she had escorts, although I assumed most of them were gay.

Toward the end of her life a burglar broke into her house and pistol-whipped her. She was an elderly woman by then, and it sent her into a downward spiral. When she was in the hospital dying, I called, and she asked me not to come and see her; she wanted me to remember her as she was. I felt I had to honor her request. As we talked, she told me she was wearing the four-leaf clover necklace I had given her. Barbara was cremated wearing it, and her ashes were scattered over Lone Pine. The fact that a piece of me remained with her at the end was and is some consolation for her loss.

Occasionally, on screen, Barbara had a wary, watchful quality about her that I've noticed in other people who had bad childhoods; they tend to keep an eye on life because they don't think it can be trusted. After her mother was killed by a streetcar, she had been raised in Brooklyn by her sisters, and from things she said, I believe she had been abused as a child. She had lived an entirely different life than mine, that's for sure, which is one reason I found her so fascinating. I think her early life was one reason she had such authenticity as an actress, and as a person.

Barbara was the first woman I ever loved.

# FIVE

# "MAINLY, IT WAS THE WIG."

On location in Tarpon Springs, Florida, with J. Carroll Naish and Gilbert Roland in *Beneath the 12-Mile Reef.* (*BENEATH THE 12-MILE REEF* © 1953 TWENTIETH CENTURY FOX. ALL RIGHTS RESERVED.)

Each of the major studios was like a royal court that was in competition with the other royal courts. Each studio had a social lion who maintained a prestigious individual salon, and it wasn't necessarily the studio head. Then there were the salons that owed no special allegiance to any studio but cherry-picked from all the elites, such as the one maintained by Bill and Edie Goetz.

At Fox, the elite circle was presided over by Clifton Webb. I worked with Clifton on *Stars and Stripes Forever,* a biopic about John Philip Sousa, then *Titanic,* and I was invited into his group. Clifton's friends included people like Noel Coward and Charles Brackett, Billy Wilder's partner, who never got much credit from anyone, especially Billy. Charlie was a kind, well-educated, very bright gay man who was fairly deep in the closet.

Clifton lived with his mother, Mabelle, who was a total character and ruled the roost. The father had left when Clifton was very young and he was out of the picture, if he'd ever been in it. Mabelle had opened a dance school in Indianapolis, and she and Clifton gave dancing lessons together. He teamed up with Bonnie Glass and formed a very successful duo that followed in the footsteps of Vernon and Irene Castle. I never saw Clifton dance on the stage, but people who did told me he was a magnificent talent, the equivalent of Astaire but with a fey manner that he managed to get away with and always high-style: white tie and tails. Certainly, he had a major career, starring in shows like *Sunny* and Irving Berlin's *As Thousands Cheer.*

Clifton and Mabelle were completely devoted to each other; Clifton would dance with her at parties. She was outrageous and would order Clifton around. "We are going to sit *here*," she would announce, "and then we are going to move over *there*." Mabelle was always at the head of the table, and Clifton was very respectful of her, although he had his eccentricities as well: he had an African gray parrot he would wrap in a napkin and put in a brandy snifter at the dinner table.

It was as if they were competing to see who could be the most like Auntie Mame. They both had a larger-than-life quality, and the bond between them was very thick. Sometimes too thick. One time Noel Coward called Clifton, and Clifton was going on and on about Mabelle, as he tended to do. And Noel said, "Dear boy, if you want to talk about her, do it on your nickel."

Clifton was gay, of course, but he never made a pass at me, not that he would have. I never saw Clifton with a man; I never knew of Clifton being with a man, or having a lover.

Clifton had a very rich deal at the studio, and his house reflected it. It was Victor Fleming's old place, and Clifton had done it in a bright, comfortable style, in the mode of Billy Haines—the go-to decorator in that era. I remember that at one point Clifton did the bar in a Greek style, full of things he brought back from the location of *Boy on a Dolphin*. The word was that Clifton earned the same money that Darryl Zanuck earned. He didn't get the stock that Darryl got, but he earned the same money. Clifton had a string of enormous successes. There was *Laura* and *The Razor's Edge*, then *Mr. Belvedere* and two sequels, *Cheaper by the Dozen*, *The Stars and Stripes Forever*, and *Titanic*—all big hits.

I was learning that this kind of moviemaking was typical of Darryl. He never had the money that MGM or Paramount did, so he couldn't buy stars, he had to make them. If he didn't have enough stars to make a movie, he had the extraordinary ability to make the movie itself the star. Darryl had the vision to see real possibilities in an effete stage star and to build very effective vehicles around a personality centering on asperity and waspish intelligence—hardly the stuff of mass audience entertainment then or now, but somehow Darryl and Clifton made it work.

Clifton was very social; he gave wonderful parties, so he had a lot of leverage by dint of his position as well as his commercial cachet. It was Clifton who introduced me to Noel Coward. Noel was playing Las Vegas, and Clifton threw a lunch for him. Eventually, everybody else left, and I was alone with Noel. And he said, "Come and sit over here." So I went over and sat down, and he put his hand on my leg.

"Are you by any chance homosexual?" he asked.

"No, I'm not."

And he said, "Ah, what a pity." His hand came off, and that was it. After that, he couldn't have been more of a gentleman, and I always adored him.

Living with Barbara, hanging around with a social set that was a generation older, I was very consciously styling myself after an earlier era and in a sense swimming against the tide, which in that era consisted of Marlon Brando and Monty Clift. But my interest in associating with people my age was no more than nominal. I wanted to see the great stars I had watched at the movies up close. I wanted to learn their secrets; I wanted to learn how they did what they did.

One day in New York I walked into "21" with Gary Cooper and Clark Gable. The restaurant . . . stopped! It was like a freeze-frame in a movie. Diners froze in midbite, waiters froze in the midst of waiting. It was as potent a demonstration of the power of great stars as anything I've ever seen.

Clark Gable always liked me because I had caddied for him, and I had been shooting with Gary Cooper and knew his family quite well. I idolized Clark and watched every move he made; Gary I admired for being such a terrific actor, such a wonderful man.

In many ways they were alike, but in other ways they were different. Gable had been born poor, while Cooper was a judge's son from Montana who never dressed in anything but Brooks Brothers. Both of them, however, had a way that suggested they came from the earth. Gable loved to hunt, loved to fish, loved automobiles and beautiful women. So did Coop, but offscreen he always gave the impression of being terribly chic.

Gable's personality was closer to what he played than Cooper's was, but they both read, were interested in what was going on, and didn't hover around Hollywood. Neither of these men was sitting in his dressing room worrying about his next picture or who was up for what part. They got out of town. Coop would go to Sun Valley with Hemingway, while Clark liked his duck blinds and skeet shooting.

Beneath their likes and dislikes, they were alike in their tremendous craft. They had a way of taking the material that was written for them, much of which was very slight, and making something out of it because of the depth of their behavior. They took the material and filtered it through their own personalities. Because they were their own men and weren't trying to be someone else, the strength of their own character was bestowed on the characters they played. They didn't have neuroses, or if they did, they didn't inflict their neuroses on the audience.

That craft didn't come easily, and the self-confidence they projected was not something they were born with. I watched Coop work in a western he did for Fox called *Garden of Evil*.

He put himself under tremendous stress when he worked; during a take his knuckles were white. But he concealed that stress magnificently; a lot of the time it looked like he wasn't really doing any acting at all. Now, here was an actor acting, and you couldn't see him acting. That is hard to do, the highest achievement in the business, and Coop never got enough credit for his ability.

Every actor's goal is to make it look like it's the first time he's ever done that scene—to make it look fresh. These men were masters of that. You were never aware of Gary Cooper acting, but he could move you to tears. As an actor, and as a man, I admired him without reservation.

Making friends with so many older actors gave me an invaluable tutorial in how to handle the paraphernalia of the business. Take, for instance, Hedda Hopper and Louella Parsons, the two women who invented and defined the trade of gossip columnists. They were both tricky, and you had to know how to play them. Moreover, although they had been around for years—Louella had started in the silent days!—they were still important because they were so widely syndicated: Louella through the Hearst syndicate, and Hedda through the *Los Angeles Times* syndicate.

You had to pay court to Hedda and Louella; if I had an interview with Hedda, for instance, I went to her house. I would go to the racetrack with Louella all the time, but you quickly learned that either of them could turn on you. One time Hedda got upset at me over something, and it was thought necessary that I come back from Catalina and go directly to her house to get things straightened out.

Years later, when I went to Europe for four or five years and then came back, Louella was very pissed off and called me an expatriate, which was a dirty word in her vocabulary. It was as if by going to Europe I had been disloyal to Hollywood and, more importantly, to her.

As my star continued to rise at Fox, I came to realize that the relationship between an actor and a studio was complex, and not always in the actor's best interests. After *Titanic*, I was making a movie for Robert D. Webb called *Beneath the 12-Mile Reef,* when my costar, Terry Moore, suddenly realized she was pregnant. The father was Howard Hughes. She got very weepy and told me about the situation. Obviously, she told a few other people as well, because the studio blindsided both of us by releasing a story that we were engaged! They never called, they never told me they were going to do this, it just appeared in the papers.

I was livid; for one thing, I was very involved with Barbara and called her from Tarpon Springs every night, while Terry was calling Hughes every night. Terry was also a much younger woman, and Barbara was—how to put this delicately?—not pleased about that. Beyond that, the studio was trying to railroad Terry and me into a marriage for its own convenience. The studio evidently thought that I was terribly suggestible, I would succumb to the pressure, and the resulting marriage would be great for the movie, great for my career, and, not coincidentally, great for the studio.

It was at that point that I realized the true nature of the transaction between an actor and a movie studio. Fox was very interested in me in terms of generating publicity for a movie or a series of movies. The studio wanted to create momentum for me as an actor, as a personality, but it had a very limited interest in what was best for me as a human being. I was looking for a home, and the studio was looking for a saleable commodity.

It was a difficult but necessary lesson, and I'm glad I learned it early.

So everybody was in the loop but Terry and me. She was in tears not only about being pregnant but because she was being pressured to marry somebody she didn't love. And I started getting congratulatory telegrams from people about my impending marriage!

There was nothing to do but be blunt. I told Harry Brand there was no chance of my marrying Terry, not then, not ever. Fox never actually retracted the stories so much as let them dry up.

Being part of events like this made me realize that there is no more brutal, front-runner's business in the world. The pressures can be staggering. I remember being on the set of *Love Is a Many Splendored Thing* and watching Jennifer Jones work. I noticed the hem of her skirt vibrating. I looked down and saw that her knees were quivering like aspen leaves. She was absolutely terrified! Over on the side, behind the big lights, I could see a pair of shoes that belonged to her husband, the great producer David O. Selznick. He was hovering, making sure that his Jennifer was all right. But it was clear that Jennifer wasn't all right, and never would be. As experiences like these began to accumulate, I realized that it was mandatory to have some kind of meaningful life outside the movie business.

So the marriage to Terry Moore didn't happen. For that matter, neither did the baby.

Other than that, *Beneath the 12-Mile Reef* was a very positive experience. I came to admire my costar, Gilbert Roland, tremendously. He had come across the Mexican border when he was a boy, accompanied only by a friend named Polo. He began in the business as an extra for $2 a day and a box lunch. He told me that in the mid-1920s he and another young extra named Clark Gable used to stand outside Musso & Frank's restaurant on Hollywood Boulevard, watching the swells eat great food and dreaming of the day when they'd be able to do the same thing.

The dream came true for Gil, just as it was coming true for me, which explains why I felt such an affinity with him. The dream came true for his brother too, who went by the name of Chico Day. Chico followed his brother to Hollywood and became probably the most respected unit manager and assistant director in the movies. He even worked for Cecil B. DeMille on the 1956 version of *The Ten Commandments,* one of the most demanding jobs ever for one of the most demanding directors ever.

Gil began his rise out of the extras ranks when he became the costar and lover of the silent screen star Norma Talmadge and broke up her marriage to producer Joe Schenck. A few years after that he married Constance Bennett. Gil was good in silent pictures as a dashing lover—he played Armand opposite Talmadge's Camille—but his accent limited him in talkies. Nevertheless, his performances in *The Bullfighter and the Lady* and *The Bad and the Beautiful* were quite good.

I admired the fact that he maintained—and for nearly sixty years: his last movie was *Barbarosa,* in 1982! As a man, he had immense dignity and showed great loyalty to his friends. He was close with Antonio Moreno practically all their lives. If Gilbert Roland was your friend, you had a man you could count on, in any situation.

*Beneath the 12-Mile Reef* grossed $4 million—a very big hit. Harry Brand's publicity department claimed that I was getting more fan mail than Marilyn Monroe, although I'm not sure I believe that. I do know that during one month in 1953 I was on seven different magazine covers. My agent negotiated a new contract that bumped my salary from $350 a week to $1,250 a week.

I'm not going to pretend that there were an awful lot of negatives attached to being a young star in Hollywood. The perks are just what you might imagine them to be: every reporter wants to talk to you, and every girl wants you, not that I could indulge. Because of Barbara, I was off-limits to the girls. During the four years we were together, I had a couple of one-night stands on location but was otherwise loyal.

When you're hot, the good times never really stop coming. Because of my friendship with Leo Durocher, I even got to work out with the New York Giants. Sal "The Barber" Maglie offered to pitch to me. Durocher took me aside and said, "Don't move. Whatever you do, just don't move." It was a good thing he told me that, because Maglie's pitches were something else. Initially, the ball came right at your head, so the instinct was to duck down. The problem was that at the last second the pitch would dive down and away and catch the corner for a strike. If you ducked, the ball would nail you on the skull. I can assure you that standing in the box against him took courage because he was authentically scary—the equivalent of Bob Gibson or Roger Clemens in a later era.

One of the negatives that occurs to every actor is miscasting, which finally came to roost on my doorstep when Darryl cast me in the title role of *Prince Valiant,* an adaptation of Hal Foster's beautifully drawn comic strip that I had loved as a child. During the production, I was happy to be working for director Henry Hathaway; I thought the picture was good, and I loved the romance of the subject matter. I was working with James Mason, another one of my favorite actors, and I thought I was sensational. I had no idea it would become for me what "Yonda lies the castle of my fadduh" was for Tony Curtis.

If I'd been paying a little more attention, I would have

known something was wrong. Mainly, it was the wig. One day Dean Martin visited the set and spent ten minutes talking to me before he realized I wasn't Jane Wyman. Then I sat in a screening with the guys in the studio doing impersonations of the Singing Sword, not to mention me as Prince Valiant. And then I had to listen to jokes about the wig, which I now think made me look more like Louise Brooks than Jane Wyman. And I got upset about the ridicule, so much so that I still have a block about that movie.

But life teaches you many things, and one of them is that something good can come out of the worst experiences. I got a couple of lifelong friends out of *Prince Valiant* (Janet Leigh and the great cameraman Lucien Ballard), and I also got to know Sterling Hayden, who was so much more interesting as a man than, with a couple of exceptions (*The Asphalt Jungle, The Killing, Dr. Strangelove*), he was on screen. Sterling was a purist about life, with an interesting political point of view that was very much on the left. He had originally wanted to be a carpenter, and he was one of those rare guys in the movie business who genuinely didn't give a shit about the movie business.

Sterling was exceedingly well read—his tortured autobiography, *Wanderer,* should be required reading—and he was without question one of the most accomplished sailors I've ever seen in my life. I saw him take his twin-masted schooner and land it single-handedly at a dock in Santa Monica. He had a feather-light touch at the helm. On a boat, he was the artist he always wanted to be.

Another person I got to know well and to admire about this time was Claire Trevor. I had gone to school with her sons, Peter and Donald, but I really got to know Claire and her husband, Milton Bren, through our mutual regard for boats. Milton had begun as an agent and become very successful in real estate and home building. Because of the fortune Milton made, Claire was able to back out of the movie business and only worked when she wanted to.

Claire was very much her own woman, and I came to admire her honesty and directness. She was a straightforward, creative human being who became a very good painter. She was also terribly underrated as an actress, as anybody who has seen her in John Ford's *Stagecoach* or John Huston's *Key Largo* can attest. Neither part was original—a whore with a heart of gold and a well-meaning but weak alcoholic chanteuse—but she gave each of these women a soul. No actress alive, not even Barbara Stanwyck, could have played those parts any better than Claire did. She was able to tend her career while having a very happy marriage to Milton, and she also had the complete respect of everybody in show business.

My realization about what Fox actually wanted from me, as well as the chance to get to know well-rounded people like Sterling and Claire, showed me how important it was to have a life outside of show business. It was a concept that would take another decade or so to ripen in my head, but I was beginning to realize that the most important parts of life didn't take place on a soundstage.

# SIX

# "THE SCENE, THAT ONE MOMENT, AND NOTHING ELSE."

A scene from *Broken Lance* with Hugh O'Brien, Spencer Tracy, Earl Holliman, and Richard Widmark. (*BROKEN LANCE* © 1954 TWENTIETH CENTURY FOX. ALL RIGHTS RESERVED.)

B eneath the 12-Mile Reef won me *Photoplay* magazine's "Most Promising Newcomer" award, which led to one of the most crucial relationships in my life.

I respected Spencer Tracy before I knew him, and not just because he was a great actor. One of the many places I had gone to school was the Hollywood Military Academy. Down the street from the Academy was a school called Town and Country, where John and Susie, Spence's kids, were enrolled. John Tracy was born profoundly deaf, and with Spence's financial backing, his wife Louise founded the John Tracy Clinic to help other children with the same malady.

Louise Tracy was a truly remarkable woman whose accomplishments and strength of character should be more widely appreciated. It was largely because of her efforts that the phrase "deaf and dumb" was gradually banished from the language. There's no such thing as "deaf and dumb," and Louise was one of the first to know it. The Tracy Clinic has done fantastic work for the deaf for decades now; when I was single, I made the Tracy Clinic my heir, and I'm proud to say that I serve on the board of directors of the Tracy Clinic to this day.

I first saw Spence when I was a kid. He was playing polo at the Riviera Polo Field, directly across from where I lived for more than twenty years in Brentwood. Spence had been hit by a ball and was bleeding, so they stopped the game to patch him up.

Years later, when I won the *Photoplay* award, he was there accepting an award as well. I went over and introduced myself. "I saw your picture," he said, referring to *Beneath the 12-Mile Reef.* On the basis of that, he okayed me to play his son in a big western Fox was planning called *Broken Lance*. I thanked him and he said, "Ah, it's nothing."

The first day we worked together on *Broken Lance,* we were to ride into the shot together. My line was, "We better ride down there, Pa." When I said the line, he broke character and said, "I couldn't hear that." So I said, "Boy, that's something, when I underplay you." So we rode in and did it again, and the second take was a print.

A few hours later, it was lunch, and I was going by his trailer. "Come here a second," he called out to me. I trooped inside, and he said, "Shut the door." He then proceeded to ream me out.

"You don't imagine that you can underplay me, do you? What are you even thinking about things like that for? Are you thinking at all? You shouldn't be thinking about any of that, you should be thinking about playing the scene. Not about whether you're underplaying, overplaying, or anything else. Concentrate on what you're going to do! *The scene, that one moment, and nothing else.* Don't learn the tricks of the trade. Learn the trade!"

"But I was only kidding. . . ."

"Don't kid about it. Ever! Now get your ass out of here."

Jesus! I realize he had no patience for a young actor's bullshit, but he really beat me up. I was very shaken, but sometime after that he came up and said, "How are you doing now?" He put his arm around me, and at that moment I realized he liked me a lot. We became very close for the rest of the picture, as well as on *The Mountain*—where he requested me as his costar—and for the rest of his life.

As an actor, Spence didn't analyze. He didn't worry about where it comes from and where it goes. He never got in his own way. He would do only one or two takes, not because he was lazy, but because he felt they were always the best. His attitude

was: block it, rehearse it, do it, move on. He possessed simplicity, the most valuable thing an artist can have and the hardest
thing to achieve.

Once, I had to hit him in a scene, and he told me not to
pull it. "Be sure and really hit me," he said. "It never works if
you pull it." And that's what acting with him was like. He was
completely alive, and he never faked it, never pulled it. He had
an absolute authenticity of emotion that transcended things
like technique or acting styles.

He was a wonderful, wonderful man, and to have him put
his arm around me both actually and symbolically, to care for
me and be interested in me, was a transformative experience.
Spence became more than my friend and mentor; he inspired
me and, once again, gave me a sense of self-esteem. Because this
great actor and great man touched my life, I finally felt that I
had a father in more than a biological sense.

Broken Lance had a very fine cast. Besides Spence, there was
Richard Widmark, E. G. Marshall, Katy Jurado, Hugh
O'Brien, Earl Holliman, and Jean Peters. It also had a good
script by Philip Yordan that was ostensibly based on an old Fox
movie called *House of Strangers,* which had starred Edward G.
Robinson and Richard Conte. Our picture was a lot better. For
one thing, it had more content. I played Joe Devereaux, the
half-breed son of Matt Devereaux (Spence) and his Comanche
wife (Katy Jurado). The theme of race prejudice—Devereaux's
three sons from his first marriage hate his second wife and his
mixed-breed son—was added to the nominal western plot of an
old-guard pioneer fighting against the tide of civilization. Yordan also was adding in a touch of *King Lear,* although with
sons instead of daughters—not that a lot of people noticed.

I felt an attraction to Jean Peters, but nothing happened

because I was with Barbara. Later, when Barbara and I broke up, I developed what I can only call a crush on Jean. We never had an affair, because she was already interested in Howard Hughes. Actually, Hughes was passionately interested in her, and Jean . . . well, Jean acquiesced to his passion.

If Jean wasn't working, she had to stick close to her dressing room or hotel room just in case he telephoned. Hughes was the reason Jean retired from the movies in 1957, but Hughes wasn't the reason she and I didn't get together. That was strictly because of Jean Peters, who was not one of those ladies who hopped from bed to bed. She was a loyal woman. That meant that we were friends and had fun together, but it never went beyond that. Unfortunately.

*Broken Lance* was another hit, as it deserved to be. The director, Edward Dmytryk, gave *Broken Lance* mythic overtones it was strong enough to support. It's a film I remain proud of.

Fox had me alternating between A pictures and B pictures at this point. Despite my feelings about *Prince Valiant,* it was a hit, as was *Broken Lance.* In the spring of 1954, *Photoplay* named me the "Fastest Rising Star of the Year." I was in good company— Marilyn Monroe and Alan Ladd won the established star category.

The good times kept coming. That summer of 1954, *Life* magazine ran a story entitled "The Stronger Sex" that ran down the prospects of the next generation of leading men who were supposed to take over from Gable, Cooper, and Stewart. There were three young actors called "the Big Three for Bobbysoxers": Rock Hudson, Tony Curtis, and yours truly. The photographer got us all to pose on a ladder, struggling for a higher rung against each other. Ranked on the level beneath Rock, Tony, and me were John Erickson, Steve Forrest, Tab Hunter, and Robert Francis.

From two lavish pictures, each with an A-list director, I

went into *White Feather,* with Robert D. Webb as director and Debra Paget and Jeffrey Hunter as costars. It was a variation on *Broken Arrow,* with me as a government agent trying to convince the Indians to move onto the reservation. Bob Webb was Henry King's second-unit director, a good man and a good sailor, but he didn't get a lot of opportunities. The studio clearly didn't regard him as a peer of Henry Hathaway or Eddie Dmytryk.

Then came a loan-out to United Artists for *A Kiss Before Dying,* back to Fox for *Between Heaven and Hell,* and another loan-out, to Paramount for *The Mountain.*

*A Kiss Before Dying* has become a cult film over the years, and it erased a lot of the jokes about *Prince Valiant.* I played a lower-middle-class college student with a clinging mother (Mary Astor). He's determined to get into society, even if it means killing anybody who gets in his way, including his pregnant girlfriend. It was sort of *An American Tragedy* recast as a thriller. (When Alain Delon later played a totally emotionless killer in René Clément's *Purple Noon,* he would be compared to me, which was immensely flattering.) In Ira Levin's original novel, the actual murders take place offstage, as it were, but the movie's high point is my pushing a pregnant Joanne Woodward off the top of a building with a complete lack of emotion. We shot that scene in Tucson, and at the time that building was the tallest structure in Arizona.

It's an interesting character, because the audience understands his motivation but not his thought processes. He doesn't have any dialogue explaining himself, which is a technical problem for an actor. I saw him as a social climber with something askew in his head. My primary problem was to keep the charm level up so that the other characters would never guess I was a killer, and being charming while killing people presents certain problems. It wasn't a terribly pleasant shoot, because the location was so obscenely hot; the ending, where the truck goes over the side and I get killed, was shot in Globe, Arizona, in 120-degree heat.

Gerd Oswald directed *A Kiss Before Dying*. He was a first-rate talent who never got the credit he deserved and was locked into low-budget pictures for all of his career. His father was Richard Oswald, a very innovative director in Germany around the time of World War I. Gerd was European in the best sense—very much into textures, backlighting, and backstory. He also directed me in a television version of *The Ox-Bow Incident* that was a hell of a piece of work and didn't need to make any apologies to Bill Wellman's original film. Gerd loved making pictures, and whether it was a theatrical or TV film mattered less to him than having it be something of quality, something he could sink his teeth into.

I enjoyed making *A Kiss Before Dying,* and I think it's a good film, but for me the most exciting thing about that movie was doing the interiors at the old Selznick studio. Before Selznick had it, it was the DeMille lot, and it had been built for Thomas Ince, but as far as I was concerned, this was where *Gone with the Wind,* the original *A Star Is Born, Notorious,* and all the great Selznick movies had been shot. Sue Moir, my girlfriend at the time, and I would walk around the place at night. It was just like the scene in *Sunset Boulevard* where William Holden and Nancy Olson take a walk around the back lot at Paramount. For me, the place was still alive with the ghosts of the great stars who had worked there.

*A Kiss Before Dying* was done on loan-out to United Artists, and that was a good thing, because the pictures I was making at Fox were beginning to suffer. The reason was simple: Darryl was having a beaut of a midlife crisis and pulling back from the studio. This came to a head in 1956, when he left Hollywood, set up an independent operation in Paris, indulged himself with a series of exotically beautiful mistresses, and made a series of terrible flops for Fox (*Roots of Heaven, Crack in the Mirror*) that would be broken only by *The Longest Day*.

When Darryl was running the studio, I did what he told me to do. I admired him, I trusted him absolutely, and I also felt great loyalty to him. If he wanted me to be in a movie and I didn't like the script, I found a way to like the script.

But when Darryl left the studio, Buddy Adler took over. Buddy was a gentleman, and I liked him, but I didn't think his judgment was the equivalent of Darryl's, either for me or for the studio in general. Fox was having trouble, as all the studios were at that point; TV had sliced away a lot of the audience for movies, and everybody was having trouble adjusting. I can't complain about my bad fortune; Fox wasn't taking care of other people any better than they were taking care of me.

Ty Power left Fox to freelance and did very well, thank you, until he died so terribly young. I genuinely believe that the best years of Ty's career were ahead of him. Not only was he one of the kindest men in show business, always helpful and friendly to young actors, who were, after all, being developed as younger versions of him—but he was also terribly ambitious and wanted to be the best actor he could be. But, with very few exceptions, such as *Nightmare Alley,* his good looks prevented him from being taken seriously. He only got a chance to exercise his serious ambitions on the stage, where he always did serious plays such as *The Dark Is Light Enough* and *John Brown's Body*. Unfortunately, stage work vanishes, and Ty is remembered for his movies, which captured only a portion of his gift.

*Between Heaven and Hell* was a goulash about World War II with Terry Moore, Broderick Crawford, and Buddy Ebsen. Not good.

And then Spencer Tracy came to my rescue with *The Mountain*. It's a story about two brothers struggling to get to the site

The movies had me in their clutches by the time I was five. (COURTESY OF THE AUTHOR)

*(Above)* My father, young Robert Wagner, in northern Michigan, where we experienced some of our best times. (COURTESY OF THE AUTHOR)

*(Right)* My mother, Hazel Boe "Chatty" Wagner, at her most beautiful, and most pensive. (COURTESY OF THE AUTHOR)

*(Above)* Jill's title for this photo is "He married them all!" The ballet class was in session from 1948 to 1950. Natalie is on the far left, next to the ballet master; on the far right is Stefanie Powers. Next to Stefanie is Jill St. John. (COURTESY OF THE AUTHOR)

*(Left)* The greatest star of his generation, and one of the finest men you'd ever want to meet. The inscription reads: "To R.J., who taught me how to putt a decent golf ball—thereby saving me unknown $. Clark." (COURTESY OF THE AUTHOR)

*(Right)* Two bulwarks of my life; on the left is my sister, Mary Lou; on the right is my best friend, Bill Storke. (COURTESY OF THE AUTHOR)

*(Below)* In *The Halls of Montezuma,* with Richard Widmark, the first movie in which I got billing. The inscription reads: "For Bob. Pansy Baker, always on the wireless. Yours, Dick." "Pansy Baker" was the radio call sign we used in the film, as well as the way we referred to each other for the rest of Dick's life. (*THE HALLS OF MONTEZUMA* © 1951 TWENTIETH CENTURY FOX. ALL RIGHTS RESERVED.)

*(Left)* With Dan Dailey, in John Ford's *What Price Glory,* as close to a fraternity hazing as I ever got.

*(Below)* My love, Barbara Stanwyck, Clifton Webb, and myself at a dinner party at Jean Negulesco's house, about 1952. (COURTESY OF THE AUTHOR)

(*Above*) My parents were always supportive of me. (© twentieth century fox. all rights reserved.)

(*Right*) My mother and me taking a "stroll" on a photo shoot. (© twentieth century fox. all rights reserved.)

*(Left)* My first boat, on which Natalie and I had many dates, at Balboa. (COURTESY OF THE AUTHOR)

*(Below)* Young studs of Hollywood, as photographed for *Life* magazine: Rock Hudson, Tony Curtis, and myself. (PHOTO BY SHARLAND/TIME LIFE PICTURES/GETTY IMAGES)

*(Left)* With Janet Leigh in *Prince Valiant.* Don't I look fetching? (PRINCE VALIANT © 1954 TWENTIETH CENTURY FOX. ALL RIGHTS RESERVED.)

*(Below)* On the set of *The Mountain* in Chamonix in the French Alps, with Spencer Tracy and Anna Kashfi, later Mrs. Marlon Brando. (COURTESY OF PARAMOUNT PICTURES)

of a plane crash in the Alps—the older brother to save people, the younger one to pillage the crash. The critics would say that Spence looked too old to play my brother, or that I looked too young to play his. I didn't care. I would have played any part, in any script, for Spence. Another selling point was that the location work would be done in the French Alps—my first trip to Europe!

Spence and I flew to Europe together. Although Spence had gotten heavy in middle age, he still had considerable physical stamina. We got to France two weeks before we started shooting, and we had to get acclimated to the heights we would be working at. On our first full day there, he went on a three-mile hike; on the second day he upped it to eight miles, and on the third day he walked for ten miles.

Spence's alcoholism was a Hollywood urban legend even then, but I can truthfully say that I saw him drunk only once. But that one time gave me an insight into his very complicated character.

We were on location for *The Mountain,* and we were in a cable car, heading up to a mountaintop location at Chamonix, near Mont Blanc in the French Alps, where the weather changes constantly. It was a single cable, from top to bottom, and it was a brand-new installation. We were about halfway up when the car suddenly detached from the cable. The car was not moving, just perilously hanging from the protective iron covering over the wheel mechanism on the car, and we were swinging wildly in the wind. It was at that point that the front window of the cable car shattered, and I swear I thought we were about to drop thousands of feet to the ground.

I had been anxious about going up in this thing anyway, which was why Spence was in the car; he had gone up to reassure me that it would be okay, and now we were hanging there with our lives flashing in front of our eyes. They finally sent a work car down, and they somehow got our car back on the cable, and we continued up the mountain. It was the most physically frightening experience I've ever had in my life.

Now, what people don't understand about the movie business is that there are times when it's like working in a coal mine. It pays better, but it's still labor. Despite our near-death experience, we had a movie to make, so we put in a full day's work. The location on the mountain was very difficult work, dangerous for the crew as well as the actors.

While Eddie Dmytryk and I and the crew were working, Spence got back in that cable car and went down. When I returned to the hotel after shooting was done, he was in the bar, and he was completely drunk—gone! It was startling, because he had become an entirely different person. The bartender made some remark, or Spence thought he did, and Spence went after him. I held Spence back, then he picked up a glass and heaved it at the bartender. I put up my hand to stop the glass, but it shattered and sliced my hand very badly. Frank Westmore, my makeup man and dear friend, played doctor and stitched it up. It was a very ugly, violent scene, complete with blood on the floor—mine.

The next day Spence had no memory of any of it. He didn't know he got into a fight with the bartender, and he didn't know my hand had been slashed open by the glass that he'd thrown. "Jekyll and Hyde" is a conventional metaphor, but in this case it was absolutely true. Sober, Spence was Dr. Jekyll and a very dear man, but alcohol turned him into Mr. Hyde, complete with a hair-trigger temper. The strange thing is that on some level Spence was blocked from fully acknowledging his dual nature; when he had played *Dr. Jekyll and Mr. Hyde*, it was one of his least successful performances because he couldn't quite access Mr. Hyde—he was acting the character rather than being it. He had to be drunk before he could let the animal loose.

That one instance aside, Spence was always a wonderfully kind and generous man. I would name my first daughter after Kate Hepburn, and I was privileged to be a part of their relationship. She gave Katie two dolls that she had made, one of herself and one of Spence as he looked in *The Old Man and the Sea*. They also gave her a crib. I brought the baby to see them, and they just glowed as they looked at her.

Spence and Kate were like an old married couple in that they had a wonderful humor with each other; they played to each other. You could feel the affection and love they had. And she was so wonderful with him; they had a way of deferring to each other, but ultimately she would defer to him. She would say that he was like a big bear that would put his paw out and slap her down, but gently. Spence was the only person in her life who could tell her she was full of shit, and she loved that about him.

I realize now that the people I was drawn to in the movie business were all older. I respected them enormously because of their accomplishments, but it was more than that. I wanted their secrets.

Was I looking for surrogate fathers?

Absolutely.

I see a lot of my life as a search for the closeness and intimacy of family. Making movies gives you some of that feeling. (Barbara Stanwyck was the same way. Maybe that's why we were so close.) At the beginning of a picture, everyone is so close. People become fast friends and swear undying loyalty. Sometimes they fall into bed. And then, eight or ten weeks later, it's "Where did everybody go?" It goes from intensity to . . . nothing. It's probably because of my particular emotional chemistry that I remember the offstage part, the relationships, more than I do the films. I remember the times we had.

# SEVEN

# "SWEET JESUS! IT WAS HOWARD HUGHES."

At a premiere with Tony Curtis, Janet Leigh, and Jean Peters, just before Howard Hughes spirited Jean away. (COURTESY OF THE AUTHOR)

Some people who have gone through a quick rise to stardom report feeling a loss of control, but I never felt that. I was doing exactly what I wanted to do.

It's possible that I had too much of an allegiance to the trappings of my stardom. Once, around this time, I was in a convertible with Watson Webb and Rory Calhoun. I was studiously going through a pile of my fan mail when Rory grabbed it and heaved it up and out of the car. It scattered through the air like confetti, and Rory thought my reaction was the funniest thing he'd ever seen.

Watson Webb was a descendant of two great fortunes. His father, James Watson Webb Sr., was a descendant of Cornelius Vanderbilt. His mother was the daughter of the founder of the American Sugar Refining Company. After Watson graduated from Yale in 1938, he decided to avoid going into either of the family businesses. Instead, he went to Hollywood, where he became one of Zanuck's most trusted film editors. He was very comfortable editing film in the conventional style of the time, but he was also adept with much edgier, more violent movies. Among the pictures Watson cut were *The Dark Corner, Kiss of Death, Broken Arrow, A Letter to Three Wives,* and *The Razor's Edge.* The last picture he edited had been *With a Song in My Heart,* after which he quit Fox and dabbled— in directing, in investing, in philanthropy, in being a great friend.

Watson had a house in Brentwood, and he also had a place at Lake Arrowhead that he had bought from Jules Stein, the founder of the Music Corporation of America—MCA. Watson was a total blue-blooded gentleman. Everybody assumed he was gay, but he was so discreet that there was no real way of telling, which was precisely the way he wanted it. Years later, when he stepped up and lent me a hand at a desperate time, he would put me forever in his debt.

I think I began to kick in as a professional about the time of *Broken Lance*. When I started at Fox, I had been under the illusion that you became an actor by practice. It was, I thought, like learning to play tennis or golf: you went to the pros and let them teach you.

It took me a while to realize that I had to learn to use myself to get where I needed to go. The main thing I had to learn was to get out of my own way. "How do you do it?" I had asked Spence, but it doesn't happen that way. I was twenty-one years old when I worked with Cagney and Ford, and it was very hard to get the fact that I was working with Cagney and Ford out of my head. I was still overwhelmed by the reality of the filmmaking process and hadn't yet learned to play the reality of the scene.

In other words, my primary problem as an actor was self-consciousness. The great trick of acting is to make it look easy, as if you're not acting at all. If the audience thinks to themselves, *Jesus, I could do that,* then you're succeeding. In line with that, the test of an actor is not whether he can cry, but whether he can make the audience cry.

For the most part, my social circle disdained "the Method," but I've always been in favor of whatever makes an actor comfortable in his skin and frees him up—something that helps get an actor where he needs to go. I went to the Actors Studio in New York, and I observed. I could see them looking at me and rolling their eyes. They thought I was an asshole—the pretty kid who had made *Prince Valiant* and been laughed at.

That just made me determined to be better. I didn't want to be a joke; I wanted to be real. There was a snobbery about some of the people who gravitated to the Method that I objected to. They loved to talk about acting, then talk some more, but I'm not sure acting should be talked about that much. You can learn a lot more by doing than by talking, and acting, after all, is doing. And by doing, you learn.

For instance, I watched Cary Grant working on *An Affair to Remember* for Leo McCarey. He came offstage after doing a scene and told me, "I learned something interesting today. I learned how to breathe in a scene."

Now, this is 1956, and Cary Grant was, well, Cary Grant; he'd been doing it with a matchless grace for nearly a quarter-century at that point, and he had just realized that a lot of times when you're acting you're unconsciously holding your breath waiting for your cue, and that's not a good thing.

Cary, of course, is the ultimate example of what I'm talking about. He had to work very hard to acquire the sense of ease that he displayed as an actor. The process by which Archie Leach of Bristol, England, became Cary Grant of Hollywood can't be broken down by endless conversation. Yet Cary wasn't just smooth; he was emotionally real and always present. Watch him in a scene and notice how focused he is, how intently he listens to the other actor. To acquire all that skill and to make it look easy is enormously hard.

The great thing about the studio system, of course, was that it was a classic apprenticeship system. I watched Gary Cooper and Cary work, and I always had this subliminal feeling that, if I worked hard enough, someday I'd be standing where they stood. But I never had a sense of entitlement, which a lot of young actors—and a lot of young people—do today.

After Barbara there were a lot of women, but the one who stands out was Elizabeth Taylor. I had met her at one of Roddy McDowall's parties before I was in the movie business, and like every other male animal around the world, I was crazy about her. People always talk about her spectacular beauty or her violet eyes, but emphasizing those features overlooks her emotional appeal, which I think is centered on her vulnerability. She is a wonderful woman in a very unusual way—great humanity and great sensuality are not commonly packaged together, but when they are, the whole world knows it.

Some beautiful women are passive in the bedroom. They're gorgeous, they know they're gorgeous, they know that you know they're gorgeous, and they don't feel the need to do anything above and beyond being gorgeous.

Elizabeth was not one of those women. Being with her was like sticking an eggbeater in your brain.

I loved her, and I think she loved me. But on the practical level, Elizabeth was not the woman I needed in my life. With Elizabeth, there was a great deal of maintenance. This is not a woman who gets up in the morning and fixes breakfast. By the time she comes downstairs for breakfast, it's time for dinner. She's not floating in the pool with you on a lazy Sunday afternoon, handing magazines back and forth. Elizabeth's life is built completely around Elizabeth, and she needs a man to service her life 24/7.

She also has the most spectacularly bad luck in terms of illness I've ever encountered, and it needs to be emphasized that Elizabeth is far from a hypochondriac. Just as there are people who are accident-prone, there are people who are illness-prone, and Elizabeth is certainly one of them. One time when I was visiting her, she was getting into a car and the man helping her slammed the door. It blew out her eardrum. Just thinking about Elizabeth's physical troubles is exhausting; I can't imagine what it must be like to have to live with them.

In any case, this was a period when I was enjoying my freedom. I first saw Anita Ekberg when she came to RKO as a starlet. This was long before Federico Fellini made her, Marcello Mastroianni, and the Trevi Fountain immortal in *La Dolce Vita*. I took one look at Anita and was reduced to the level of a hormonal schoolboy. Luckily, she responded to me the same way I responded to her. The fact that she had been staked out by Howard Hughes was irrelevant to me.

Anita and I were enjoying ourselves in an apartment in Westwood when there was a knock on the door. I looked out the window and . . . Sweet Jesus! . . . it was Howard Hughes. His truculent reputation preceded him; he was not a man you wanted to get into an argument with. I threw on my clothes and went out the back door, with Howard Hughes running after me. I remember very distinctly that I was running across the lawn when I kicked a sprinkler head, opened up a very nasty slash in my brand-new shoes, lost my balance, and tumbled ass over teakettle. I was not only young, I was nimble; I sprang up and kept running.

I would like to go on the record as saying that an afternoon with Anita Ekberg was worth the destruction, not just of a pair of shoes but of an entire wardrobe and probably a Mercedes-Benz showroom as well.

During the few months when I was hot and heavy with Anita, my mother noticed that she wasn't seeing me much. "What are you doing with your weekends?" she asked me out of the blue one day. My mind was a million miles away—probably on

Anita—and I blurted out something about playing tennis at the Bel-Air Hotel.

She gave me a strange, amused look and pointed out that the Bel-Air Hotel didn't have tennis courts.

Busted.

I got a copy of Frank Nugent's script for *The Searchers,* which John Ford was going to direct for Warner Bros. The part of Martin Pawley leaped out at me. It was a part I could play, and I knew it; had he hired me for *The Searchers,* Ford could have knocked me on my ass on a daily basis. I just loved that script; I had enough sense to know that it would make a wonderful movie, especially with Duke Wayne as Ethan Edwards and Ford directing. The greatness of that picture, its dramatic strength, was already evident on the page. I could see it, and I knew Ford's visual splendor would put it over the top.

You'll remember that Ford had called me "Boob" and treated me like a dog on *What Price Glory?* No, let me rephrase that. There are no conditions under which I would treat a dog as badly as John Ford treated me on that picture. Actually, Ford liked dogs a lot more than he liked actors. I knew all this, and I swallowed my pride and scheduled an appointment with Ford.

There's a certain reality of show business that the public doesn't understand: it's a business for whores, especially when it comes to actors. We have to put ourselves out there for those few good parts that come along, even if those parts are controlled by people we don't like, and who may not like us. But we put on our best clothes and smile and go out and try to sell ourselves. Not pleasant, but reality.

I took a deep breath and went to see Ford.

"You'd like to play the part, wouldn't you?" he said.

"Yes, Mr. Ford."

He didn't waste my time or his. "Well, you're not gonna play it. Jeff Hunter's going to play it."

I knew John Ford well enough to realize there was no way you were ever going to argue him out of a casting decision, or anything else. I thanked him for his time and got up to leave. I got to the door and Ford spoke up.

"Boob?"

"Yes, Mr. Ford?"

"You really want to play the part?"

"Very much, Mr. Ford."

"Well, you're still not going to!"

That was John Ford, and whether the actor in question was Duke Wayne, Jeff Hunter, or me, you learned to accept him for what he was: a great artist with a personality that could keep you up nights—for years.

One day near the end of 1956, Spencer Tracy took me over to Humphrey Bogart's house. I had known Bogie for years because of our shared passion for boats and the sea. Bogie was distinguished as an actor by an unusual combination of dramatic power and a light touch—he could suggest dramatic and character points gracefully, and he could bring humor to heavy material. Bogie called his boat the *Santana,* and she was a sleek thing of beauty—a yawl. On board the *Santana,* Bogie was pure—not an actor on a boat, but a sailor on his boat.

Everybody in Hollywood knew that Bogie was dying, shrinking day by day from cancer. Every afternoon he would be bundled into a dumbwaiter and brought down to the first floor of the house for an hour or two of conversation with his friends, after which he would be bundled back into the dumbwaiter and return to bed.

It was an amazing experience—a salon held by a dying man.

Bogie must have been in terrible pain, but he never let it show. The mood was light and mostly humorous. The conversation was about boats, pictures, and people—who was doing what. Even dying, Bogie had humor, and he gave me a touch of the needle. He asked Spence, "What the hell are you doing giving this kid costar billing?"

I took it as a straight line. "Listen," I said, "when we work together, I'll be happy to give you costar billing." He laughed.

When he died in January 1957, there was no coffin, no body at the funeral. The centerpiece was simply a model of the *Santana*. People have always paid tribute to Bogie's professionalism, the way he was a stickler about his work—one of the traits he shared with Spence. But he was also a nicer man than he liked to let on. And that model of the *Santana* showed that there was something else he took almost as much pride in as his acting: being a good sailor.

# EIGHT

# "AND THEN I MET NATALIE."

At the train station in Los Angeles, on our way to being married in Arizona.
(COURTESY OF THE AUTHOR)

These were years in which I didn't have a steady girlfriend, so I named my new boat *My Lady* with more than a touch of irony. I didn't have a steady lady, I had a boat. *My Lady* was a perfect bachelor's boat, a twenty-six-foot Chris Craft. Ray Kellogg, the head of special effects at Fox, helped me take her out for a shakedown cruise. I docked her in Newport, near Claire Trevor's boat. I was happy in my career, and I was happy aboard *My Lady*. I thought I had everything I wanted.

And then I met Natalie.

The first time Natalie Wood saw me, I didn't see her, or at least I don't remember seeing her. It was the spring of 1949, at Twentieth Century Fox, and Natalie was making *Father Was a Fullback,* with Fred MacMurray.

As she told the story, we passed each other in a studio hallway. We didn't speak, but she always said I smiled at her. As we passed, she turned around and watched me go by, but I didn't turn around. I have to take her word for this episode, which she mythologized over the years, because I honestly don't remember it.

She was ten years old, I was eighteen, and she told her mother, who was walking with her down the hallway, that she had seen the man she was going to marry. And she also told the screenwriter Mary Loos, who was on the set of *Father Was a Fullback,* that she had just fallen in love with an incredibly handsome man, but she didn't know who he was.

As the years went by, I would occasionally see Natalie around town, at parties and at premieres, but she never seemed like she was particularly interested in me, let alone interested in marrying me. What I didn't know at the time was that she had retained Henry Willson as her agent simply because Henry had also been my agent, which was all she needed to know.

For the most part, we moved in entirely different social circles. While she was making *Rebel Without a Cause,* she was having an affair with Nicholas Ray and hanging around Jimmy Dean and Dennis Hopper, and I was with a much older crowd who generally regarded Nick and Jimmy as the barbarians at the gate.

We talked about that period a lot in later years. There was nearly a thirty-year age difference between her and Nick Ray, so the relationship was kept quiet, but I think she was looking for a father figure, and Nick was always happy to play the part of the all-knowing guru. Her family had been very opposed to her doing *Rebel;* they didn't understand the part, or the film, but Natalie had worked with Jimmy Dean in a General Electric Theater TV show right after he shot *East of Eden* but before it was released. She knew about his gifts, which were primarily those of brilliant inventiveness and unexpected power. They had bonded before they did *Rebel Without a Cause.*

Natalie sensed what a break *Rebel* could be for her. She always had a wonderful ability to recognize life-changing moments when they presented themselves. Besides that, she was desperate to get away from the girl-next-door parts that Jack Warner was putting her in, and she was equally desperate to get away from her family, who had viewed her as a meal ticket since she was a toddler, which oppressed her practically as well as emotionally.

So *Rebel* spoke to all sorts of needs that Natalie had—career as well as family. Not only that, but within the film itself was a recognition that the families we make for ourselves are often far more meaningful than the families we are born into, which was something that would also have appealed to Natalie at that point in her life. At that stage, all she wanted was to get away from her biological family, so Nick, Jimmy, and Dennis Hopper formed a new family for Natalie.

I met Jimmy Dean a couple of times; I especially remember having drinks with him one night at Patsy d'Amore's, but I can't claim any insight into his character. Natalie never specifically alluded to it, but my impression of him was that he was bisexual; certainly, that was the scuttlebutt around town. At that point, Jimmy was always charging around on a motorcycle with Pier Angeli. I had worked with her sister, Marisa Pavan, on *What Price Glory?*, but for the most part he and Natalie were with an entirely different group than I was.

After Natalie made such a breakthrough with *Rebel Without a Cause,* Jack Warner showed his complete lack of understanding of what he had by teaming Natalie with Tab Hunter for a couple of pictures. To say that they didn't strike any sparks was an understatement. By this time, Natalie was clearly maturing into something special. She had that same riveting, sexual quality that Ava Gardner or Elizabeth Taylor did, but in a smaller, subtler package—more of a gamine than an earth mother.

The first time I really remember talking to her was in June 1956, when we were both attending a fashion show at the Beverly Wilshire Hotel and we were asked to pose for a few photos together. Again, she was pleasant and quite beautiful, but she made no particular moves in my direction that let me know she had maintained a mad crush on me.

A month later, on July 20, I took a leap and invited Natalie to the premiere of *The Mountain*. What I didn't know at the time was that July 20 was her eighteenth birthday. I remember being unusually nervous before I picked her up. It was a big studio premiere, but that wasn't it; I was excited about taking Natalie out, and I was also anxious about what Spencer Tracy would think of her. I needn't have worried; he liked her very much.

At dinner afterward, we both sensed that things had changed. Time had altered the emotional dynamic, and we sparked to each other. I sent her flowers the next morning; then I called to tell her I had had a spectacularly good time. A little later, we went out again, this time for lunch, and she kept me waiting for three hours.

With anybody else, I would probably have left, but with Natalie . . . I waited. I think she was impressed by that, and by the fact that I wasn't angry. The next night we went out again, to *My Lady,* and this time the sparks flew upward. It was December 6, 1956, a date we would remember all our lives. In her journal, Natalie wrote, "Our first serious date."

I remember the instant I fell in love with her. Natalie had the most incredibly expressive brown eyes, dark and dancing and deep. One night on the boat, Natalie looked at me with love, her eyes lit by a Coleman lantern that was on top of the table. That was the moment that changed my life.

I was soon a part of Natalie's family, who proved to be some of the most clinically interesting people I've known. Natalie's mother was particularly bizarre. Her name was Maria, but everyone called her "Mud," which I think was Natalie's shortening of "Muddah," a comic version of "Mother."

I think Mud genuinely came to love me, but she had spun a terrible web of dependence around Natalie. Basically, Mud was afraid to let Natalie out of her sight, because Natalie was the bread-winner. It all began when Natalie was a child actress. Mud told her that a serial killer prowled movie theaters and stabbed young girls in the back. Result: Natalie didn't like to leave the house to go to movies when she was a child. Natalie also developed a genuine fear of flying, although she eventually learned to cope with it.

Mud didn't just tell Natalie these things as a means of controlling her; she was herself genuinely prey to irrational fears. For example, if a fire engine went by her house, Mud would rush over to see if Natalie was all right. That actually happened, and more than once. She was an interesting character, but more interesting at a distance. She was one of those people who always had to create tension. Everything was a drama. God, she was exhausting.

Mud wanted to control Natalie's money and control her parts. She wanted to control who could be at one of Natalie's parties, control who Natalie dated, control everything. For a long time she was a chaperone for Natalie, and a formidable one, always the first to announce, "Let's go home."

Around the time of *Rebel Without a Cause,* Mud finally relented and allowed Natalie out of the house by herself. But if Natalie went out on a date, Mud would look at her dress when she got home to see if it was wrinkled. And if Natalie didn't get a part, it wasn't because she was wrong for it, or hadn't tested well; it was the agent's fault, or the director's, or the producer's. Natalie lived in a cocoon, and the lives of the entire family revolved around her: Mud was the mother of Natalie Wood, Lana was the sister of Natalie Wood. Natalie struggled against these totally unhealthy relationships for most of her life.

For some reason, her mother wasn't threatened by me. From the beginning, Mud responded to me very positively, as did Nick, Natalie's father. But Nick was an alcoholic, and it was obvious that on the psychological level he had been cast off and didn't matter. That particular family was a total matriarchy—a Russian matriarchy.

Mud was a White Russian who had been born in southern Siberia in 1912 and came to America in November 1930. Her first marriage was already on the rocks by the time she arrived in California, but Nick Gurdin, whose real name was Nikolai

Zacharenko, was introduced to Maria by her first husband. Nick and Maria married in 1937, and Natalie was born in July 1938. Although Natalie believed Nick was her father, for all of her life Maria harbored a secret belief that Natalie was actually the result of a long-standing affair she had been having with a man named George Zepaloff.

Whether this was just another one of Mud's romantic fantasies or the truth is irrelevant, because Mud lived in her fantasies far more than she lived in reality. From her point of view, I think I was better than any of the alternatives that had presented themselves because I was the sort of man she had dreamed of for her daughter. I was successful, famous, presentable, well connected, and I didn't take any shit. I wasn't one of the guys Natalie had been running around with. I was legitimate.

So Mud was not averse to our relationship, although she was very averse to Natalie leaving her sphere of influence. When Natalie told her she wanted to move out, Mud said, "What's going to happen to us? Where are we going to go? How are we going to live?" The usual questions you'd get from somebody who'd been supported by her child since she was six years old.

Natalie had fallen in love with me, I think, but she wasn't sure, and there were the suspicions that had always been encouraged by Mud, who had always told her to be wary of anybody outside the family who tried to get close to her. There would be episodes when she'd pull back, or even test me. Natalie was a full-blooded Russian and could be very moody and inscrutable; her Russian moods could drive me up the wall. I noticed that rejection could trigger her moods, or a perceived betrayal—the suspicion of having been lied to, or of someone being devious in some way. The bright lamp would suddenly switch off, and she would become gloomy and interior.

One night after dinner she asked me to drop her off at the

Chateau Marmont so she could see Scott Marlowe, an actor she'd had a brief affair with. I didn't know that Marlowe was basically gay and not really a threat, but I was still furious that she'd make such a request—it was diva behavior, something that's never enticed me.

We didn't see each other for a while after that, but we had patched things up by March 1957, when I had to go to Japan to make *Stopover Tokyo*—or, as I prefer to call it, *Stopover Acting*. Just before I left, I gave her a gold charm bracelet with WOW, CHARLIE engraved on it. It was a line of Brando's from *On the Waterfront,* and we used to call each other "Charlie." Once I got to Japan, Natalie and I burned up the long-distance lines talking to each other, but that wasn't as easy then as it is now. It could take an hour or two to get a connection from Tokyo, so I spent a lot of time in my hotel room. One night I couldn't find her. I called her mother and asked her if she knew where Natalie was.

"I think she's with Nicky Hilton," she answered. "They went to Mexico." Nicky Hilton was Elizabeth Taylor's first husband and easily one of the sleaziest people in Hollywood. He was a handsome but extremely nasty piece of work, and he lived off his father's hotel business. I was just furious. I ripped the phone out of the wall and heaved it right through an open window. Outside, it was pouring rain.

I was sitting there fuming when, ten minutes later, there was a knock on the door. A very wet Japanese man with an umbrella was standing there holding my phone. It had hit his umbrella, he had picked it up and noticed the room number on the dial, and he had very kindly brought it back to me. Since Natalie was stepping out with Nicky Hilton, I consoled myself with Joan Collins.

*Stopover Tokyo* was the only movie directed by Richard Murphy, a good screenwriter. If you haven't seen it, don't trouble yourself. The only compensation turned out to be the location. Japan was a fascinating place to be so soon after the war, and Joan was lovely to spend time with, but the film itself was a lot more fun to make than it is to watch.

Once I got back from Japan, I was able to quash the Nicky Hilton thing, and Natalie and I got very serious very fast. We spent many days and nights on board *My Lady* in the Catalina isthmus, with our single, small Coleman lantern illuminating our faces as we barbecued steaks for dinner. The boat's table broke down into a double bunk, and overall *My Lady* was perfectly comfortable for two people, although too small for four. Not that we cared; when we were together, the presence of other people was superfluous. Natalie found that she was quite comfortable on board a boat, so *My Lady* became our designated getaway.

In August 1957, Natalie was going on location for *Marjorie Morningstar,* and I went with her. The company was shooting at Schroon Lake in the Adirondacks, and Natalie and I lived together for the three weeks they were on location. Warner Bros. obviously felt that publicity about our relationship wouldn't be helpful, because nothing leaked to the press. Mud was there at Schroon as well and served us breakfast in bed, which she probably didn't do with Nicky Hilton.

After *Marjorie Morningstar* was finished, Natalie and I began to have serious talks about our future. We both realized that every day we had to be apart was a day we were uncomfortable. Put simply, we wanted to be together. The only possible problem we could both agree we had was our conflicting careers. We agreed that we should never be separated for more than a couple of weeks, which meant that movie shoots and publicity tours would have to be carefully scheduled.

On December 6, one year after our first serious date, Natalie got a present for me, an ID bracelet. I took her to dinner at

Romanoff's, but I hadn't said anything about our anniversary, so I think she was worried that I had forgotten it.

I opened a bottle of champagne, poured two glasses, and handed one to Natalie. At that point, she noticed the diamond and pearl ring at the bottom of the glass. I told her to read what was engraved on it. MARRY ME, it said. She was totally surprised and immediately said, "Yes!" I ordered more champagne. At the bottom of her glass was a pair of pearl earrings. Another glass, and another charm for the WOW, CHARLIE bracelet. On the back of the charm was engraved TODAY WE'RE ONE YEAR OLD.

The next day Natalie wrote in her journal: " 'Two lonely stars with no place in the sun found their orbit—each other—and they were one.' I sent this to R on the anniversary of our first love. It also turned out to be the day that we were engaged to be married, and the start of our real life."

My father ran true to form. When I told him that I was leaning toward asking Natalie to marry me, he told me he didn't want me to get married, not to anybody. He wanted me to wait until I was at least thirty. My response was to mutter, "Fuck you!" under my breath and do what I wanted to do.

Natalie and I were married a few weeks after that dinner, on Saturday, December 28, 1957. She was nineteen, I was twenty-seven. Warner Bros. wanted to control the wedding because of Natalie; Fox wanted to control the wedding because of me. I realized that if we left it up to the people we worked for, we would be married at the Hollywood Bowl, with the Los Angeles Philharmonic serenading us with "The Wedding March." The hell with that.

So we snuck out of town and got married in Scottsdale, Arizona. The church was the Scottsdale Methodist Church. Barbara Gould was Natalie's maid of honor, and my father was my best man. (He liked her a great deal, and I confess that I still wanted his approval.) There were only about a dozen people in the church, among them Natalie's sister Lana, Mary Loos and her husband Richard Sale, my business manager Andy Maree and his wife Pru, and Nick Adams.

Natalie wore an ankle-length gown that was made of white lace and encrusted with hundreds of tiny seed pearls. Instead of a traditional veil, a mantilla of the finest lace covered her head. Natalie was my girl, and now she was my wife, so of course I was enchanted by her looks, but that day she surpassed herself. She was far beyond beautiful, she was exquisite, like a stunning portrait by Velázquez, except Velázquez never had a subject as beautiful as Natalie.

After the ceremony, we had a party at the Valley Ho resort and left. I had a train car pick us up and take us across the country to Chicago; then we changed trains to go to Florida. I had booked a place in Stuart, Florida, where we were going to go fishing. Well, Stuart was terrible, totally unromantic. We were there only a couple of nights; then we got on the train and went to New York, to the Sherry-Netherland.

On the way back, a fellow in Chicago told me we were being given a Corvette to drive back home. I showed up at the dealership, and the manager said he hadn't heard about the gift, but I could take the car. We're movie stars, right? Doesn't the world always open its arms for movie stars? It seemed like the most logical thing in the world.

So Natalie and I piled into the Corvette and drove across the country. The Corvette was gorgeous—metallic gray finish with red leather interior—but it paled next to Natalie. Our drive across country was intimate, enveloping, and great; radio stations would announce that Natalie Wood and Robert Wagner were on Highway 32 outside of Lubbock, and a half-hour later there would be dozens of cars tailing us.

Except for times like that, during long stretches of the drive it felt like we were the only people alive, which was very much the way we both wanted it. Unfortunately, I found out that the gift of the Corvette was a practical joke cooked up by a guy at Warner Bros. named Frank Casey. It wasn't a gift at all, and since I had put thousands of miles on the car, I ended up having to buy it from the dealership in Chicago, which struck me as a heavy joke.

After we got back to Los Angeles and began married life, we didn't exactly integrate our very different social circles. Natalie's friend Nick Adams hung around a little bit, but mostly the group Natalie had been hanging around with disappeared, and we started associating with Frank Sinatra and his circle and the rest of my friends. When it came to dogs, my other great love, Natalie had poodles, which are not my favorite breed, but because they were Natalie's they were just fine with me.

We got back to Los Angeles in time for Christmas and spent the holiday at my apartment on Durant Drive. At that time there was a wonderful jeweler out here named Ruser, from whom I had gotten the apartment. Ruser had a superb engraver named Al Lee, and that first Christmas I started to give Natalie jewelry—bracelets and charms with things engraved on them that were particular to us and wouldn't have as much meaning to anybody else. We never needed a specific holiday to lavish gifts on each other; a simple vacation would be as good a reason as any, or the anniversary of our first date.

I tended to give gifts that were small in size—I still love to give jewelry—but I found that Natalie liked to work large. She had a knack for fantastic gifts—she gave me a Jaguar XKE once, and another time it was a Mercedes coupe—and they were always complete surprises. We'd walk out of the house and there would be the car. "It's yours," she'd say.

From the beginning, Natalie made me spectacularly happy. It's so unusual to be in perfect sync with another human being, to have everything understood by both of you simultaneously and to feel no need to explain anything, but at this point in our lives that's what we had; it seemed like we even stepped on sidewalks at the same time.

I called her "Charlie," "Nate," or "Nat." Sometimes I called her "Bug." Mostly she called me "RJ," although occasionally she would call me "R." I think the bond between Natalie and me was so strong because we were in similar places psychologically, even though I was older. I was in flight from my father, and she was in flight from her mother. And we were discovering together, not just each other, but our talent and our place in the movie business.

Natalie's great gift was her spectacular sense of life as well as her humor. One of the things I loved about her was that she was so genuine with other people. If she liked someone, she took time with that person. She was generous with herself, and when she turned her face toward you, you were the only person there. She didn't scan the room looking for someone else more important, which is a trait most actors and actresses have down to a fine art. And one other thing: she was fun. God, she was fun.

Natalie was passionate on the subject of Vivien Leigh, her favorite actress, and the movies she could watch over and over were *Gone With the Wind* and, particularly, *A Streetcar Named Desire*. God, she loved that movie, and she loved all of Tennessee Williams—his particular poetic take on damaged souls. She liked to read a great deal, mostly novels, and liked to keep current on what was popular.

Her favorite designer for movie wardrobes was Edith Head, whom she trusted implicitly in terms of design. Natalie might have seen Edith as a sort of surrogate mother. Edith wasn't there advising her about every little thing, but Natalie respected her intelligence a great deal. Edith knew the movie business backward and forward and, unlike Mud, was very objective. Certainly, she and Natalie talked about a lot of things besides wardrobe.

For Natalie's personal wardrobe, she was always willing to experiment with different people and different looks, with the proviso that some things were not going to change—her love for Jax pants, for example.

When it came to music, she liked vocalists, some jazz and romantic dance music. And yes, she was a good dancer. Her taste in music was very current, whereas mine tended toward throwbacks—big bands and my passionate attachment to jazz. This, I think, was where the gap in our ages was most evident.

We found that it was very easy to get acclimated to each other's tastes. The only thing about Natalie that initially brought me up short was her choice of perfume: Jungle Gardenia, which was Barbara Stanwyck's favorite as well. I asked Natalie about it, and it turned out that more than ten years before we were married, when Natalie was a child actress, she had made a movie with Barbara called *The Bride Wore Boots,* and she had fallen in love with Barbara's perfume. She decided when she was an adult she would use Jungle Gardenia as well. Well, okay, but it was always a bit disconcerting to me. However, I knew that when Natalie made up her mind, whether it involved a young contract actor she passed in a hallway or a perfume, she got her way, so I didn't try to get her to change.

At this stage of her life, she was very ambitious and fascinated by actors who were doing things she wasn't. She always had a great desire for the authenticity of New York—that's where she met Jimmy Dean before they made *Rebel Without a Cause*—and she was fascinated by the actors who were working in television drama, the shows that Sidney Lumet and John Frankenheimer were directing, because they were so much more raw and passionate than the movies she was making.

For that matter, Elia Kazan excepted, they were more raw and passionate than the movies anybody was making. Those TV shows were far in advance of Hollywood in terms of their choice of material and the handling of that material, and they really pointed the way to the kind of movies Hollywood would increasingly make in the 1960s and '70s. The vast majority of those '50s TV shows would never have been made by Jack Warner.

Natalie's fascination with New York translated into a fascination with young Method actors, guys who played the same brooding notes as Brando and Monty Clift but didn't actually have their talent. Scott Marlowe, for instance. In Natalie's mind, New York was always a sort of acting promised land.

I found her to be outwardly much less conflicted than most of the parts she played. She was naturally inquisitive about how things worked, and she was also very interested in how other people lived. I came to realize that she was extremely intuitive and perceptive about people—about who was honest, who was dishonest. She seemed to live in a perpetual state of joyful discovery, and since she had never met people like Fred Astaire or Clifton Webb, there was a real sense that she was coming into a new world. Her parents had kept her on a short rein, so by marrying me she gained, for the first time, a sense of real freedom.

We didn't really talk about having a baby; we were very young, and we wanted to enjoy our togetherness before anything else. A child wasn't completely out of our minds, but we didn't work at it. We thought we had plenty of time, and besides, there were our careers. Natalie in particular was working all the time, going from one picture to another, as was I.

As a woman, Natalie had that radiance that made her one of those women everybody loved. She was everything I had imagined, and she immediately became the preeminent component of my life. My memories of those first years with Natalie are almost unmarked by any genuine stress between us. Those first years, as well as our later remarriage, had a purity of emotion that was never affected by any transient arguments.

# NINE

# "HE NEVER SPOKE ABOUT AVA, NOT EVER."

A surprise party for my thirtieth birthday that Natalie threw for me at Trader Vic's. The only guest was Spencer Tracy. What a present!

J ust about the time Natalie and I were getting serious, I had made *The True Story of Jesse James,* a remake of a Henry King picture from 1939 that the studio assigned to Nicholas Ray. I was looking forward to working with Nick Ray on a western, but he was a very strange man. He was bisexual, with a drinking problem and a drug problem—a very confused and convoluted personality, even for a director, few of whom were as obviously tormented as Nick. I found Henry Hathaway, for instance, to be all about action; I don't think he ever gave me a direction that involved the character's state of mind. Hathaway thought in terms of direct lines of physical move-ment. But Nick was the complete opposite—he hardly ever gave you a physical direction. It was all about emotions, and that's what he tried to put into the movie.

The problem was that Nick was always anesthetized; he'd stare off into space and then he'd say, "Try this. No. Wait. Don't." He liked acolytes; I have this mental snapshot of him wearing cowboy boots, surrounded by actors sitting around him on the ground. I remember thinking that he looked a little too comfortable. He was terribly enamored of Kazan, but he completely lacked Gadge's focus. Every morning we'd all won-der how Nick was going to be today, which is no way to make a movie. I liked working for him—he was as close to the avant-garde as Hollywood got at that time—and he was very interest-ing in his various pathologies. I always enjoyed working with Jeff Hunter as well, and the picture turned out okay.

After Natalie and I got back from our honeymoon, I began *The Hunters,* with Robert Mitchum, directed by Dick Powell. I adored both of them. Powell was one of the great guys of all time, and Mitchum and I became fast friends. He insisted that I call him "Mother Mitchum." One day we cooked up a juvenile practical joke—we hired a girl to sit on a bench at lunchtime without any underpants on. We were in Arizona, at an Air Force base, and from the reaction you'd have thought the men of the United States Air Force had never seen a woman's private parts before. As word spread, we gradually brought the entire base to a halt. The fact that it was juvenile didn't make it any less funny; actually, it made it funnier.

Mitchum and Dick Powell had worked together on a picture the year before, the very good *The Enemy Below*, so they already had a rapport. Mitchum wasn't drinking at the time, although he did smoke a little grass. His marijuana bust in the 1940s hadn't fazed him in the least; grass had remained his preferred method of relaxation.

Let me say something right here: Robert Mitchum was one fine actor. He belonged to that small tribe of actors who are more interesting in concealing emotion than expressing it. Most actors lunge to show you every card in their hand. That wasn't Mitchum's way. But that smooth, implacable surface hid things only up to a point. On those occasions when he let loose, in movies like *The Night of the Hunter* or *The Friends of Eddie Coyle*, the effect was powerful and startling.

*The Hunters* was based on a fine novel by James Salter, but the script was far more conventional than the book, and in any case, beautiful prose can't be directly translated into a movie. What's left is the underlying story structure, which is often very ordinary.

Mother Mitchum wasn't the only legend I got to know about this time. Fox had a project called *Lord Vanity*, a novel by Samuel Shellabarger, a first-rate historical novelist whose books—*Captain from Castile* and *Prince of Foxes*—had served as excellent vehicles for Ty Power. The proposed cast for *Lord*

*Vanity* included Errol Flynn, me, Clifton Webb, and Joan Collins. Of course, I was terribly excited by the opportunity to work with Errol Flynn, one of a handful of truly legendary Hollywood characters. Flynn was making a much-heralded comeback at the time as a somewhat debauched character actor; his performance in *The Sun Also Rises* was being talked about for an Oscar.

I went over to Warner Bros., where Flynn was making *Too Much, Too Soon.* I was looking forward to telling him about the time he picked me up hitchhiking on Sunset Boulevard years before. I asked about the location of his dressing room. "Around the corner," they told me. I went around the corner, and there was a wooden building that looked like a little schoolhouse and could be wheeled around the lot.

The door was slightly ajar, and I said, "Mr. Flynn?" as I opened it. There he sat, facing the door, with his legs spread. Between his legs was a blond girl giving him what looked to be a very expert blow job. Flynn looked up, and his eyes locked with mine, which I'm sure were very wide. He slowly shook his head emphatically from side to side. I didn't say a word, not even "Excuse me." I just closed the door. Very tightly.

Unfortunately, *Lord Vanity* was never made. It might have made for an interesting picture; it would definitely have made for an interesting experience.

The marriage of Natalie Wood and Robert Wagner sent the fan magazines into overdrive. There weren't as many as there had been when I was a boy, but there were still about a dozen that catered to a predominantly female audience: *Photoplay, Modern Screen, Motion Picture,* and so on. The keynote of the fan magazines at any period was a throbbing, melodramatic view of show business. Every date was a possible marriage, every marriage was a coupling of titans, and every movie was *Gone With the Wind*. The fan magazines are all gone now, but the attitude still survives on TV shows like *Entertainment Tonight* and *Access Hollywood*.

Natalie and I were the latest model off the assembly line. Preceding us were Janet Leigh and Tony Curtis, and Debbie Reynolds and Eddie Fisher. I realize now that the fan magazine sensibility could subtly affect your attitude about yourself. What's DeMille's line in *Sunset Boulevard*? "A dozen press agents can do terrible things to the human spirit." Among other things, all that publicity can make you feel bulletproof when in fact you're not.

In this period, we were mostly living on my salary, because Natalie had refused all the scripts Jack Warner sent her after *Marjorie Morningstar.* The only picture she regretted turning down was *A Summer Place,* not because it was particularly good, but because it was particularly successful. Warner was infuriated and put her on suspension.

It wasn't just Jack's tacky taste in projects that made her angry. She was also grossly underpaid. Finally, in early 1959, Warner gave Natalie a new contract that started at $1,000 a week and ran up to $7,500 a week. The most important thing, as far as Natalie was concerned, was the provision that for every picture she made at Warner's, she could make another picture for somebody else. She didn't trust Jack Warner and believed she'd have to do her quality work for someone else.

She was right, more or less. The first picture she made back at Warner's was *Cash McCall,* a programmer with Jim Garner that was strictly designed to exploit his new fame stemming from the *Maverick* TV show.

I first met Frank Sinatra when I was about twenty-four, shortly after he had broken up with Ava Gardner. Like most guys of my generation, I had tremendous admiration for him as a man and as a musician. He was such a tremendous influence, as much as Brando was in another sphere—the dialogue, the Jack Daniel's, the manner, everything. And in his work he was like Brando in another way: the combination of an overtly tough masculinity on the surface and, just beneath that, total emotional openness. My friendship with Frank easily broadened to include Natalie, and we both became part of his circle.

One day we were all in New York when Natalie casually mentioned that she had never seen the East Coast, so nothing would do but that Frank had to charter a Beechcraft, and the three of us took a flight up the East Coast so that Natalie could see that part of America from the air.

Frank was an enormously exciting man to be around, but I don't believe that he was ever content. He was very restless, both physically and in every other way. He wanted to get out there and get it done, and he didn't have a lot of patience—or rather, he was somewhat patient with recording, but not patient at all with movies. If you were making a movie with Frank, you had to be on your toes, because he'd only do a shot once or twice, and he would get really pissed off if it didn't go well. As I gained more experience, I would begin to see what he was talking about, because there is an awful lot of wasted motion in motion pictures.

Looking back, I don't think Frank was comfortable with movies in the same way he was with music. With his music, he was in control. He knew what sound and what emotion he wanted before he walked into the recording studio. But there are so many more people standing between an actor and the audience than there are between a singer and the audience. He knew that a movie was going to be taken and edited in a way that he couldn't control, and I don't think he ever quite learned how to assert himself in movies the way he did in music.

That said, people think that because he would shoot only one or two takes he didn't take it seriously, but that wasn't the case at all. Spencer Tracy didn't like a lot of takes either, and nobody thought he was casual about the work. Frank was very conscious of his lack of training; he was never sure that he would be able to reproduce an effect more than once or twice because he had to rely on emotion more than craft. He was very serious about his work; he went over his wardrobe, the look of the film, the dramatic arc. He didn't just pick up a script, look at it, and shoot it. He prepared; I saw him in thrall to the words of *The Manchurian Candidate*.

As for his temperament, Frank would reliably be set off by someone not fulfilling their obligations in the manner he thought proper. Any kind of dishonesty or bullshit would infuriate him. And people were afraid of him because his explosions were not pretty.

He never spoke about Ava, not ever. It wasn't a subject you could bring up, and he certainly never brought it up himself. Even casual references—"Ava and I were here one night," that sort of thing—were conspicuous by their absence.

He adored Dolly, his mother. I was with him when he gave her a house, and it was touching; he so wanted her to be pleased. Dolly was one tough little broad—she would have been the first to tell you so—and probably the only woman Frank was ever submissive toward. He went to a great deal of trouble for her, and he wanted everything to be just right—he had personally bought and supervised the installation of the chandeliers and everything else.

Frank catered to Dolly, and it was so touching to see him that way. He was such a dutiful son that it's appropriate that they're now buried together in Palm Springs, although it's impossible to believe that the ceaseless energy that constituted Frank could be contained in a small cemetery plot. When you listen to his music or watch his movies, there it is again—as vibrant as ever.

My next picture was *In Love and War,* written and directed by Philip Dunne, who was a top-quality human being and screenwriter but only a medium-quality director. Darryl's absence from the lot was definitely having a negative effect on my career. My costars were Jeff Hunter, Hope Lange, Brad Dillman, and Dana Wynter. Dana later married the lawyer Greg Bautzer, who was one of the great cocksmen of the movie industry and a behind-the-scenes player who had a great deal of clout within the business.

Greg was my lawyer, and a good one, but he was a very volatile man—a couple of drinks and he was off to the races. Booze made Greg pugnacious, and he'd take a swing at anybody. Between the women and the liquor, Greg was not your typical lawyer.

Somewhere in here was a guest bit in a silly picture called *Mardi Gras,* which was only notable as the last movie directed by Edmund Goulding, who was, shall we say, an interesting man: a married, gay, former boxing champion.

The year 1959 brought *Say One for Me* with Bing Crosby and Debbie Reynolds, directed by Frank Tashlin. There was a period when it was not fashionable to say nice things about Bing Crosby as a human being, but I had a great deal of affection for him. As for Frank Tashlin, he was another issue entirely. For one thing, he didn't want Natalie visiting the set, which I thought was rude and unprofessional.

Much more important than that was Tashlin's attempted intercession for a friend of his who had written some songs that Tashlin wanted featured in the film. Sammy Cahn and Jimmy Van Heusen, two great talents on whom both Bing and Frank Sinatra relied, had written the songs for the film, and here was Tashlin trying to use me as a guinea pig for someone nobody had ever heard of. "Jesus Christ," I told him, "I'd rather have Sammy Cahn and Jimmy Van Heusen write my material than your friend."

He didn't appreciate my response, and I didn't appreciate his suggestion, so things were a bit chilly between Mr. Tashlin and myself—not that I cared. The movie was about a caddish nightclub owner on the prowl for a nice dancer played by Debbie Reynolds, and I did a little singing and dancing. I wasn't Astaire, but I wasn't terrible. Bing played a priest. Again. It was basically a riff on *Pal Joey*, but a riff that was too little, too late.

Bing and I spent a lot of time talking about golf, and he gave me some pipes he had brought back from England. He also gave me a beautiful Labrador I named Conroy, after Bing's character in the film. Conroy loved to walk out onto the edge of a diving board and leap into the pool. Then Conroy would do something dogs rarely do, which is swim underwater. If you were underwater with him, you could see his mouth drawn back in a huge grin. He was never happier than when he was swimming underwater. Hysterical.

Debbie Reynolds was going through a very bad time; the Eddie Fisher–Liz Taylor affair had just broken wide open. Debbie wasn't exactly falling apart, but she had her ragged moments. The sad part was that her career was on fire, and the circumstances were such that she couldn't really relax and enjoy it. Debbie was fragile and kept to herself, so I spent most of my time with Bing and the wonderful character actor Frank McHugh, who was part of that old Hollywood Irish mafia at Warner Bros.

When we weren't working, Natalie and I enjoyed the Hollywood social scene. The great restaurants and clubs that had been opened in the 1930s were still thriving. In this period, our favorite restaurants were Romanoff's—Spencer Tracy was always at Romanoff's—and Chasen's, Patsy d'Amore's for Italian food, and Don the Beachcomber's for Polynesian. Dave and Maude Chasen were great, warmhearted people who served great food. I particularly liked their chili, the great seafood platter with iced shellfish, and the hobo steak. Chasen's also had Pepi, the best bartender in town, who made the best martini, which featured both orange and lemon peels. For the pièce de résistance, Pepi would light the martini!

To give you some idea of why Chasen's was so loved, years later Jimmy, the captain at Chasen's, was the second man to hold our daughter Courtney because, after she was born, Dave Chasen sent down a big hamper of food to Natalie's hospital room, and Jimmy delivered it.

My bachelor apartment had been too crowded for two people, so Natalie told her parents they had to move out of the house Natalie had paid for so we could move in. We wanted a big house in Beverly Hills, but between the two of us, we weren't really making enough money to afford a big house. Natalie knew how her parents would react. "You won't believe what you're going to hear," she told me.

Sure enough, Mud and Nick acted like they were characters in a Victorian novel, dispossessed and thrown onto the street by ungrateful children. Actually, Natalie just found them another place to live. A little later, in the summer of 1959, we finally took the plunge and bought a house. It was at 714 North Beverly Drive, a very nice neocolonial house that cost $90,000—I wonder what it would bring these days?

Natalie was a show business kid, and for most of her life she hadn't been terribly interested in anything beyond whether or not she got a part. But after we were married, she became very interested in interior decorating and decided to do the house over completely. Remember the Cary Grant movie *Mr. Blandings Builds His Dream House*? For the next three years, that was my life. Walls were taken down, walls were put up; floors were covered in marble. Plumbing contractors put their grandchildren through college on what we spent.

Natalie had an enormous marble bathtub installed on the second floor, but it was too heavy, and the floor started to give way. We had to repair and reinforce the floor, but even when that was done, hot water took so long to get to the tub that it wasn't really hot. We added an outdoor lanai and swimming pool, which was filled with saltwater.

As if the reality wasn't bad enough, the fan magazines, which were heavily invested in portraying us as intensely glamorous "America's sweethearts," exaggerated everything. They said we had Old Master paintings (Natalie's good taste in art didn't come until much later); they said Natalie had a collection of stuffed tigers (she had a couple of poodles); they said we had two saltwater pools (we had one). All this publicity just made the reality worse. We would end up spending more than $75,000 redecorating that house, and it never really was finished.

I hadn't been too fond of the movies I'd been doing, and Natalie felt the same way about her career. We decided to join forces and do a film together, which seemed like a good idea for both creative and commercial reasons.

*All the Fine Young Cannibals* was done on loan-out to MGM. The studio had originally planned it as a vehicle for Elizabeth Taylor and Elvis Presley, but at some point they dropped out and we dropped in. We made more money together for the movie than we could have made making two separate movies, but it was the wrong movie for the wrong studio.

*All the Fine Young Cannibals* was a big, juicy soap opera, the sort of film that Douglas Sirk had been making at Universal for Ross Hunter, but MGM didn't have the facility at making and selling that kind of picture that Universal did. MGM hired Michael Anderson to direct our movie. He had recently had a big hit with *Around the World in 80 Days* and proved a good man and a good director.

Toward the end of the picture, Michael had to leave for another assignment, so Vincente Minnelli came on and directed the last two weeks of the shoot. Minnelli had a nervous habit of constantly puckering his lips as if he were going to kiss someone, and he was very fidgety about things like drapes and props. He was quite particular in every way imaginable, even though it wasn't his picture and he was working without credit. I was surprised by how effete he was, obviously bisexual at the very least.

I enjoyed making the picture, and I especially enjoyed the music of the picture. Uan Rasey blew the horn for me, and it was such a kick to spend time with him. Uan is still alive and still playing, even though he's lost his eyesight. When he's not playing, he's giving trumpet lessons.

I noticed that, compared to Warner's or Fox, things were pretty sparse at MGM at this point. We were one of the few films in production, and the studio didn't seem to know its audience anymore. For instance, one of the film's major components was black people; it was Redd Foxx's first picture, and there was an interracial affair between Pearl Bailey and me. But MGM cut the love scenes between us because they were worried about bookings in the South.

Compare this to the way Universal emphasized the racial aspect of its remake of *Imitation of Life* just the year before, and considering the fact that the year we did our movie the hot pictures were *Psycho* and *The Apartment,* and you realize how badly MGM was falling behind the times. The studio was just hanging on, and it ended up semi-sabotaging its own movie, which is by no means an unusual event. Instead of being a really good movie, *All the Fine Young Cannibals* was just an ordinary movie with a couple of good scenes.

It was the first time I had worked with Natalie, and it was as great as I had hoped. We always tried to make it realistic. It would seem that being together 24/7 with someone could get a bit claustrophobic, but it didn't feel that way. It was great to work on a scene at home, go to the studio together, and talk some more about the work. It was an immersion experience with the woman I was head over heels in love with, so of course I loved it.

I got to know some of MGM's old guard while making the movie, guys who had stalked through the jungle with Louis B. Mayer. Eddie Mannix had been Mayer's number-two guy, and Benny Thau had been the head of talent and even ran the studio for a time in the 1950s. Both of them were superficially nice guys, but you definitely wanted them for you, not against you.

In recent years, there have been a lot of questions about whether or not Eddie had George Reeves, his wife's lover, murdered. I knew Eddie, I knew his wife, and I knew George Reeves. Is the murder scenario possible? Yes, it's possible. Eddie certainly had the connections needed to have someone taken out, and I think he also had the emotional capability. He was a tough little guy, as was Billy Grady, the head of talent at MGM—all tenacious bastards.

As for Benny Thau, after the MGM years he had an office at William Morris, but Benny was controlled by false ego; he couldn't stand to come to work at a company that wasn't his. Years later, Benny ended up in the Motion Picture Home. I ran into him and asked how he was doing.

"I'm doing fine, RJ. Listen, I want you here tomorrow, for lunch."

"Well, Benny, I'm working tomorrow, I can't make it for lunch."

"Well, when can you make it? I want you here." Benny was used to giving orders, and there was no one left to give orders to. It was another negative lesson about the perils of the movie business.

# TEN

# "THAT FUCKING CUNT
# WILL NEVER WORK IN
# MY STUDIO AGAIN!"

Natalie. (COURTESY OF THE AUTHOR)

*ll the Fine Young Cannibals* didn't break my streak of losers, but as far as the public was concerned, Natalie and I were living the movie star life and loving it. In October 1959, Frank Sinatra threw a major bash at Romanoff's to celebrate Natalie's twenty-first birthday as well as her fifteenth anniversary in the movies. There was an orchestra, Frank and I both toasted her, and Spencer Tracy hugged her. Then Frank, Dean Martin, Sammy Davis Jr., and I formed a quartet and sang "Happy Birthday" to her. I admit I was the weak link in that particular vocal chain.

At Fox, I could feel the temperature falling. Buddy Adler had died, and the studio was now being run by Spyros Skouras, whose background was as an exhibitor. It was a field that had served Louis B. Mayer and Jack Warner well in that it gave them an education in exactly what put people's asses in seats. But Skouras was a walking, talking disaster, and he had just begun production on *Cleopatra,* the biggest runaway production of all time. *Cleopatra* would bring the studio right to the edge of the precipice, so he certainly had more important things to worry about than me.

When I would go in to complain, the studio minions would say something on the order of, "What the hell are you beefing about? You're making thousands a week, and there are hundreds of kids out there earning nothing. We've done all right by you so far. We know what we're doing."

Actually, Darryl Zanuck had known what he was doing, but nobody else at the studio had his touch. The studio was making a mistake by keeping me a bright-eyed and bushy-tailed juvenile and not letting me play an adult, and I suppose I had been at least somewhat complicit in this as well.

That was one reason Dick Powell and I began developing a picture called *Solo,* about a jazz musician, somewhat in the mold of *Young Man with a Horn*. But it was increasingly clear to me that the studio was much more interested in catering to a new group of leading men: Brad Dillman, Richard Beymer, Tony Franciosa. They may have been comparatively untried, but they hadn't been touched by failure either.

If my career was sputtering, my marriage was still solid. We were having a great deal of fun, and we continued to learn together. When Jack Warner bought *Gypsy* for Natalie, we went to New York to see the show. It was clear that it was a perfect vehicle for her and that she'd be sensational in it. Warner and Natalie gave a press conference announcing their plans for the picture, and afterward we were sitting in Jack's office, at 550 Fifth Avenue. Natalie went down the hall to pose for some stills, leaving me sitting there with Jack Warner.

"Would you like a drink?" Jack asked, and I said yes. He poured us both a Jack Daniel's. So there I was, sitting on Fifth Avenue having a drink with Jack Warner. I distinctly remember thinking, *Life is good.*

"Great, great property for Natalie," he says. "It will be a wonderful picture."

"She'll be wonderful in it, Jack."

"Who do you think should play the mother?"

"Well, Jack, in my estimation there's only one person in the world who can play the part."

"Who's that?"

"Judy Garland."

And suddenly all the good feelings vanished as Jack Warner began screaming. "That fucking cunt will never work in my

studio again! Fuck her! She's a pain in the ass, a no-talent cunt."
And that was just for starters. It was a stunning transition, because Jack Warner was a man who always effected the air of a
jovial comedian. Jack Warner wanted to be liked, but he was acting like he was going to pick me up and throw me out the window, Jack Daniel's still clutched in my hand.

As he continued ranting, it became clear why he was so
angry. Right after the premiere of *A Star Is Born,* he had gone to
a party at Judy's house on Mapleton Drive. When he walked in,
he had a vague feeling of déjà vu. Instead of dissipating, it got
stronger, and then he realized what it was. Judy and Sid Luft
had taken the furniture that had been used for the sets of *A Star
Is Born* and moved it into their house. Judy Garland had stolen
furniture from Jack Warner! He'd been brooding about it for
years, and his anger had been building, and all it took was the
mention of her name to set him off. His attitude was, "She
fucked me and I'm going to fuck her!"

Warner's outburst was a window into the ferocity of that
generation of movie moguls. This had happened six years before, but as far as Jack was concerned, it was the day before
yesterday. There was no sense of letting bygones be bygones,
and there wasn't even a sense of respect for Judy's talent and
the fact that she would have been far superior as Mama Rose
than Rosalind Russell, who got the part. These men were so
competitive! Most obviously with each other, but it went deeper
than that. They didn't want anybody getting ahead of them,
on any level. Not another producer, and certainly not an actor,
no matter how talented, no matter how much they needed that
talent.

I have learned that in a long life we all eventually play the part
of the betrayed, and we all eventually play the part of the

*(Above)* With Elvis Presley in the commissary at Fox. Nicholas Ray is sitting next to me, and Alan Hale, Jr., is on the far right. (COURTESY OF THE AUTHOR)

*(Left)* With Jayne Mansfield at a premiere, 1956. (PHOTO BY DARLENE HAMMOND/HULTON ARCHIVE/GETTY IMAGES)

*(Above)* Natalie and me on our wedding day, thrilled with each other and the world. (COURTESY OF THE AUTHOR)

*(Below)* The official wedding photo. My parents are on the left, Natalie's parents are on the right, and Lana Wood is next to me. (COURTESY OF THE AUTHOR)

*(Above)* Frank Sinatra, Dean Martin, and many others helped me surprise Natalie on her twenty-first birthday. (PHOTO BY MURRAY GARRETT/GETTY IMAGES)

*(Below)* A test scene from the proposed swashbuckler *Lord Vanity,* in which Joan Collins and I were to have costarred with Errol Flynn and Clifton Webb. Can you tell which is Joan and which is me? (© TWENTIETH CENTURY FOX. ALL RIGHTS RESERVED.)

*(Left)* With Steve McQueen on the London set of *The War Lover.*

*(Below)* With Mart Crowley in Venice, 1961. (COURTESY OF THE AUTHOR)

*(Above)* With the amazing *Pink Panther* gang: Claudia Cardinale, David Niven, and Peter Sellers in Rome, 1963.

*(Below)* Paul Newman watches Jay Sebring give me a haircut on the set of *Harper*. The man with the beard is the great cinematographer Conrad Hall; on the right is director Jack Smight.

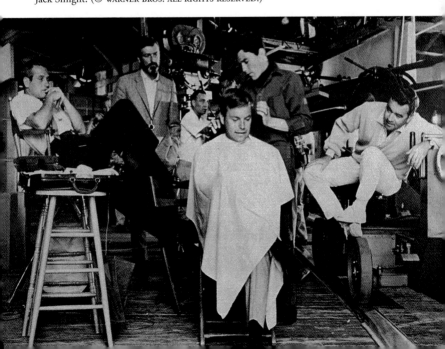

*(Above)* On the set of *The Biggest Bundle of Them All.* You'd never know that both Vittorio de Sica and Edward G. Robinson were furious at Raquel Welch for her chronic tardiness. (© TURNER ENTERTAINMENT CO. A WARNER BROS. ENTERTAINMENT COMPANY. ALL RIGHTS RESERVED.)

*(Below)* Roddy McDowall's photo of my new family. Next to me are Peter Donen, Josh Donen, Marion, and Katie. (PHOTOGRAPH BY RODDY MCDOWALL, COURTESY OF THE AUTHOR)

*(Above)* With Frank and Tina
Sinatra in the south of France
at the Colombe d'Or
in St. Paul de Vence.
(COURTESY OF THE AUTHOR)

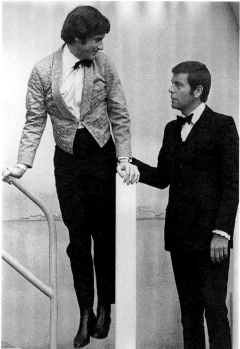

*(Left)* With Roddy McDowall
on the set of *It Takes a Thief.*
(COURTESY OF UNIVERSAL
STUDIOS LICENSING LLP)

*(Above)* With Bette Davis in an episode of *It Takes a Thief,* the beginning of a beautiful friendship. (COURTESY OF UNIVERSAL STUDIOS LICENSING LLP)

*(Right)* Natalie and me on the windswept day of our second marriage. (COURTESY OF THE AUTHOR)

betrayer, and neither is pleasant because both roles involve pain—inflicting it or absorbing it.

By the spring of 1960, I began to feel pressure building on our marriage. With the exception of *Gypsy*, Natalie felt that she had been put on the back burner by Jack Warner, and she was right: Fred Zinnemann hired Audrey Hepburn for *The Nun's Story*, and Josh Logan hired Leslie Caron for *Fanny*. Finally, Natalie caught a break when Elia Kazan asked her to be the leading lady of *Splendor in the Grass*.

It didn't start out that way. Kazan's first choice was Diane Varsi, but she quit the business. Then he thought about Jane Fonda, but it was William Inge, who wrote the original script for *Splendor*, who suggested he look at Natalie. Jack Warner wasn't happy about it and actually tried to talk Kazan out of using her; Natalie had defied him when she went on suspension after *Marjorie Morningstar*, and God knows, Jack could hold a grudge.

For Natalie, this was her ship coming in. Kazan was unquestionably the best actor's director alive, and he'd made *A Streetcar Named Desire*, which contained Natalie's favorite female performance. A lot of people thought Kazan was nuts to hire her; one reporter told him that she'd been good in only two movies. "Then I say she's got it," Gadge said. "Two pictures is a hell of a lot of pictures." While the script was by William Inge, not Tennessee Williams, it had both authority and emotional authenticity.

Natalie was so hungry for the part that she even agreed to test for it. She told Kazan that she wanted a new career, and Gadge recognized her power as an actress and her willpower as a person; she got the part. What was unsaid but clearly indicated by the fact of that screen test was that she was willing to put herself completely in his hands—one of those things that every director wants to hear.

Fox had postponed *Solo,* so I was able to accompany Natalie to New York, where all of *Splendor in the Grass* was shot, beginning in the spring of 1960. We rented an apartment on Sutton Place that Bill Inge found for us—he lived in the same building. The exteriors were shot on Staten Island and in upstate New York, which stood in for Kansas, and the interiors were shot at the Filmways studio.

Elia Kazan, who became a good friend of mine, said in his memoirs that Natalie and Warren Beatty began an affair on *Splendor in the Grass,* that I was on the set, and that my humiliation was a terrible thing to see. I was indeed on the set when they were on location, but I honestly didn't see any evidence of an affair.

There's another scenario: Beatty had nothing to do with our breakup, and Natalie didn't begin to see him until after we split. I choose to believe the latter. Now, it's within the realm of possibility that the affair began earlier, but I don't think that's what happened for one simple reason: she would have told me.

Here's what all the speculation about this period of our lives fails to take into account: both of us were serious about the marriage, and we were always straight with each other.

Let me put it another way: I never knew Natalie to tell me a lie. Affairs were not part of our equation. I had been faithful to her, and she had been faithful to me. If she had been sleeping with Beatty, she would have told me. Mart Crowley, who was with Natalie throughout *Splendor,* also thought nothing happened until much later. As a matter of fact, she initially disliked Beatty because she thought he didn't bathe enough—scruffiness supposedly equaled authenticity, at least according to the Actors Studio.

I do know that *Splendor in the Grass* constituted a critical time for Natalie. The material was emotional and sensual, she worshiped Kazan, who properly set a very high bar for her performance, and Warren Beatty was . . . attractive. A good actor, a great sense of humor. He even played the piano.

Perhaps the core problem was in something Kazan said years later: "So many actresses, you feel they have a private life, a husband and kids, and acting has a place. But, with Natalie, acting was her whole life." At this point in her career, I think Kazan was right—Natalie's success or failure as an actress was more important to her than anything else. Including me.

Whether or not Beatty made the crucial difference in our marriage breaking up, I do not know. I do know that with Natalie, I always had a fear of a third party coming between us. Anytime you are involved with a beautiful woman, you can see that other men respond to her the same way you do. You have to have a lot of self-confidence to cope with the ultimate questions: Would she like him better than me? Would he please her more than I can?

Because of Natalie's innate radiance, she couldn't help attracting every man around her, so there was always a certain unease on my part. And when *Splendor in the Grass* came around, there was an added sense of fear. When such a fear is combined with the feeling that you're not being responded to in the way you expect, things can get very edgy, very fast.

After she finished *Splendor in the Grass* on August 16, she had exactly two days off before beginning rehearsals with Jerome Robbins for *West Side Story*. The Mirisch brothers, who were producing the picture, offered her one of two deals: a flat salary of $250,000, or $200,000 plus 5 percent of the profits. I advised her to take the percentage instead of the extra $50,000, but Abe Lastfogel pointed out that musicals had been in a downward spiral for years and there was no guarantee that *West Side Story* would do any better than *Les Girls* or any of the other musicals that had been laying eggs. The only successful musical in the recent past had been *Gigi*.

"Take the $50,000," Abe said, and she did. *West Side Story* is still playing, still earning money. She spent the rest of her life regretting the deal, but that's the business—even the brightest agents and managers make mistakes. In the future, whenever she was offered a percentage instead of flat salary, she took the percentage, with very good results.

It was around this time that Natalie began to put together the support system that was with her for the rest of her life. Mart Crowley was a go-fer on *Splendor in the Grass,* and he would go on to write *The Boys in the Band* as well as be a mainstay for me on *Hart to Hart.* She met Howard Jeffrey when he worked on *West Side Story.* The triumvirate was completed by the actress Norma Crane. Unlike many stars' friends, Mart, Howard, and Norma weren't competitive with each other at all, perhaps because they were all different kinds of people. Although they were Natalie's friends before they were mine, I grew to love them as well.

All these people benefited from being close to Natalie, because one of her greatest gifts was kindness. Natalie paid for Mart's first six months of analysis. When Tom Mankiewicz, who also became part of our circle, bought his first house, she used her decorator's license to get dealers to sell him stuff cheap. Then she threw a housewarming party and invited big shots whom Tom didn't even know, but who she knew would bring him presents that he really needed.

As she began work on *West Side Story,* Natalie was under so much pressure; her career was approaching white heat, and mine was no more than lukewarm. What made things even worse was that making *West Side Story* was miles of bad road. Jerome Robbins was incredibly demanding and difficult, so much so that he threw the shooting an entire month behind schedule. The producers waited until October to fire him because it was imperative that the musical numbers be superlatively shot, and Robbins did almost all of those. The book scenes were less important, and those were finished by codirector Robert Wise.

Natalie was furious about Robbins's firing and threatened to quit the picture unless he was reinstated. Both Abe Lastfogel and Robbins told her that was foolish, and she went back to work. Then she got furious all over again when the producers overdubbed her singing with Marni Nixon's. All this turmoil couldn't help but be reflected in our married life, and things continued to deteriorate, even after the movie was finally finished.

None of the arguments were about anything that could be objectively regarded as important, but Natalie's intensity and my fears magnified every trivial disagreement into a critical blowout. In February 1961, Mart Crowley moved into an apartment we had over the garage. He thought our marriage was hanging by a thread, and not a sturdy one. As for me, Abe Lastfogel had arranged a three-picture deal at Columbia. The first one up was a comedy called *Sail a Crooked Ship,* written and directed by Irving Brecher, from a novel by Nathaniel Benchley. Irv had written for the Marx Brothers and was one of Groucho's best friends. Irv was and is a delightful man, very attuned to comedy, and he surrounded me with funny people—Ernie Kovacs, Frank Gorshin, and Frankie Avalon among them. But he was a much better writer than he was a director, and the movie itself, while not bad, simply wasn't strong enough to lift me out of the trough I had fallen into, and I knew it.

My insecurities were mounting, as were our disagreements. We argued. We made up. We argued again. I would give Natalie gifts to apologize for the argument, and then we would argue again. And the pressure mounted. It had gotten to the point where we were almost never alone. There was always an agent on the phone, or the studio, or a publicist. Everybody was fluttering around trying to keep her together; she was very nervous, and all of this was taking place away from me.

I can see now that I was not that sympathetic or understanding about Natalie's needs. She told me that she wanted to go into analysis; she was overpowered by the pressure of her work, going from one movie to another, and the movies were getting bigger and bigger. She felt that therapy would help her. After all those years of Jack Warner giving her films from the back of the cupboard, she was suddenly getting major movies; it became a case of "Be careful what you wish for."

And I was standing there saying, "What about us? They're just parts in a movie." What I really meant, of course, was "What about me?"

I was excluded from almost everything that was happening to her, and I was jealous. I wanted us to spend more time together, and she wanted to stay on the merry-go-round, even if it was going faster and faster. And I felt that her going into analysis implied a failure on my part.

In June 1961, we got into a terrible, terrible argument. There was a lot of yelling that ascended to screaming. The argument culminated in Natalie running to her parents, which was a measure of her desperation, because her parents had spent her life running to her.

That same week we announced that we were going through a trial separation but had no plans for a divorce. We had been married for three and a half years. From the coverage in the papers, you'd have thought we'd killed the Lindbergh baby.

In our own minds, we had always been an ideal couple, and the media had picked up on that and spread it around the world. We were about to endure the sort of coverage that was being thrown at Elizabeth Taylor, Richard Burton, and Eddie Fisher, which was no help at all.

Looking back, I can see that some of the attitudes of Robert

Wagner Sr. were coming out in his son—it was "pull-yourself-up-by-your-bootstraps-a-man's-gotta-do-what-a-man's-gotta-do." Utterly stupid, not to mention counterproductive, but that's the way I felt.

It wasn't really professional jealousy I was feeling. I've always known that the movie business is completely cyclical—roll a seven and the waves part; roll snake-eyes and the waves close over your head. I was never one to sit there and whine, "How come I'm not working for Kazan?" It was the fact that Natalie was less and less of a presence in our life, and I didn't handle it well. Had I had more maturity, or taken some steps back, the divorce might not have happened.

The irony is that I was threatened by the idea of analysis. I told her, "Try to do it on your own," but she couldn't. Nobody could. We were both paralyzed by our individual insecurities. We still loved each other—I don't think we ever stopped loving each other—but we could no longer communicate with each other. Our emotional vocabulary had deteriorated.

Warren Beatty really came into the picture after she left the house. That summer, when I read about the two of them as the hot young couple around town, I wanted to kill that son of a bitch. The one thing I did not want to have happen was have him move into my life and break up my marriage. That was the absolute bottom. I felt as if the ground I had been standing on was being systematically cut from beneath me. I was also totally humiliated, in a way I'd never felt before and, thank God, have never felt since. *Life* magazine was calling Beatty "the most exciting American male in movies," and my last four or five pictures had been flops. How would you feel?

At one point, after their affair made the papers, just after Dorothy Kilgallen wrote, "The way Natalie Wood and Warren Beatty are carrying on . . . it's a wonder they have time to eat," I was hanging around outside his house with a gun, hoping he would walk out. I not only wanted to kill him, I was prepared to kill him. I was living out of a suitcase, staying with Mart Crowley some nights, John Foreman and his wife other nights. At the same time, I was opening up our house on Beverly Drive and walking around at night, sleeping in our bed, smelling Natalie on the sheets. I was, in short, a mess—on the verge of a complete emotional meltdown.

Maintaining a troubled marriage with two people is difficult but possible; maintaining a troubled marriage with three people can't be done. I was desperate, ripped wide open, and going slowly downhill. I drank a lot in this period, although I didn't tip over into alcoholism. I don't have the compulsive personality that alcoholics have; if they're not drinking, they're gambling or snorting or eating, and I've always been able to control my appetites. I poured my sorrows into bottles, not cases.

One night I went by the house to get some things. The house was empty, and a mood of desolation washed over me that was just overwhelming. I thought everything was coming to an end—my marriage, my career, the life I had painstakingly built up for the last dozen years, all of it leaking away. I remember thinking that if I couldn't kill Beatty, maybe I should kill myself.

There was a knock at the front door. I didn't answer it. Then there was a knock at the side door. Persistent. Finally, I opened the door. It was our old friend John Foreman. He came in and said, "What's going on?"

"I just don't think I can make it," I said. And John held me and stayed there with me and helped me. It was John who got me into analysis, which slowly enabled me to put the pieces of my life back together.

After John talked me into going to see somebody, I thought of trying the LSD therapy that Cary Grant swore by, and I went to see the same doctor. He scared the living hell out of me.

While I was talking to him in his office, I could hear moans coming from a back room, and I noticed there were suspicious stains on his rugs. While we were talking, he was spinning a record around on a turntable and trying to play it with his fingernail. Finally, he said, "I don't know if you're capable of this therapy," which was precisely the decision I had come to on my own. On the other hand, he helped a lot of people besides Cary.

Throughout this perilous, ragged time, John and Linda Foreman held me together. I was at their house every afternoon, drinking and crying. Sometimes I crashed at Mart Crowley's place, some nights I spent on Guy McElwaine's couch. Other times, I would just sit in a near-catatonic trance. Bob Conrad was very helpful at this point, but it was really a man named Gerald Aronson who made the difference. He was my therapist, he made himself available to me at any time, and he helped get me through some of the longest nights of my life.

Throughout this time, I remained crazy in love with Natalie. I did not want a divorce, but she was very involved with Warren and felt that she had to give things some space—in other words, spend more time with Warren. Friends did what friends always do in this situation—you get variations of the "there's lots of fish in the sea" speech, and they introduce you to lovely single women.

I couldn't have cared less. I was only interested in a reconciliation with Natalie, and I had no interest in starting something else that could possibly derail a reconciliation down the road.

*Solo,* the movie Dick Powell and I had developed, was supposed to be a serious picture about a jazz musician. Dick had gotten André Previn to compose the jazz score, and the picture was shaping up as something special. But Fox had reshaped it into a project that could have been made by Sam Katzman; now there were supposed to be a lot of currently hot rock-and-roll stars doing numbers, and they wanted me to work opposite Jayne Mansfield. In other words, it was supposed to be a follow-up to *The Girl Can't Help It,* which neither Dick Powell nor I wanted to get anywhere near. I went on suspension.

The last thing Fox offered me was a western with Elvis Presley called *Flaming Star.* If I'd done that, it would have taken the "jaws of life" to free up my career, because nobody ever paid attention to any other man in an Elvis Presley picture—Colonel Tom Parker made sure of that.

Between my career and my marriage, it was game, set, match. It was at this point that I decided to leave it, all of it, and go to Europe and start over. I had loved living and working there when Spencer Tracy and I made *The Mountain,* and going back gradually became a goal in my mind. The most charitable view of my situation would be that I was standing still; a more realistic view was that I was losing ground, and fast. I had to move, had to do something to alter the chemistry of my life and career. It was either flip out or flip the page. I chose the latter.

What was happening all around me made it that much easier. Hollywood was falling apart, and Fox wasn't doing well either. The mood on the lot was different because the people who had been there in 1949 weren't around much anymore. There had always been a family feeling at Fox—the same wardrobe people, the same technical crews. If a grip worked at Fox, he had fifty-two weeks of work a year, or close to it. Likewise, it seemed like my dear old friend Joe MacDonald was always the cameraman. It wasn't so unionized that a carpenter couldn't put an electric plug in a wall or a lighting man couldn't lift a piece of lumber. There was a certain esprit de corps; everybody worked together to make the film. We worked a full day on Saturday, and if a picture was supposed to be shot in thirty-five days, you better believe that it was finished on that thirty-fifth day, no more, no less. Overtime? Forget about it.

But by the late 1950s, business was down, the crews were being let go, and people were hired by the picture. All the crews and costumers, who were devoted to their jobs and to the studio and to the picture, had to start freelancing, and I think the quality of the movies was subtly affected. It was the beginning of a crucial transition in the business—from several generations of people whose concern was what was happening on the studio floor to several generations of people who were more interested in the programming and the marketing.

Darryl was still in Europe and had no intention of coming back anytime soon. I had been making movies for twelve years and was no longer the fair-haired boy, to say the least. I believed that if I went to Europe, where the most interesting movies were being made, I could get the kind of work I wanted to do and perhaps start my life over again. As for Natalie, I was still holding out some hope that we might be able to reconcile somewhere down the road.

Abe Lastfogel was my agent, and I told him I wanted out of Fox. Abe agreed that it sounded like a plan, so we went to see Spyros Skouras. "I don't know what we're going to do with the company," Skouras began. He seemed to be honestly distressed about the way things were going, even though he was one of the primary reasons behind the deteriorating situation. But at this point, that wasn't my problem. I told him I wanted to leave the studio; I had had it.

Skouras said that he wanted to keep me at Fox and wanted to renegotiate and keep me on—maybe at the same salary. Abe started talking about a raise. While they were talking, I flashed back to a conversation I'd had with Spencer Tracy. "Get out," he said. "The quicker the better. Leaving MGM was the smartest, not to mention the most lucrative, decision I ever made."

It was at that point that Skouras revisited the Elvis picture, and I said that wasn't what I wanted to do at all. I held firm; Abe and I told Skouras that I wanted out. Skouras said he didn't understand any of this; hadn't the studio taken me from nothing, from a $75 a week contract actor to someone whose face was known around the world?

"Spyros," said Abe, "I think we need to move on."

"The bottom line," said Skouras, "is that we want him here."

"That's not our bottom line," Abe said.

And then Skouras uttered the magic phrase: "If he doesn't stay here, I will see that he doesn't work anywhere." Well, Abe didn't scream, but he got extremely angry, as angry as I ever saw him. "How can you speak about him like that?" From pretending to be fatherly, Skouras had slipped right into pretending to be a gangster, and he didn't have the personality for either part. We left that office with my release from Fox.

I've always retained a sense of surprise about that meeting. Perhaps I was naive, but I had thought the meeting would be consummated with more grace. I would have been perfectly happy to let them have an option for a picture or two in exchange for my release—there is always room for negotiation in a negotiation—but Skouras poured gasoline on what was actually a modest flame.

It was always about power with those guys. Skouras wanted his way, not because there was a good reason for it, but simply because it was his way. Fox wasn't going to do anything for me that it hadn't already done, and we both knew it. The difference was that he couldn't admit it.

I began to sell everything I had that could be sold. What I couldn't sell or put into storage I gave away; I even gave away

Conroy, the wonderful Lab that Bing Crosby gave me. Natalie and I divided everything down the middle. The house we had bought for $90,000 and dropped nearly $100,000 into sold for around $185,000—we managed to avoid a bloodbath, the only bloodbath I had been able to avoid for a long time.

On my last day in Los Angeles, Abe and Frances Lastfogel drove me to the airport. Abe was very paternal and supportive during the ride, which, God knows, I needed. As for my father, he was consistent—he stayed in La Jolla that day. He wasn't crazy about me relocating to Europe, but then he hadn't been crazy about me becoming an actor either.

It was a quiet departure. I just got on the plane and left. About all I took with me were my clothes and a few belongings. I had no intention of coming back anytime soon, but then I had no real sense of what was actually happening: the great movie studios were in their death throes. Nobody really believed that the studio system, the way Hollywood had run and defined itself ever since Cecil B. DeMille opened up a little studio on the corner of Vine and Selma in 1913, was self-destructing. Sure, TV was tough competition, but hadn't it produced more jobs for more actors?

I had no sense of the old order dying; rather, I was focused on the wonderful pictures that were being made in England, France, and Italy. I meant to get into some of them. No, that isn't correct. I *had* to get into some of them. This wasn't about want, this was about need; it was a question of survival.

On the trip to the airport, on the plane to London, I tried hard to cling to my residual optimism, as I have all my life. I believed that the future had to be better than the recent past. All I had to do was be there. All I had to do was strike a match.

A heartbroken actor in Rome, on the terrace of his new apartment, 1962.
(PHOTOGRAPH BY ARALDO DI CROLLALANZA)

# PART TWO

# ELEVEN

# "I MISSED HER LOVING ME."

With my friend and mentor Darryl Francis Zanuck on the set of *The Longest Day*. (*THE LONGEST DAY* © 1962 TWENTIETH CENTURY FOX. ALL RIGHTS RESERVED.)

I set up shop in London, where Kate Hepburn helped me get a house. After a month or two, the situation with Natalie hadn't appreciably altered. She was still involved with Warren, and the press was whooping it up like jackals, with me as the prey. In Hollywood, we hadn't had any contact after the separation—everything was handled through intermediaries—but she was never out of my head.

In September 1961, I called her from the apartment of the producer James Woolf. I told her that I had an opportunity to be in a movie, but that a movie, any movie, was less important to me than being with her.

"I'm supposed to go to Florida," she said. I knew that Warren was making a movie there with John Frankenheimer.

"What do you want to do?" I asked her.

There was a pause, and she finally said, "I'm going to Florida." I hung up. It had all been awkward; I would much rather have talked to her face-to-face. There was nothing else to say, and now there was nothing else to do. The legalities were all handled through third parties, and for a long time we were out of contact. When she was nominated for an Oscar for *Splendor in the Grass,* I wrote her a note: "I hope with all my heart that when they open the envelope, it's you."

God help me, I was still in love with her. During all the time we were apart, she never left me. Every person has a favorite lover, the person who transforms your life and makes it better than it ever had been before. For me, that was Natalie.

Leaving meant she didn't have the problem of dealing with me and feeling guilty—about Warren, about her career going up and mine coming down. I didn't miss the public us, the "RJ and Natalie" thing. That never entered the picture. *I missed her loving me.* She was one of those girls who had a gift for life. She was the sort of woman everybody loved, a wonderful human being with great humor and empathy, and we had found everything together. Other than Barbara Stanwyck, she was the first woman who lived up to my idea of what a woman could be.

But I had to face reality. Natalie filed for divorce in April 1962, and it was granted that same month. I stayed in Europe, and my attorney didn't contest it. We had been married three years and seven months—not a long time, but up to that point, the best years of my life.

The second picture under my deal at Columbia was *The War Lover,* with Steve McQueen. It was all right, although Steve and I both felt it could have been better. Neile, Steve's wife, was on the set, and she was a great stabilizing force for him. Steve had just finished *The Magnificent Seven* for John Sturges and was approaching stardom cautiously. Steve didn't like Shirley Ann Field, and I did, a lot, especially offstage, so I worked with her in most of her scenes. She was a lovely girl who had caught a big break with Olivier on *The Entertainer* and didn't really follow it up, but she helped take my mind off Natalie for a time.

I found Steve very self-conscious, and very competitive, even about small things. For instance, Steve was about five-nine, smaller than me, so he made sure to never have his wardrobe hanging next to mine where anybody could see it. It's the sort of thing that strikes me as wasted effort—why not use that emotional energy for something constructive? Steve was such a complicated man: always looking for conflict and never really at peace. That kind of personality can be very wearing, to say the least.

But Steve was a good friend at a difficult time in my life. The subject of Natalie came up often, and he knew I was brokenhearted. He was very sympathetic, and I grew to like Steve a lot; I think he trusted me as much as he trusted anybody, which wasn't all that much.

Later, when I was married to Marion, my second wife, the four of us became close, and Steve and I would ride our motorcycles in the desert together, then have dinner and drink. He loved antique airplanes; he had a hangar near Santa Barbara where he kept his biplanes.

While I was making *The War Lover,* Darryl Zanuck called and asked me to be in *The Longest Day,* his epic about D-Day. He didn't have to ask twice. Working on *The Longest Day* was great fun, but it was also one of those films filled with a purpose—to tell a great story that had never been told before. I was thrilled to find that my scenes were to be shot at Point du Hoc, and Darryl directed them himself. Most of the actors were on "favored-nation status"—meaning we all got the same money—so there was very little competitiveness.

It was all very felicitous; I had been through such a terribly dark time, and it seemed that the clouds were lifting. It was at this time that I flew from London to Paris to shoot my scenes for *The Longest Day.* I was rushed through customs, and there were about three hundred people to meet me at the Georges V. Hey, I'm an actor. I love it; I think I'm doing just great. I took my sweet time getting through the crowd, signing autographs and milking it, and I finally got to the front desk. I said that I'd like my suite, and the man behind the desk said, "What's your name?" I looked at him somewhat coldly and said, "Robert Wagner."

That night I went out with Eddie Fisher and Elizabeth Taylor, who were taking a break from the early stages of *Cleopatra.* We had a sensational time. Too sensational. By the time I got back to the hotel, I was thoroughly blitzed. I walked up to the desk and asked for my key. The man behind the desk said, "What's your name?" I grabbed him by the lapels and said, "You son of a bitch, my name is . . ." And then I looked at him through my alcohol haze and realized that this was not the same man. And then I looked around the lobby carefully and realized that this was not the Georges V. I dropped the man's lapels, apologized profusely, then found my way to the right hotel. Easily one of the most embarrassing moments of my life.

I know that Eddie Fisher ended up as something of a joke, but he had a wonderful way with women, and on the basis of the times I spent with them, he and Elizabeth were good together. The thing about Eddie professionally was that he had absolutely no sense of rhythm, which makes singing pretty difficult. He started drinking because he thought it would relax him and make him as loose as Dean Martin. He could never understand how guys like Dean did what they did. But then, they had rhythm.

*The Longest Day* reunited me with Mother Mitchum, who was as he had been. We were walking down the Champs-Élysées together when a woman came up to him and said, "Mr. Cooper, would you autograph my passport?" He took her passport and wrote, "Fuck you, Gary Cooper."

The thing about Mitchum was that you never knew which direction he would go. He was extremely bright, and his responses could be variable: he could laugh something off, or he could get very dark and wintry. Like the time in the 1940s when he got caught smoking marijuana. Now, when has a movie star actually done time, before or since? But Mitchum was not just bright, he was brave as well. When he got busted, he said, "Fuck it," took the fall, and did the time. As far as he was concerned, it was no big deal.

I think that element of authentic strength and danger was

what made him so compelling on screen. The general theory about Mitchum was that he really didn't give a shit. Not true. He gave a shit—he just didn't want to get caught giving a shit.

The thing about the movie business is that it's full of legendary characters, not all of whom are famous. One of the reasons *The Longest Day* was such great fun was Ray Danton. Ray was one of those actors who put his energy into his life, not his career. At the time we did *The Longest Day,* Ray was shacked up in a hotel with two very beautiful girls. There were two-way mirrors in the bedroom, and the hotelier was making a great deal of money charging people to watch Ray make love to two women at once. Ray never knew how much money this guy was making off his remarkable prowess!

Years went by, and Ray was now directing television. He directed a couple of episodes of *Switch* with Eddie Albert and me. Sharon Gless and Ray hit it off professionally, and she kept him with her as her star rose on television. When Ray developed terrible kidney problems, she kept him working on *Cagney and Lacey.* Ray no longer had the stamina to direct, but he could hold script, and Sharon made sure that Ray always had a job so he could keep his medical benefits.

It goes without saying that Sharon is a special lady. Occasionally, things happen in this business that make you realize there are people who live by a higher law than the one of the jungle.

When I got to London, I started taking out Joan Collins again. Joan was always companionable, always fun. As a matter of fact, I was the one who introduced Joan to Anthony Newley, whom she eventually married. We had gone to see *Stop the World, I Want to Get Off,* which Tony wrote and in which he starred, and that brought Joan and me to a screeching halt. I asked Joan to come to Rome with me, but she didn't want to go because (a) she didn't like to fly, and (b) she wanted to be with Tony Newley.

So I went on ahead and met Marion Marshall in Rome. Marion had divorced Stanley Donen and had two wonderful sons, Josh and Peter, as well as a magnificent apartment in Rome. I was immediately enthralled with Marion and her boys, and very soon we had a life together.

Marion was a year older than I was, and she had been a successful model before she got to Fox around the same time as Marilyn Monroe. When Marion married Stanley Donen in 1952, she quit acting to raise their two kids—Peter, who was born in 1953, and Josh, who came along two years later. The marriage broke up in 1959.

Marion was the right woman for me at the right time, and she gave me a lot. For one thing, she began to heal the wounds left by the divorce from Natalie. For another thing, my friends told me that she gave me an international quality that hadn't been there before. She was a refining influence in matters of clothes and attitude.

And magically, things started to happen in a positive way for me, which was certainly a switch from the last couple of years. Besides my new love for Marion, Josh and Peter became my sons every way but legally. And a wonderful, empathetic agent named Carol Levi began handling me. Carol was based in the William Morris office in Rome and understood exactly what I wanted from the next phase of my career.

Carol helped get me cast in *The Condemned of Altona*, a fine picture with Sophia Loren directed by the great Vittorio De Sica. *The Condemned of Altona* was based on a play by Jean-Paul Sartre, and Vittorio was without question one of the best directors in the world. I was back doing what I wanted to do: making good pictures, working with great directors.

Years before we did the De Sica picture, I had met Sophia
Loren when she came over to Fox after shooting *Boy on a Dolphin* in Europe and the studio set up a publicity event for her.
Buddy Adler was running the studio then, and we were all supposed to toast her for the cameras, but I had neglected to get a
glass of champagne. Sophia promptly handed me her glass. A
small thing, but I would learn that Sophia is more than an actress, she is a woman of true graciousness. She sees more than
her reflection in the mirror; she sees the people around her and
acts accordingly.

There's a famous still of Sophia looking askance at Jayne
Mansfield's breasts. That picture was taken at Romanoff's. I
was on my way there when I passed Jayne in her car. Her window was down, and she was applying rouge to her nipples. I
knew her, so I stopped the car. "Looking good!" I said, but
what I really wanted to know was what the hell was she doing?
It turned out to be a setup to draw attention away from Sophia,
who was the hot new girl in town. It worked, for that one night,
but Sophia had the career that Jayne could only dream about.

During *The Condemned of Altona,* I fell madly in love with
Sophia. Who wouldn't? Most nights she would cook for me,
and on top of everything else she's a splendid cook. She was
very loyal to Carlo Ponti, although she was never short of
admirers including Cary Grant who she got to know during
*The Pride and the Passion.* Sophia had never had a father in her
life—her own father disappeared when she was quite young—
and Carlo had found her at a very young age and carefully built
her career, and she wasn't about to betray him. I could certainly
appreciate that loyalty; I could also respect it. Sophia mostly
lives in Switzerland now, but we talk all the time.

As much as I adored Sophia and Vittorio De Sica, I grew to
detest Maximilian Schell. He'd won the Oscar for best actor the
year before for *Judgment at Nuremberg,* and seemed pretty

enthralled with his own accomplishments. Of course, Sophia had also won an Oscar, for *Two Women,* but you would never have known it. Her attitude was that of a professional going to work—no more, no less.

The night before we shot a crucial scene, Schell came to my hotel room and gave me a big talk about our playing brothers and how we had to get into the essence of the scene we would be shooting. The next day Schell was behind the camera giving me the off-camera lines for my close-ups, and the entire time I was acting he was shaking his head.

Brothers, my ass!

It was stunningly unprofessional, not to mention calculatingly rude, and the first and only time I've ever seen anybody pull anything like that. What was really upsetting him was the fact that Sophia and I were very close, and he didn't like that.

Schell's rudeness became his modus operandi; one day, when he was doing a scene with Sophia, he asked me to leave the set because he found my presence disconcerting. We were in Livorgno at the time, and I seriously thought about taking a club to his head, but Carlo Ponti talked me out of it. Of course, Schell being Schell, on those occasions when I've run into him in later years, he's all over me with bonhomie. "Oh, darling, it's so good to see you"—it feels like showbiz bullshit.

I had been looking forward to working with Fredric March, an actor I had admired tremendously for years, even when he was desperately trying to steal scenes, as with his furiously fanning himself in *Inherit the Wind.* Unfortunately, Freddy was a bit disappointing. If you asked Freddy about a picture he'd made twenty years before, he'd reach into his pocket, pull out a little card that had a complete list of his credits, and refresh his memory. He was very much the Master Thespian, and he gave Vittorio De Sica fits.

Freddy was playing a character based on the founder of the

Krupp munitions dynasty, and the picture opened with his character being given a fatal cancer diagnosis. Every day Vittorio would tell him, "Freddy, do not play self-pity. Do not fall into that trap." And every single day Freddy would play self-pity and Vittorio would have to pull him out of it.

Freddy had a reputation of being incredibly, tastelessly bold with women, and the reputation was completely deserved. It was a remnant of the early part of the century, when leading men sleeping with their leading lady was practically contractual. Once he reached over to look at a brooch Marion was wearing, and he very obviously copped a feel of her left breast while pretending to admire her jewelry. The man was sixty-five years old, but he would have fucked mud if someone had held it for him.

Spencer Tracy had worked with Freddy on *Inherit the Wind,* and when I got back to Hollywood, I asked Spence about him. All he would say was, "He wouldn't put down that fucking fan."

But Freddy had been around for nearly forty years and picked up a lot of experience along the way. He gave me some good political advice. The company was planning to shoot in East Germany, and the American embassy didn't want American citizens going across into a Communist country. Freddy took me aside and told me, "Look, you don't want to be lumped in with Vittorio and Abby Mann and the rest of these left-wing guys. It's a stigma; it won't do you any good." On balance, he was probably right. Freddy had been a man of the left all his life and had gotten into some trouble during the blacklist era because of it. He was thoughtfully trying to save me from trouble I really didn't need.

In contrast to Max Schell, Vittorio De Sica couldn't have been warmer or more welcoming. During production, he would stand right next to the lens so that he could see what the camera was seeing. He let me watch him work in the editing room and took me completely under his wing. One day he showed me a scene he had shot where I was on camera left and I didn't have enough authority. "See," he said, "be on the right side. And be more powerful. I want you to drop your voice." And he put his hand on my chest, where my voice needed to be placed. Vittorio sent me to Professor Scurri, who helped me get away from the California voice I had been struggling with for a decade. And Vittorio reshot the offending scene, to much better results.

To be in Rome in the early 1960s was to be in the middle of an atmosphere of luxurious creativity. It was palpably *alive,* in the same way London would be a few years later. There was absolutely nothing about Rome I didn't like—the people, the piazzas, the entire Italian attitude toward life. The Italians work in order to live, not the other way around.

The premiere of *The Condemned of Altona* was in Milan, and the picture was very well done and received fantastic reviews. When the movie premiered, Sophia insisted that I escort her. I remain proud of the picture—the European version. In America, Fox lost its nerve and edited the picture severely, and most of the atmosphere and all of the quality disappeared. A few years later, Fox would do the same thing to Luchino Visconti's *The Leopard,* which contained a performance by Burt Lancaster that was truly majestic—a career performance. It was a better picture than ours, but by the time the studio had finished cutting and redubbing it, the magic was gone—just as with *The Condemned of Altona.*

From working with Vittorio De Sica, my next picture was with Blake Edwards. Marion and I were in Paris when we ran into Blake, and Blake promptly cast me in his new picture. Then John Foreman came over to Rome, and I was once again in a family atmosphere, where I've always been happiest.

It was June 1962, and Marion and I were in Rome. One night we were having dinner at the Hostaria dell'Orso, when Natalie and Warren walked in. It was one of those moments that can be classified as awkward, with the potential to become excruciating. Generally speaking, the movies do these scenes better than life.

The conversation was polite and stilted—"How's your mother?" "Fine, how's yours?" "Fine." After the exchange of pleasantries was over, we looked at each other.

"Miss you," I said.

"Miss you too."

Both Marion and Warren were standing there while we had our little moment. Maybe they minded. I don't really know, and I guess I don't really care. Neither of us could say what we were feeling, but there was a strong vibe in the air, and I could sense she was just as aware of it as I was. Afterward, I dropped Marion off at her apartment, went back to my place, and sat down and wrote Natalie a letter. I told her how much I valued our relationship; I told her that she would always be in my heart.

As soon as I was finished, I went back to her hotel—the Grand. I stood there, scanning the building, wondering which room was hers, hoping I'd see her outline against the shades. Finally, I went in and handed the letter to the concierge and told him to give it to Miss Wood. He walked over and put it in her mailbox. I went back to my apartment, and first thing the next morning I went back to the Grand. She had checked out early. The letter was still in the mailbox, unopened.

Over the next eight years, we would run into each other a number of times, although that was the only time it happened when I was in Europe. These moments were always intense—it was as if everybody else in the room froze and the sound died away and we were the only two people still moving, talking, and breathing.

# TWELVE

# "I HAVE A FROZEN COCK."

With David Niven and my friend and publicist George Kirvay, at
David's house at St. Jean-Cap Ferrat in the south of France.
(COURTESY OF THE AUTHOR)

I f you loved David Niven—and everybody did, with the tragic exception of his second wife—you called him "Niv." I had first met Niv years before, on Bogart's yacht, the *Santana*, and we immediately struck up a friendship. Later, when he was having an affair with that wonderful woman and actress Deborah Kerr, Natalie and I spent a great deal of time with both of them. So the Cortina d'Ampezzo location of *The Pink Panther* was as much a reunion as it was a film set.

I loved David. I loved the way he lived his life. I loved the way he left Hollywood and went to Europe, which was one of the reasons I did the same thing. And when we met up in Europe, David became another mentor for me. He took me to his tailor, he took me to his shirtmaker. David dressed in Turnbull and Asser, not to mention Schifanelli. He would put on a gorgeous dress shirt and roll the cuffs back—a marvelous sense of style, elegant and casual at the same time. Along with Marion, he helped give me a new style for my new life, and at a time when my confidence had flagged, he worked hard to give me a sense of my own possibilities.

Now, at Cortina d'Ampezzo, there was a chairlift that went up to the top of the mountain, with a restaurant at the top. The height went from two thousand feet to eight thousand feet, and it was a beautiful place. One day in particular began with stunning weather, so David and I went up the mountain to have lunch. We were dressed casually in slacks, but once we got up there, the bad weather moved in, and it got cold. Really cold.

As we came down after lunch, Niv was sitting in the chairlift saying very matter-of-factly, "My cock is frozen. I have a frozen cock. Frozen solid." When we got down to the hotel and bar, Marion was waiting for us. David explained his predicament and asked Marion to sit on his lap and save the life of his favorite friend. Having a strong maternal disposition, Marion sat in his lap and saved a very valuable part of David's life.

Niv ordered a brandy. And then he told me to follow him, and we went into the john, where he unzipped and dropped his unit into the brandy snifter to try to save it from frostbite. I was staring at something I never imagined on the eleventh hole at Bel-Air.

It was at that point that the bathroom door swung open, and in came a man in a military uniform. And he looked at David with his cock in a brandy glass, and me staring at it, and stopped dead, with a stunned look on his face. At which point Niv looked up and said, "I always give it a little drink from time to time."

I just fell over laughing and was so hysterical I literally wet my pants. From that day on, Niv always referred to Marion as the family bird-warmer because she had sat on his lap and warmed him up.

He was a special, special man.

Niv specialized in a smooth, blithe manner and an authentic wit and joie de vivre. Beneath that was a lot of pain that he worked very hard not to let anybody see. It wasn't that he was protective of himself; I think he thought that there was quite enough misery in the world, and he saw no reason to add more.

After David came back from the war, during which he helped plan the raid on Dieppe and was attached, among other places, to Montgomery's army, he resumed his career in Hollywood. On May 19, 1946, he and his wife, Primmie, were at a party at Tyrone Power's house. Rex Harrison, Lilli Palmer, Patricia Medina, and Richard Greene were also there. Soon after they started to play a hide-and-seek game called "Sardines" that had to be played in the dark, there was a terrible thud. Ty Power put the lights on, and everybody realized that Primmie had mistaken the basement door for the bathroom door and taken a terrible fall down the stairs—twenty feet, headfirst. She was at the bottom of the basement steps, unconscious.

They got her up the stairs, and while they waited for the ambulance, Primmie opened her eyes and said, "I feel so strange . . . even when I had babies I never felt so. . . ." And then she closed her eyes. "We'll never be invited again," she said. Primmie died two days later, at the age of twenty-eight. David was left with his two boys, David Jr., who was three and a half, and Jamie, who was six months old.

People who knew David at the time said he was completely devastated. David would talk about how he loved her, how cruel it was, and how he was never happy again. Clark Gable, who had lost Carole Lombard in a plane crash in 1942, when she was just thirty-three and they had only been married three years, helped him through it, just as in time David would help me.

Part of the reason David was always in some secret pain was his second marriage, a year and a half after Primmie died, to a woman named Hjordis Genberg. It was a classic rebound mistake, made partially because David didn't want to marry any of the actresses who pursued him relentlessly after Primmie died. I think he wanted a wife for himself and a mother for the boys.

Hjordis was quite beautiful, but that's a genetic accident; for the qualities that stem from character, she hadn't had as much luck. Niv's eventual nickname for her was "Nej," which is pronounced "Nay," and is Swedish for "no," which she said all the time. Perhaps the early years were good, but by the time I met David in the mid-1950s, he was having affairs, as was Hjordis, who was also emptying a lot of bottles in the bargain.

David's method for coping with all this was to pretend that nothing was wrong. He was a good, involved father, allowing for the fact that he was a successful actor and away making movies a lot. Otherwise, he was very concerned about his boys' future and welfare.

David met Deborah Kerr when they were making *Bonjour Tristesse,* and they immediately had a great simpatico. They were the most wonderful couple I ever spent time with. They had the same sense of humor, the same sense of effortless continental style, and together they were a joy. Besides Deborah, the location of the Preminger movie exposed David to the Côte d'Azur, and he fell in love with that as well. A couple of years later, he bought his villa at Cap Ferrat, where he lived for the rest of his life.

Sometimes a hit has a tangible feel to it, because you're having so much fun, and *The Pink Panther* was like that. Blake Edwards was a very spontaneous director, and extraordinarily gifted. Blake loved Laurel and Hardy, as did I; the essence of their comedy was the idea that the buildup to the joke is as important as the joke. A deliberate rhythm can make a joke much funnier than rushing to the punch line. Watching Blake gently impose that rhythm on his actors was one of the joys of making *The Pink Panther.*

Blake would arrive on the set and announce, "All right, let's rehearse. Let's try this. You do that. See if that works." The dialogue was on paper, but Blake rehearsed a great deal, as you have to with physical comedy. And he shot a lot of takes. The mood was elevated, very happy, so it was a pleasure to work with him. When Peter Sellers replaced Peter Ustinov—Blake had wanted Sellers from the beginning—and the two of them started to work on Inspector Clouseau, there was such a feeling of creation. It was no slipshod thing—it was magical!

The only blight on the great experience of *The Pink Panther* occurred during a sequence when I was hiding in the bathtub with Capucine. The scene called for me to emerge from beneath the suds and between her legs, but the prop man first had to create the suds, which is hard to do under bright lights. He told me he had used baby detergent, but he had actually used the strongest detergent he could find. It burned and lacerated my eyes, it burned Capucine's vagina, and it burned her under her arms.

I was in terrible pain, and I was scared. An ophthalmologist washed out my eyes, but I had to keep my eyes covered for an endless three weeks, opening them only to put in eyedrops. For those three weeks, Josh and Peter led me around. Back in Hollywood, some thought was given to writing me out of the script so that no production time would be lost, but David, Peter, and Blake refused to continue unless they could shoot around me while my eyes got better. After three weeks, my eyes were fine again. Because of my friends, I kept my job, which at that point in my life was of critical importance. The fact that the picture was an international hit was also a great help.

Most people in show business have some level of talent. Peter Sellers had a level of genius. It was Peter who helped break me of a bad habit I had fallen into. As *The Pink Panther* wore on, I began to develop a nasty case of stage fright. It didn't have anything to do with the injury to my eyes; it was that my confidence was still a quart low, and I was working opposite Peter Sellers and David Niven, for God's sake! They were so good, so seamless in their work, and I began to wonder if I was in their league. At first, I got a slight case of the shakes, and then it manifested itself as not being able to look the other actors in the eye.

This was an entirely new experience for me. When I had been starting out, I was nervous, of course, but stage fright goes far beyond nervousness. Stage fright limits your concentration because you're not thinking about the scene—you're not thinking about anything other than how terrified you are. It's emotionally disfiguring.

Very little in life can be done tentatively. Certainly, acting can't. It's like telling a woman you're in love with her when you're not. The lie shows, and even if the audience can't tell, you can, and you feel like a total fraud, which only increases your inner terror—"They're going to find me out!"

One day Peter said to me, "What the hell are you doing with your eyes?" I was hooding them slightly, because I was afraid of the camera. Peter was the only one who noticed, and he forced me to confront it. I went to David with what was happening, and he said it was something that had to be worked through. David ran scenes with me numerous times so that I would be as comfortable as possible.

All this happened toward the end of the shoot, which, other than the incident with the detergent, had been an entirely wonderful event. It's possible that I was upset about saying good-bye to a group of people who had become a sort of surrogate family for me. In any case, I knew the stage fright was something I was going to have to address.

Peter was always a little crazy, but I must say that I never found him that nuts. I did have to talk to him at one point: he liked amyl nitrate when he was getting oral sex, and I told him that unless he was careful he was going to blast his heart right out of his chest. Amyl nitrate extends the orgasm for a very long time, and it can be dangerous. And that's what eventually happened: he had a massive coronary while making Billy Wilder's *Kiss Me, Stupid*. After that, he got really crazy, but for some reason it never bothered me.

A few years after *The Pink Panther* I was doing *It Takes a Thief,* and Peter guest-starred for me, playing a man with a nautical shop. As always, he was great fun. He gave me a gold cigarette lighter, which I have kept by my bed for more than forty years.

This run of pictures put me right where I wanted to be—in a different world than I had been in back in Hollywood. And if

I was a member of an ensemble rather than carrying the picture, that was fine with me, so long as the picture had some chance at quality.

Next up was *The Biggest Bundle of Them All*, with Raquel Welch and Edward G. Robinson, which also gave me a welcome reunion with Vittorio De Sica.

Eddie Robinson, of course, was just a wonderful actor, and he was also the most cultured and elegant of men. He had amassed one of the finest art collections in Hollywood when a toxic divorce forced him to sell most of it off. He sold Van Gogh's *Sunflowers* to Stavros Niarchos, with the proviso that once Eddie got back on his financial feet he would be able to buy it back for the same amount of money Niarchos had paid him.

A few years later, Eddie had the money, but he could never get Niarchos on the telephone. It doesn't matter how much money a chiseler may have—he's still a chiseler. Eddie went on to rebuild his collection. He converted his garage into an art gallery, and he was the proud owner of a three-panel *Water Lilies* by Monet.

Raquel was a very difficult woman; her career was at white heat, she was only twenty-five or twenty-six years old, and as a result she was terrified. Her fear manifested itself in her constant lateness. She would be in makeup for hours while she kept everybody waiting. It was the same behavior that gradually alienated people from Marilyn Monroe, who was probably driven by many of the same fears.

Yet, as difficult as it was working with Raquel, I liked her and felt sorry for her. She didn't seem to have the tools she needed to handle her life. She asked me once about a painting she was interested in buying, and I told her a story that Eddie Robinson had told me, about how purchasing a painting can change your life.

Eddie had been a struggling young actor in New York when he scraped the money together to buy a small Cézanne. He took it home and hung it over his mantel, then realized it didn't look quite right. He changed the mantel, and the painting did indeed look better. Then he realized that the room wasn't quite right, so he got new furniture that was more in keeping with the painting and the mantel. This went on until he moved to an entirely different apartment, just so he could properly showcase the Cézanne.

"You can't worry about the value of the painting appreciating," I told Raquel. "You just have to make sure that the painting feeds you in some way; you have to buy something you genuinely like, that you want to see every day. And if you can find a painting like that, then you have to have the right place to display it, and that's how a painting can change your life."

I told her all this, and she looked at me and said, "I don't have any of that. How can I get that?"

Well, it helps if you have someone you trust to lead you through things. I had been lucky—Barbara Stanwyck, Clifton Webb, Natalie, and a lot of other special people had lent me their good taste until I could develop my own. Raquel wasn't that lucky.

I found her oddly vulnerable, but Vittorio De Sica and Eddie Robinson weren't buying it. Waiting for her drove them both crazy, because professionalism and courtesy was the absolute bedrock for that generation of actors, irrespective of nationality. One day Eddie Robinson finally exploded and read her the riot act. He excoriated her for being unprofessional, for being rude, for being inconsiderate, for being less than all the other people she was working with, for thoughtlessly subjecting other people to her indifferent ethics. He just kept going. It took him six or seven minutes, and he was amazingly eloquent; he never repeated himself.

Raquel's response was to cry a little bit and continue to keep everybody waiting. One day we had been sitting there waiting . . . waiting . . . waiting. She finally came out of her trailer and walked past us. Vittorio muttered, "She's so strong, it would take six oxen to pull a hair from her cunt."

In the spring of 1963, Marion, the boys, and I came back to America. Marion and I were married on July 22, 1963, in the Bronx Courthouse. My best man was Bill Storke, the dear friend who flowed through my life for more than fifty years. We trusted each other absolutely, and Bill made me godfather to his son Adam, who became—horrors!—an actor. Staying close to and loving Adam as I do has enabled me to stay close to Bill, even after he died in 1996.

In October, Marion and I moved into a small ranch I bought in Tarzana that had originally been built by Robert Young. It was a beautiful place, not far away from the old Edgar Rice Burroughs house where he had entertained us with the jungle sounds he piped into the trees. The Tarzana ranch had eight acres of land and gardens—now all that beautiful land is covered with houses.

I remembered how much dogs and horses had meant to me when I was a boy, so I made sure that Peter and Josh had access to both. Those first couple of Christmases with Marion, Josh, and Peter, in Rome as well as America, were wonderful. Seeing Christmas through the eyes of a child makes it a more important experience than it can ever be with adults. Christmas is better with children than it is without them, and I don't think it matters all that much where you are.

I devoutly believe that it's not the house, it's who's in it. It's not what's under the tree, it's who you're with. I was with my new family, and that's why it was so good for me.

# THIRTEEN

# "MY HEART STOPPED
# WHEN I SAW HER."

PHOTO/DOMINICK DUNNE

My second wife, the beautiful Marion. (PHOTOGRAPH BY DOMINICK DUNNE)

arion and I had some initial problems in relation to her two children, Josh and Peter. Her ex-husband, Stanley Donen, lived in England and there was a custody battle which ended up being very lengthy and costly—the trial transcripts were eventually five feet high. Between the court case and the purchase of the Tarzana property, I was financially strapped and very much on the edge.

The low point came when I had to post a $40,000 bond into an interest-bearing account for the court. I had about $30,000 in AT&T stock, but I didn't want to sell it, and I didn't have $40,000 in cash. It was the last thing on earth I wanted to do, but I went to my father, explained the situation, and asked him to give me a loan.

To make a long story short, he wouldn't lend me the $40,000. He liked Marion but hadn't wanted me to marry her because she had two kids who were half-Jewish because of Stanley. Refusing the loan was his way of registering his disapproval. I wouldn't say that my father was an anti-Semite, but like many people from his time and place, he felt that Jews were definitely déclassé.

I went to Watson Webb and explained the situation. Wat listened, nodded, sat down, and wrote me a check for $40,000—the equivalent of several hundred thousand dollars today. Wat came through for me because he understood what it was like to have a father who didn't believe in you.

Ultimately, Marion retained custody. Stanley didn't even bother to appear at the final hearing. All this crushed Marion and brought her to the edge of a breakdown, which was, of course, the point.

I've mentioned Marion's marvelous sense of style, which rubbed off on me, but her greatest gift to me was undoubtedly our daughter Kate, who was born in May 1964 and was named after Kate Hepburn. Having a child is a common experience, but that doesn't make it any less astonishing. As I looked down at Katie for the first time, I felt a surge of responsibility and an entirely different level of love than anything I had ever felt before.

There was a sense of healing in that emotion. I had lost Natalie, much of my career momentum, and, a couple of weeks before Katie was born, my father—a relationship that was never completely resolved.

At the end of his life, my parents were living in La Jolla. One day my father ordered something to be delivered from a drugstore. He hung up the phone and said to my mother, "Can we afford this?" At the time he had several million dollars.

Soon afterward, he had a cerebral hemorrhage. He had always been an incessantly busy man, but for the most part he had settled down. "I want to die in that chair," he had told me, pointing at his favorite easy chair, and he nearly did.

After the stroke, a neighbor who was a doctor gave my father some shots to stabilize him, and he was taken to Scripps, where everybody waited for me. It was a serious stroke, similar to the one that hit Joe Kennedy. Had he lived, my dad would have been in a wheelchair and unable to speak. I knew he wouldn't want to live like that, so I told the doctors to take no unusual measures—a decision with which my mother agreed. My father died and was buried at Forest Lawn.

I believe he had a premonition that something was going to happen, because he had made a special effort to talk to me and my sister just before he died, which was unusual for him. My father being my father, everything was in perfect order, so there were no problems with his estate, which went entirely to my mother.

And then we opened up his safety deposit box and discovered a marriage certificate that predated his marriage to my mother. I was stunned; neither my sister nor I had any idea he had been married before. I think my mother knew, because she never batted an eye. Now, you would think that a son who was having terrible marital problems and who was, moreover, in terrible pain might be taken aside by his father and told, "Look, this happened to me too, and you can survive it."

But that conversation never happened. Robert J. Wagner Sr. was a Catholic, a thirty-second-degree Mason, a man of severe temperament. When I would express my feelings about him to my mother, she would simply say, "He loved you, but he loved you in his way." In many ways, he still haunts me.

Because he and I were, at bottom, very different kinds of people, we never shared the emotional intimacy that I desired, but I remain proud of his strength, his will, and the values of hard work that he gave me. He *defined* his own life; judged on the terms he chose, his life has to be considered a great American success story.

So the birth of Katie so soon after the death of my father was a special blessing and a promise of renewal, as every child is. But she was also something more: a chance for me to be a more loving father than my father had been. The moment I looked down at Katie in the hospital for the first time was the moment I realized that a parent's love for his child is one of the few things that is permanent in life. I had finally found something I could count on.

A few nights after Katie was born, I was celebrating at La Scala when Natalie and Mart Crowley walked in. Natalie came over and congratulated me. She seemed very happy, but Mart Crowley told me later that she was actually terribly sad. Partly this was because I had been able to move on and establish a viable marriage with someone else; Natalie herself had bounced around after she and Warren broke up. Most recently, she'd just split up with Arthur Loew. Beyond that, Natalie was telling friends that she had decided she was ready to have a child, but there was no suitable father in sight.

I didn't know about all that; what I knew was that my heart stopped when I saw her. At the same time, I felt a terrible, conflicting disloyalty to Marion, who deserved a husband totally focused on her.

Professionally, I was open to anything during this period. Although I hadn't been on a stage since high school, when I was offered a production of *Mister Roberts* at the Pheasant Run Playhouse in St. Charles, Illinois, just outside of Chicago, I leaped at it. We opened in January 1965, and I think it was something of a career starter for me, especially emotionally.

For one thing, I loved that play, even though any actor

who plays the part is inevitably compared to Henry Fonda, just as anybody who plays Stanley Kowalski has to fight the ghost of Marlon Brando. For another, I found that I loved being onstage. Understand, I was scared beyond all imagining, because the rhythm of a stage performance is so different. Films are made thirty seconds at a time, and the arc of a performance is shaped with the director and, especially, the editor. Onstage, once the curtain goes up, the actor is completely on his own. There are no retakes, and the performance has to be sustained and shaped, and the dialogue remembered, for two and a half hours every night, not to mention twice on matinee days.

The critical moment was my entrance on opening night. It was the first time for the audience, but it was also the first time for me, so the illusion of spontaneity was not going to be a problem. But I was stunned when the audience applauded before I opened my mouth. Jesus Christ! What did they expect from me? What did they want? *What if I disappointed them?* I hadn't expected the applause, and it threw me. But I loved doing the play, and it was a pretty big success. Years later I would scratch the theater itch again, for years at a time, when I did *Love Letters* across the country and in London.

My first film back in America was *Harper* with Paul Newman, which was a joy. Jack Warner didn't want me in the movie because he now had a grudge against me. Years before, I had taken a position he hadn't liked about Natalie's participation in a publicity tour for the studio. I hadn't wanted her to go, and he threatened her with suspension. So now I was in the position Judy Garland had been in—except that I hadn't stolen any furniture, so the hole wasn't as deep. John Foreman and Paul both insisted, however, that I make the picture, and I did *Harper* as the heavy, which is always great fun for an actor.

*Harper* was the first of many films John Foreman would make with Paul Newman. Foreman had been an agent, one of the founders of CMA. From his partnership with Paul, he also developed a partnership with John Huston. Anjelica Huston has always said that John Foreman was responsible for her career, because he was willing to cast her in *Prizzi's Honor.*

John Foreman was a wonderful man and always adventurous in his choice of material as well as adventurous in his life— probably too much so. Eventually, a lot of people turned on him because John was not a man who was shy about expressing himself. But John was a fighter, and a believer. Once he set his course, nobody could deter him, and the best testament to his instincts is the roster of the pictures he produced: *Harper, Butch Cassidy and the Sundance Kid, Prizzi's Honor. . . .*

While we were shooting *Harper* at Warner Bros., Natalie was making *Inside Daisy Clover* there at the same time. One afternoon, while the lights were being set, the screenwriter William Goldman and I walked over to her set. They were making a musical number—"You're Gonna Hear from Me." It was a crowded set, and I climbed up on a ladder to get a better angle. After the director called, "Print," Natalie was on her way to her dressing room when she passed by the ladder.

"Hi," I said.

"Hi," she said, looking up.

"That looked good."

"You think?"

"I do. Yeah."

"Hope so. Bye."

"Bye."

It wasn't what was said—it almost never is. It was the meaning behind the words and the look in her eyes. I knew I had the same look in mine. Every time I saw Natalie was like the first time I saw her. Not in that hallway at Fox, but the first time I really saw her. She took my breath away.

# FOURTEEN

# "FRED!...FRED!...FRED!"

With Fred Astaire, the greatest dancer of them all. (COURTESY OF UNIVERSAL
STUDIOS LICENSING LLP)

Taken together, *The Pink Panther* and *Harper* were the beginning of my comeback. In retrospect, I can see that I was never entirely out of options. I may not have been doing the things I would have wanted to do in an ideal world, and I may not have been making the money I wanted to make. But from this time on, I was always going forward, always had something on the burner. Marion was very supportive, and my friends were always there for me.

Time. The key factor is time. Things can change in a minute. A lot of young actors have come to me over the years and talked about how hard it is to make enough money for their families. They can be working, then six or eight months go by with nothing at all, and that can be terrifying. They worry about money, about having enough for their children's needs.

I tell them that the prime factors are time, listening, and the refusal to do anything other than keep going. What's Micawber's line in *David Copperfield*? "Something will turn up." In my experience, something always does turn up, but you have to be alert to it when it does.

*Find smart people and listen to them.* When Lew Wasserman sat me down in 1966 and told me how good I could be on TV, I didn't just say, "Fuck television, I only make movies!" Lew Wasserman was a very bright man, with a track record. You ignored Lew Wasserman at your peril. Ditto John Foreman. You have to listen to smart people who take the time to tell you things.

This is how I came to television: after *Harper,* my agents made a three-picture deal for me at MCA/Universal. Lew Wasserman called and said he wanted me to do one of the shows on *The Name of the Game,* an NBC show with rotating stars.

"I don't want to do television, Lew," I said. "I want to stay in the movies." At that time, there was still something of a stigma attached to TV, and I talked about that. But Lew was Lew, and we kept talking. Other people were slotted into *The Name of the Game*.

Finally, Lew shifted his tactics and said, "Look, we have a great property that's been written just for you, and you would be wonderful in it. I guarantee you that if you make the pilot and we can't sell it as a series, we'll make a movie out of it."

He explained the show to me. I was to play Alexander Mundy, a cat burglar and gentleman thief who has gotten caught. While he's in prison, a government spy agency offers to spring him if he'll work for them, with the possibility of total freedom being dangled as the carrot to keep him in line.

I've heard much worse premises for TV shows, and Lew's suggestion sounded like a good compromise to me. I checked with David Niven, who had gone into TV during a fallow period in his career and made a fortune as a partner with Dick Powell and Charles Boyer in Four Star Productions. David strongly suggested that I give it a whirl. Lew had given me the full-court press, but with David's recommendation, it was game, set, match. I made the move into television, and it proved to be wise, as well as lucrative.

I trusted Lew's and David's judgment, but there was one remaining problem—I was still feeling unsure of myself. I hadn't really addressed the stage fright I had on *The Pink Panther;* if it came back, I knew it would be even more crippling than it had been before.

I went to Gadge Kazan and told him what had happened. Gadge had forgotten more about actors than most directors will ever know, and he suggested I see a therapist, which did indeed help. The more you find out about yourself, the more you can cope with the things life throws at you. And what I found out was what I had long suspected: losing Natalie was the root cause of my insecurity as a professional.

After I agreed to do *It Takes a Thief,* I went to Cary Grant, who had played a similar part in Hitchcock's *To Catch a Thief.*

"Do you have any ideas?" I asked him.

Cary looked at me and said, "Yes, I do. Bring *you* to the part."

It was like a door opening. In the movies, I had always been concerned about playing the character. It hadn't really occurred to me to use my own personality because, like a lot of actors, I wasn't all that sure about my own personality. "Bring *you* to the part" sounded risky—what if they didn't like me? And if they don't like *you,* what's your fallback position? But Cary was a sharp man and had done rather well by bringing aspects of himself to his parts. I decided to give it a try.

Universal was at an interesting stage in its development. About two-thirds of its production was slotted directly for television. Because of its extremely heavy volume, the studio had basically reinstituted the contract system that had died out in the 1950s. Universal had three or four character heavies under contract, a half-dozen leading men, and boxcars of male and female ingenues. It wasn't surprising—Lew Wasserman was an enormous admirer of Louis B. Mayer and the way he had run MGM.

But Mayer had never offered guided tours of his studio to the public, and Lew did. Universal even built sets that were ostensibly part of the backstage apparatus of the studio but were actually just window dressing for the tours; at one point there was a set that tour guides would tell people was "Robert Wagner's dressing room." The folks would come in, walk around, and feel like they'd been in my backyard. In reality, I was never there. No one was, except the tourists. All the people working at Universal were expected to play along and be cordial whenever the trams came by, even if they were an irritating imposition.

One day on the lot the trams came by, and the guide said, "Ladies and gentlemen, there's Neville Brand on the corner!" The people in the tram waved, and so did Neville Brand. And then the guide said, "And there's famous dress designer Edith Head!" Edith took a big sheaf of sketches she was holding and shook them at the tourists like the sketches were signal flags!

The first thing I did at Universal was a TV movie, a light-hearted thriller called *How I Spent My Summer Vacation,* which had a very good cast: Walter Pidgeon, Lola Albright, Peter Lawford, and a delightful actress named Jill St. John. It ran in January 1967, and we outrated the television premiere of the Sam Goldwyn production of *Guys and Dolls.* Lew was pleased, and I was pleased.

Then Lew slotted me into a theatrical, a movie about a golf pro called *Banning.* It was a pleasure for me because I love to golf, and I was again working with the delightful Miss St. John. It was a good picture, but golf movies have never set the box office on fire, probably because the pace of the game is too slow for drama, and *Banning* was no exception.

Finally, it was time to put *It Takes a Thief* into production. Eddie Dmytryk very kindly agreed to direct the pilot, and Lew was right—I did like TV, the pace, the constant flow. I've always been a man who likes action, and TV is made for that temperament. So we made the pilot, and ABC passed on it. I headed off to Brazil, where I directed a documentary about the bossa nova called *And the World Goes On.* Soon after I got there I got a telegram: *It Takes a Thief* was going on at midseason. I couldn't believe it; what I didn't know was that the studio had recut the show and added some scenes, and the new version had sold.

At this point, I figured I was in deep trouble. For one thing, midseason shows of that period could usually be characterized as lame, halt, or blind—sometimes all three. They were cannon fodder to be thrown on the air and to fill time until the shows the networks really cared about could come on in the fall. For another, the show had been diddled with, and because of that I felt less a part of it. I steeled myself for the firing squad.

*It Takes a Thief* went on the air on January 9, 1968, and from the first episode the show was a hit. As William Goldman wisely observed many years later, "Nobody knows anything." The year 1968 was, of course, the height of a very crazy time in the world, and I think the show served as a sort of retro escape valve. From *Raffles* on—which David Niven had played, if not quite as memorably as Ronald Colman—a gentleman thief involved with intrigue in exotic locations has never gone out of style.

Roland Kibbee had created the show and stayed on to run it with me. He was always called "Kibbee," never "Roland," but under any name he was a sensational writer and a good man to work with. Because of the show's romantic nature, we had a lot of women guest-starring, which put more strain on the writers. Relationship scenes and love scenes have to be written from character, so it's mandatory to have someone who can do more than write "Long shot: The building explodes." Kibbee was perfect, and he helped make Alexander Mundy one of the best characters ever written for television.

I began alternating TV with movies, which became my modus operandi for the rest of my career and which I regard as the best of both worlds. This began a wonderful time of my life. Personally, Marion and I were solid, we had Katie, and I was professionally back on the upswing.

It was Kibbee's idea to have a semiregular on the show who was related to me. I had a wonderful wardrobe man named Hughie McFarland who had also handled wardrobe for Fred Astaire and John Forsythe. Hughie had been around show business forever, had fallen into booze, but had then become a mainstay at Alcoholics Anonymous, where he helped hundreds of people get sober. Hughie was a wonderful man, and he and Fred were very close; in the years after Fred's wife Phyllis died, Hughie had helped fill some of the lonely times—accompanying Fred to the track, going to the movies with him, that sort of thing.

When the subject of Alexander Mundy's relative came up, it was Hughie who said, "Well, what about Fred?"

I hadn't actually thought about Fred; for one thing, I regarded him as a friend, and I would have felt presumptuous asking him to be on any show that didn't star Fred Astaire. I thought about it for a minute, then said, "Well, yeah, but can we get him?"

"Well, ask him."

I was enthralled with the idea. My time with Zanuck had shown me that the secret to success in show business is to surround yourself with the best talent you can get and then give that talent room to flourish. I was never worried about being overshadowed; it was my show, and anything that made the show better would make me look better. And Fred Astaire never touched anything he didn't improve.

I talked to Universal about getting Fred, and I told them that if he was agreeable, I didn't want any problems—no haggling about money, billing, or anything. If Fred wanted to do the show, I said, give him whatever he wanted.

I had been close to the man I had seen on the eleventh fairway at Bel-Air for some time; we went to the track together and we played golf—nine brisk holes in the morning, and then off to work. When Katie was born, he gave her a gold bracelet with an inscription: I WILL ALWAYS LOVE YOU, KATIE. F.A.

You met the most interesting people through Fred—he introduced me to the great billiards player Willie Mosconi, for instance. I met Fred's mother and sister, whom he absolutely adored. Although Fred's parents were from Omaha, where he had been born, his mother radiated elegance and breeding. His sister Adele did too, but Adele had a bawdy sense of humor, with a vocabulary to match.

Actually, Adele swore like a drill instructor in the Marines. Needless to say, she was a much more outgoing personality than Fred. When she was around, he definitely retreated into the background, and he was fine with that, not that he had much choice—she took total command of the room.

But none of this had anything to do with working together. When I went over to his house to talk about the show, I told him, "This is a business deal. Do what you think best. I will love you no matter what."

Fred and I talked, and he thought it sounded like fun. But when I went back to Universal with this wonderful news, they started bitching. This, I thought, was totally insane. I told them that this man was at the top of the alphabet as well as the top of show business; they could put his name at the top of the menu in the commissary: A for Astaire. You simply couldn't treat Fred Astaire as if he were a day player.

Their objection wasn't to his presence but to the money and the perks that a great star like Fred Astaire had earned many times over. It was at this point that I told Universal that I wasn't Jack Webb and I had no interest in doing a glorified version of *Dragnet*: two-shots and close-ups, no action, no scenery, no guest stars, and everybody reading their lines off a teleprompter. One guy shuffled some papers and said they wished I was Jack Webb because, from the front office's point of view, Jack Webb was the ideal filmmaker.

That was it. I drove off the lot and disappeared. We were in production, and they couldn't find me. When they called the house, Marion told them I wasn't there and she didn't know when she would hear from me. I told my agent to tell them that when they had settled Mr. Astaire's contract and apologized to him, I would be back. After four or five days, they settled.

As always in show business, wasting money is somehow expected, but wasting time drives people crazy, and that was what drove Universal to settle. The studio had stepped on a particular sore spot of mine: a lack of respect for people who have earned respect. I can't and won't accept that. So Fred's contract was quickly settled. He got $25,000 a show, suites on location, and all the perks. And he more than met my expectations.

Once again, I had to get over the fact that I was working with a man I had worshiped since I was a child. But Fred made it easy. I had such great respect for him, and I was so proud to be working with him.

As an actor Fred was fully present, and as a man he was marvelous: substantial, honest, and totally straightforward. I never knew Fred to have a hidden agenda, and there wasn't a duplicitous bone in his body. His ethic was basic: if he was going to do it, he wanted it to be the best it could be. He knew his work, and he loved his work. And yes, he loved to rehearse. When he was on the set, my crew was his crew; everyone deferred to him, as they should have. And to have him on the show was enormously exciting; it elevated the show, and it elevated me.

Glen Larson got the idea of how to introduce Fred on the show. We shot the introduction in Venice, where Fred and I were to run into each other. We had become estranged because Fred's character, Alistair Mundy, was also a thief. I had gotten caught and let the side down. As far as Alistair was concerned, I had failed. We started production in Venice and then began moving south, toward Rome, writing and shooting as we went. I called the studio and said they should let us stay in Italy, that we could do a batch of shows and amortize the costs, and they said yes.

Now, of course, no network series could possibly do this because the costs of shooting in Europe are far too high; even then, it was highly unusual, especially for Universal, which preferred that everything be done at the studio.

We finally got to Rome, where we were shooting in a lovely villa. Fred and I had gone to lunch, and on the way back to the set the crew saw us coming in. One guy began clapping his hands rhythmically and called out "Fred!" The rhythm and the call were quickly picked up by the rest of the crew, and as "Fred! . . . Fred! . . . Fred! . . ." reverberated around the ballroom, Fred began to dance. He did incredible little combinations and twirls, kicked the piano, and danced around the ballroom to the clapping of the crew. It was pure dancing, for his own pleasure and the pleasure of the people he was working with. I just stood there and thought, *Remember this.*

What a time!

It was fascinating to act with Fred, but it was also fascinating to go to the track with him. Fred adored horses and the people who worked with them. Going to the track with Fred was like going to Rome with the pope. He knew *everybody,* from the owners to the stable boys, he could talk their language, and *everybody* liked him. Fred's politics were Republican, but when it came to people he was a true democrat. He was comfortable with anybody, could talk to anybody. People cared about Fred because he cared about people.

He loved the track, I think, because of the commitment that's necessary in racing. Everyone involved in racing, from the back of the track to the front, is totally devoted, and that was the way Fred worked. The job of the dancer is to train and rehearse a dance over and over again until the number is committed to muscle memory. At some point, the dancer reaches a point where he doesn't have to think, he can just perform. It's almost precisely the same thing a trainer does with his horse.

Acting with Fred was like that as well. We talked about scenes a lot—what we were going to do and what we were going for—and we rehearsed a lot. I found that Fred had innate intelligence, and he also had a great instinct for what worked for him and for the character he was playing. And then, when the cameras rolled, we threw all of that away; we weren't talking about it as actors, we were playing it as the characters.

If you think about it, Fred was a very brave performer; he was always trying new things, and he never played it safe. It didn't matter if it was utilizing innovative special effects for a dance number, recording a jazz album, or getting on a skateboard at the age of seventy-eight. Fred was always trying to do something *more*.

The blessing for me was that Fred's knowledge of the business and what was needed to survive it helped me become better. When I would get down about the studio or my career, he would take me aside and tell me, "Don't let them get on top of you. Don't ever get negative. There are a lot of bumps in the road; you've got to keep your chin up. The most important thing is to keep going."

None of this is profound, but all of it is true, and the fact that it was coming from Fred Astaire forced me to take it seriously. So many truly talented people fall by the wayside because they get discouraged and lose their joy, their intensity. It was Fred who impressed upon me the permanent value of maintaining a positive attitude.

We stayed close for the rest of his life. In the mid-1970s, he fell in love with the jockey Robyn Smith, who was more than forty years younger than he was. Fred asked me what I thought. "Look," he said, "everybody thinks I'm crazy to want to marry this woman. What do you think?"

I remembered how much I had loved Barbara Stanwyck; I knew that age was no barrier to love, and I told him I was 100 percent for it. Actually, I told him what Spencer Tracy had told me: "Are you happy? Then that's all that matters." By 1980, when they finally got married, Fred was eighty and Robyn was thirty-six. I believe that, while Fred was alive, she was absolutely great for him.

# FIFTEEN

# "SHE WAS WITH ME FOR THE REST OF HER LIFE."

The second time around, and never happier: Natalie's and my second marriage. My sister, Mary Lou, is next to me, and my daughter Katie is the flower girl. (COURTESY OF THE AUTHOR)

elevision helped me a lot as an actor because I didn't have time to think. It's fast and totally reactive. I couldn't be Cary Grant or Greg Peck, I had to be me, and I discovered that the audience bought it.

I became very close to Lew and Edie Wasserman. Nobody knew this about Lew, but he liked to barbecue, and he would invite me to his house to eat the chicken and ribs he loved to cook. When we weren't eating, we were playing Ping-Pong. Like most people in show business, he was very competitive at everything he did. He liked me, and we had some wonderful family times together. I always felt honored because very few actors were welcomed at his house. The influence he had on my life was tremendous: he was the archetypal big-picture guy, and he had a very specific vision of my career that, in large part, came to pass.

My career was back on the upswing, and I loved it. In 1969 I did *Winning*, with Paul Newman and Joanne Woodward. It was a good part—I was a charming but weak race car driver who seduced Joanne—and a good picture. Paul and Joanne are both quality people, and I have endless admiration for the way they've built their lives and careers. Long before Joanne met Paul, I pushed her off a building in *A Kiss Before Dying*. We had babies at the same time, and we've remained friends for a lot of years. They live in Connecticut, and I'm in California or Aspen, but we stay close.

In 2007 Paul announced that he was retiring from acting. On one level, I understood. What's he got left to prove? He was on Broadway just a few years ago, he's made a dozen great movies, he's raised tens of millions of dollars for charity. He doesn't need to sit on a set with material and coworkers who may not be up to his standards and implicitly ask for their approval. Let's face it, acting doesn't get any easier as you age, emotionally or physically.

Yet, I would bet you that if a great part comes along that Paul likes, and it's something he would be great in, he'll take the tap shoes off the wall and go into his dance. That's what actors do; that's who they are.

Paul once said about me, "If I'm in the trenches, this is the guy I want next to me." Right back at you, pal.

Throughout these years, a part of me was always with Natalie, but in the cold light of day, I never believed I'd get her back, especially after she married the producer Richard Gregson. In June 1970, Marion and I were invited to a party at John and Linda Foreman's house. Linda also invited Natalie and Richard, which was fine with me; the Foremans had maintained their friendship with Natalie just as they had maintained their friendship with me, and they always had our absolute love and trust, together or singly.

The day before the party, Marion wasn't feeling well and called Linda to tell her that she wouldn't be coming but I would still show up. As it turned out, Richard Gregson didn't show up either because he'd gone to New York on a movie matter. Natalie was six months pregnant at the time and spent most of the evening sitting down. I went over and sat at her feet. We never really discussed Subject A, but everything we did discuss had overtones of our feelings for each other. After the party, I drove her home, and we sat there for a minute.

"I guess I shouldn't come in," I finally said.

"I guess you shouldn't," she said. She got out and went in the house. I drove down the street, then had to stop. I was crying, and I couldn't see the road anymore. I sent flowers the next day, and Natalie sent me a thank-you note. She gave birth to Natasha on September 29.

To be blunt, my feelings for Natalie constituted unfinished emotional business for me, and I have no doubt those feelings affected my relationships after we divorced, not to mention my relationships after Marion and I separated and divorced.

The first time I saw Natasha was a couple of days after she was born. My mother and Natalie had always been close, and she wanted to see the baby, so I tightened my belt and took my mother to Natalie's house. My mother and I sat there while Natalie sang Natasha to sleep. (Natasha has always hated to go to sleep.) And while we sat there and watched Natalie nuzzling her daughter and singing, my mother fell asleep!

To see Natalie with her child by another man was difficult, but I realized that I had never seen her happier at any time of her life. I felt a sense of contentment for her, as well as of loss for myself.

It was while I was doing *It Takes a Thief* that I began to stray off the marital reservation. Partially, I think this was because I felt that TV was a wedge back into success for me, and I threw myself into the show in a way I hadn't done before. I was so intensely focused on the show, and on my resurgent career, that I was less focused on my marriage. Marion, Katie, and I were living in Palm Springs, which was too far for a daily commute, so I stayed at my studio apartment four nights a week.

I was literally living at the studio; on top of the twelve-hour days, I was on a nine-month schedule, because we were making thirty-two episodes a year compared to the twenty or twenty-two they make today. You'd have a final dubbing session on a Thursday for the show that was running on Sunday—the print the public saw was still wet, and this went on week after week for nine months.

The suite at Universal made it easier to indulge in behavior I had never indulged in during my previous marriage, and that I wouldn't repeat with my later ones.

The public sees the results of the pressures of show business marriages, but I don't think most people understand why so many end in divorce. For one thing, when an actor goes to work, he's usually working with very attractive people, which is not necessarily the case at the insurance office. Besides that, it's emotional, intense work; when you're acting, you expose everything you are, and there's somebody right there who's collecting it and giving it back to you, and that doesn't happen in other fields either. Take emotion, add intensity, compound it with the fact that all of this takes place in the media hothouse, and you have a dangerous combination.

Nowadays, of course, it's much worse. Because of the twenty-four-hour news cycle, people literally can't walk out the door without having a camera or cell phone shoved in their face, and there are wolf packs of photographers staking out every store, restaurant, and beauty parlor. It's insane—how can anyone live like that? Why would they want to?

TV was a much more grueling regimen than movies, but honesty compels me to admit that wasn't the problem. I had always been able to resist extramarital gopher holes before, but not this time. My relationship with Marion had been initially passionate, but that passed, and in our case friendship wasn't enough to sustain the marriage. If I had to ascribe my infidelity to one thing, I would say that it was the times. Everybody was going crazy, and I felt I had to make up for lost time. That's an explanation, not an excuse.

On some level, Marion knew about what I was doing—wives always do, although they may choose not to acknowledge it— and she got involved in a serious relationship with another man. When that happened, things cracked wide open. At one point she accused me of having an affair with Jill St. John! Her intuition was correct, but premature by more than ten years.

Marion and I separated at the end of 1970 and spent most of 1971 haggling over settlement terms. Finally, on October 14, 1971, the divorce went through.

When ABC abruptly canceled *It Takes a Thief* after three years, I was surprised and disappointed. The show was a success, the format was perfect, and it was already one of the strongest shows in the history of syndication for Universal. But there was a new regime at ABC, and they wanted to clear out some slots for their own shows. Good-bye, Alexander Mundy. I loved playing him, but there was no sense moaning about it; I kept working.

I had some time left on my contract with Universal, and they made some noises about having me work out my contract making guest appearances in other Universal TV shows. Universal was a great believer in moving its people around. If you were under contract, you could be doing *The Virginian* one month and *Ironside* the next month.

But I wasn't about to do guest shots on other people's shows. I had top-lined a successful show of my own and wasn't going to take a step back into being a jobbing actor. Universal backed off. I suspect I got away with my stand because Lew Wasserman always took my side; if I told him I didn't want to do something, I didn't have to.

For a time after my divorce from Marion, I was involved with Tina Sinatra, Frank's youngest daughter. Tina was very young, but Frank always liked me and he was okay with our relationship. One day I told Frank that I didn't think it was going to work long-term but that it was fine for the time being. He was all right with that too. When it came to matters of the heart, Frank was not judgmental and surprisingly open. For that matter, it wouldn't surprise me at all if Frank and Natalie had a thing during the period when we were divorced. She never alluded to it, but he was obviously crazy about her, and what Frank wanted, Frank usually got.

At one point, Tina and I double-dated with Frank when he was dating Jill St. John. The woman who became my wife could have been my mother-in-law. Feel free to frame whatever jokes you can imagine; believe me, I've made them all.

At the same time I was going through my divorce from Marion, Natalie's marriage to Richard Gregson exploded. He had fallen into an affair with their secretary, and Natalie was in the pool and picked up the house phone and heard him coming on to her employee. Natalie went berserk and cut her hand up trying to get back into the house and get at him. She threw him out and never wanted to see him again.

Natalie could turn off on people just as quickly as she could turn on to them, and when that happened, there was rarely any road back. I think she learned to act that way out of self-preservation, because of her family. When she closed the iron door, there was no getting it back open, and she was certainly not a woman to forgive infidelity.

It was John and Linda Foreman who provided the setting for our reconciliation. It was a party at their house, and both Natalie and I were there, unescorted. In retrospect, the fact that John invited both of us was probably not an accident. I looked at Natalie. She looked at me. As always, there was something there—a light that went on in both of us. The next day I called her and told her she looked lovely.

"I hear you're going out with Steve McQueen," I said.

"What are you doing?" she asked.

"I'm with Tina Sinatra."

"How long do you think you're going to be with her?"

"I don't know. She's a wonderful girl."

"Well, if the situation changes, maybe we could get together."

"Maybe we could. Let's see what happens. And if it happens, I hope it happens before winter."

So we were back in touch, although we didn't see each other at that point. I stepped back with Tina. She was twenty-two, and I was forty-one. Tina was a lovely girl, and now she is a lovely woman, but she wanted more out of me than I was capable of giving. Frankly, I was always a little concerned about the age difference between us. Not at that moment, but in terms of the future—I had seen relationships with a similar differential collapse as time went on, and the last thing I needed was another failure. In retrospect, I was too emotionally cautious when it came to Tina; she meant a great deal to me, and she deserved better.

Just before Christmas 1971, I dropped by Natalie's house on North Bentley with some Christmas presents for her and Natasha. There were other people there, so the things that were said were said with our eyes, which seemed to be enough at that point.

Finally, I moved out of the apartment Tina and I had in Century City and moved into Watson Webb's guesthouse for a while. It was Christmas, and I was feeling lonely. I called Natalie and told her what had happened. And then I made my decision. I went back to the house in Palm Springs that I had kept after Marion and I divorced. I called Natalie and asked her to meet me in the desert. She didn't hesitate, just said, "Yes!" and got on the next plane. She was with me in Palm Springs from then until the end of March.

Put it another way: she was with me for the rest of her life.

This began the most exciting, paradisical time of my life. At first, not a lot of people knew that Natalie and I were together again, just the Foremans and a few others. For the first couple of months, we hid out at my house in Palm Springs or hers in Lake Tahoe. Natasha stayed in Los Angeles with her governess, a wonderful woman named Nyoko, who took superb care of her. Natalie and I both knew that this was a crucial moment in our lives, and we didn't want to blow it a second time.

It was a quiet, rich time. We were alone, sitting by the pool, ordering food in, taking long walks. We talked about falling in love with each other again. At night we'd go to restaurants in town we had liked during our marriage—Don the Beachcomber's, among others. We may have been seen, but we managed to avoid being noticed. Night after night we gazed at the stars in the dark desert sky.

Natalie felt that the first time around there had been a sense that we were kids acting out a script—that we deliberately hid our weaknesses from each other because they didn't fit into the plot that we had in our heads. This time we were both determined to be more open with each other, and we weren't afraid to be what we really were.

On those occasions when people saw us together, they'd say, "Huh?" On February 10, 1972, we left Palm Springs to stay at her place on North Bentley Drive for a couple of days. Natalie threw me a forty-second birthday party at her house and invited a lot of people. That served as the official announcement that we were back together, and that was emphasized in April when we went to the Academy Awards and watched Roger Moore and Liv Ullman present the Oscar to Marlon Brando for his performance in *The Godfather*. Or, rather, they presented the Oscar to someone calling herself Sacheen Littlefeather. Marlon, in a typically eccentric gesture of contempt for his own profession, had instructed her to reject it for him in case he won.

What surprised us about that night was the explosion of cameras that greeted us around every corner and the way everybody congratulated us as if we were newlyweds. It seemed as if both the public and the people in the industry were confirming that we belonged together, hand in hand.

I had been doing well financially, but the divorce and an income tax matter had pretty much cleaned me out. It was at this point that Cubby Broccoli did me the great honor of suggesting that I should play James Bond. George Lazenby had replaced Sean Connery, but while *On Her Majesty's Secret Service* had been a good picture, it hadn't done anywhere near the business that the Connery films had. There was no formal offer, but Cubby thought I was a viable candidate to replace Lazenby. I thought about Cubby's suggestion for about two seconds, but realized it just wasn't a good fit. "I'm too American," I told Cubby. "James Bond has to be English. Roger Moore is your guy."

I had known Roger since I was under contract at Fox and he was under contract at MGM, then Warner's. Once, when I sold a car to Gore Vidal, Roger drove it all the way to the East Coast so Gore could pick it up. Roger has always been blithe, charming, hilariously funny—an adorable man.

Roger, if you're reading this, please make the check out to "Cash."

As it happened, because of her percentage of the profits of *Bob and Carol and Ted and Alice,* Natalie was in fine financial shape. She couldn't have cared less about the financial disparity between us. All either of us cared about was that we were rediscovering the most crucial relationship of our lives.

That said, there was always an odd seesaw effect in our careers. When I was hot, she would be marking time, and vice versa. At just about the time we picked up our relationship, Natalie hadn't made a picture in two years because a couple of projects had fallen through, although producers were still throwing scripts over the back wall. Because we had suddenly hit this incandescent moment, neither of us had believed would happen again, she didn't mind.

A few days after the Oscars, we boarded the *Queen Elizabeth II* for a trip to London. I had to promote *Madame Sin,* a TV movie I had produced with Bette Davis, and Natalie went along for the ride. We discovered that Arthur Loew and his wife Regina were also making the crossing, so we settled in for a fun time. Unfortunately, the morning after we sailed a terrible storm blew up. The swells were more than seventy feet high, and the winds were just about as strong as the swells were high. Natalie was nervous and wondered if there was any way off the ship. I explained that we would get blown off the deck before we could even make it to a lifeboat. She didn't even blink; she just ordered another bottle of champagne and some caviar. Because of the storm, we were two days late into Southampton, but we were alive and exceedingly well fed.

We remarried on July 16, 1972, on a chartered boat called the *Ramblin' Rose,* in Paradise Cove off Catalina Island. It was a Sunday, and we made sure to keep everything very quiet. Our attendants were my Katie and her Natasha, and the music we piped through the stereo was Frank singing "The Second Time Around." What else?

Only family and a few friends were invited. Among them were Natalie's sister Lana and her husband of the moment, who was our designated photographer. The photos were supposed to be strictly for our use, but as soon as he got off the boat he sold some of them to a tabloid. I was beyond furious—our private family occasion had been pimped out to the media, and what made it doubly insulting was that Lana's husband had sold photos he hadn't even given us copies of. It was a preview of coming attractions.

For the ceremony, Natalie wore a violet gingham gown. She was just stunningly beautiful. We spent our honeymoon around Avalon, Emerald Bay, and the Isthmus. There was no fog, just brilliant weather and smooth water for the entire time. My response that day, and for the next nine years, was gratitude—pure and simple. It was the most deeply emotional time of my life, and I don't think there was a day when I didn't spend every waking hour in a state somewhere between contentment and jubilation. My money troubles didn't really faze me because I knew that with Natalie at my side, good luck would surely follow.

Throughout our second marriage, there was an unspoken agreement between us not to go back to what had happened before. We never had that conversation. There's an actor's phrase: "in the moment." That's where we were. We both felt so fortunate that we had found each other again that regrets about the past simply didn't enter the picture.

We slid back into each other as smoothly as if we'd never been apart, and the ease of it surprised us both. We fit together perfectly, and this time no alterations were necessary. Before, we were both kids. Now, we had both been through years of therapy and we had both become parents. We were seasoned and better able to deal with the *tsuris* of show business. What was unusual, and what surprised both of us, was the emotional and sexual intensity, on the highest level you can imagine. I was always very much aware of what I had lost, but it's possible that Natalie had to go away from what we had in order to understand how much she needed it.

I found Natalie to be a very pulled-together mother, with mature views about life. We decided to have a child, and just before our first anniversary she became pregnant with our miracle baby. We were both jubilant, and she turned all of her energies to having our child. She turned down a part in *The Towering Inferno*—she didn't want to lose focus on the baby. I thought the script was far better than most disaster films, and I took a part that was offered to me because I thought the film would make money and it's always good to be in a hit.

It wasn't long before Natalie and I began to look for projects we could do together. The first thing we found was a wonderful script by Barbara Turner called *The Affair*. Aaron Spelling and Leonard Goldberg approached us about it, and we all wanted to make a theatrical picture out of it. But the project had been developed for television by ABC, and the network insisted it stay on television.

What, they wanted to know, would it take to make it happen for television? They could pay my fee, but Natalie's salary was much higher and out of the reach of a TV project. As an incentive, Leonard and Aaron gave us part ownership of three future series they were working on, and we made the movie while Natalie was pregnant.

We went through Lamaze classes together; we both wanted this child desperately, and we were both very much engaged in the whole joyous process. Natalie's pregnancy mostly took place at my house in the desert, although in December we sailed to England on the *Queen Elizabeth II*. In England, I made *Colditz* with David McCallum, a BBC series about a Nazi prison that was very successful there but didn't peek its head up very far in America. We took the kids to England with us, so overall it was a very pleasant family experience.

We came back to L.A. to have the baby, but as it turned out, I wasn't able to be in the delivery room as we had planned. Something went wrong with the placement of the umbilical cord, and we couldn't go through with the Lamaze delivery. For the health of Natalie and the baby, Natalie had to have an emergency cesarean section on March 9, 1974. It was a very dicey situation for a time, and afterward we went out and raised a lot of money for fetal heart monitors.

We named our daughter Courtney, which was the name of Natalie's character in *The Affair*. Despite the difficulties of her birth, Courtney was born healthy, and we both fell desperately in love with her. For weeks after the birth, Natalie would show Courtney off to our friends and say, "Who needs movies?"

While we had been in England, Mud moved into the Palm Springs house, but after we came back, we made sure that she was never alone with Natasha. Willie Mae Worthen, the children's nurse, had the primary responsibility, but Mud was there, continually interjecting herself into every situation. Her pathological fears and need for conspiracy kicked in, and she began telling Natasha that her grandmother was the only person Natasha could trust, that her mother and father meant well but didn't have her best interests at heart. We found that Mud had changed the locks in the house and locked Natasha in her room so that nobody could harm her.

As far as Natalie was concerned, that was it. She had lived through this kind of ridiculous behavior when she was a child, so she knew that with Mud everything was about control. She told me she'd handle it herself and she did. Natalie didn't exactly ostracize Mud—she would still be invited to holiday dinners—but we never again allowed her complete access to the children.

# SIXTEEN

# "WHY DID SHE LOVE ME?
# I THINK IT WAS BECAUSE
# I MADE HER LAUGH."

With my daughters when they were young: at Chasen's with Courtney
(PHOTOGRAPH BY PETER C. BORSARI); in Scotland, while producing Madame Sin,
with Katie (COURTESY OF THE AUTHOR); on the Splendour with Natasha
(COURTESY OF THE AUTHOR).

The first project Leonard and Aaron brought to us as part of the development deal was a project of Leonard's called *Alley Cats*. It was, without exception, the biggest piece of shit I have ever read. Even Aaron thought it was shabby. "You ought to be ashamed of yourself," he told Leonard. I told Leonard what I thought, and he told me, "The girls we have cast will be on the cover of *Time* magazine in a year."

I didn't believe him. My carefully considered opinion was that the show would be canceled about ten minutes after the first episode ran, but I got involved anyway. I brought in Ivan Goff and Ben Roberts, who had written *White Heat* for Jimmy Cagney as well as a lot of other good movies, to run the show, and I brought in Jaclyn Smith to go along with Farrah Fawcett and Kate Jackson, who had already been cast. Aaron and Leonard changed the title and put the rest of the project together. Natalie and I owned 50 percent of the show they called *Charlie's Angels*. When it finally went on the air in the fall of 1976, it was a tremendous hit from day one—the equivalent of buying stock in Microsoft. And Jaclyn was the only one of the girls who stayed with the show for the entire length of the run.

Over the years, I have spent a great deal of time in court, battling with Aaron and Leonard over their definition of profits, and I'm glad to say I've usually won, allowing the children to be brought up very comfortably. As for the two succeeding shows in the original three-show deal, another one was developed but never went forward, and the third never happened at all.

Despite Natalie's disinterest in working, it wasn't long before she had a good offer for a film called *Peeper*, with Michael

Caine. We leased a house on Foothill Road while she did the film. She had always liked Michael, and it was also something of an experiment to see if a career could be successfully juggled with motherhood. We decided to move back to Beverly Hills; I sold the house in Palm Springs, and we found our house at 603 Canon Drive. It was a two-story house in a sturdy Cape Cod style; Patti Page had bought it with some of the royalties from her recording of "Old Cape Cod." I believe we paid $350,000 for the house.

It was a large, comfortable place that Natalie decorated with her favorite French paintings, my favorite sculpture and drawings of the American West, and a lot of tropical plants. Her maturation was evident in the change in her tastes since the marble and gold period of our first house years before. Now her taste was very low-key and homey. She decorated the house in floral upholstery and needlepoint pillows. The master bedroom had wicker armchairs and a quilted floral bedspread. Upstairs were three bedrooms for the kids as well as a playroom. Over the garage was an apartment where Josh Donen lived for a time.

I fully intended to live in the Canon Drive house until it was time for the Motion Picture Home; as it was, we lived there for the rest of Natalie's life.

Disaster movies are heavy lifting for the second unit and the stunt crew, but not so much for the actors. What you basically have to do is project either fear or resolution in varying degrees. My sequence in *The Towering Inferno* was done near the beginning of the production, and it was quite dangerous—for the stuntmen. For those few of you who haven't seen the picture, a new skyscraper catches on fire, and I die a spectacularly unpleasant but flamboyant death trying to save lives. The same could be said of most of the cast.

My stuntman worked for at least a month on controlling his breathing before the scene was shot, because once he was set on fire, he couldn't breathe, not even once. If he breathed, he died. It was a very dangerous shoot, but amazingly, given the dicey nature of working with fire, not one person was hurt making that picture, although Fred Astaire had a near-miss.

They were shooting the climactic sequence, where Fred and those members of the cast who hadn't already been killed were huddled in the penthouse waiting for the cistern to be dynamited, thus putting out the fire. Fred was on the floor when they had to shift the lights. Fred was seventy-four years old when we shot the film, and he liked to stay in place after a take so he didn't have to get up, then get back down in position.

"It might be a while, Fred," they told him, and he said that was okay, he'd just stay there. But they insisted, and somebody came and helped him get up. A minute later a big 10K light came crashing down on the precise spot where he'd been sitting.

Critics never gave Irwin Allen much of a shake, but then, they never thought much of Cecil B. DeMille either, and Irwin's best pictures were like DeMille's. It wasn't about subtlety or characterization, it was about promising the audience a big show and delivering a big show. Most movies promise dollars and deliver pennies, but *The Poseidon Adventure* and *The Towering Inferno* never cheated the audience.

I loved Irwin. For one thing, he knew how to make those pictures; for another, he lived and breathed his movies and was genuinely interested in the people who worked for him. He was friendly and affable to work with, and he would take time to talk to the electricians or anybody else.

It was wonderful to be working with Fred Astaire again, even though we didn't have any scenes together. He was still Fred, still in good shape, and our friendship remained strong

for the next five years. It wasn't until after he went east to shoot
*Ghost Story* that his old friends began to feel pushed out and he
became difficult to reach. His interest in racing tailed off, something that he'd loved since he came to California to get into the
movie business. Greg Peck didn't see him after that, and neither
did I.

When he died in 1987, Greg and Veronique Peck, as well
as Bill Self—three of his oldest friends—weren't invited to the
funeral. Bill Self went anyway and stood under a tree. About
the only people from the old days who were invited were
Ava, Fred's daughter, and Fred's choreographer and alter ego,
Hermes Pan.

After Courtney was born, Natalie became totally involved
with her. She was very much into being a mother, which
meant she was less into being an actress. *Peeper* had been a
pleasant shoot, but the movie was terrible, and Natalie didn't
seem to care all that much. She began turning down job after
job, including some films she would have killed to be in just a
few years before. Her priorities had shifted to her family and
kids. There was nothing more important to both of us than
that.

Our kids meshed—my Katie and her Natasha became *our*
Katie and Natasha. Marion had opened a couturier shop on Ro-
deo Drive in Beverly Hills that proved very successful. The
shop was called "Marion Wagner" and was confirmation of her
fine taste. Katie was living with her mother, but she was over at
the house all the time and had a fine time with Natasha and the
baby. Katie fell right into the fold, and there was plenty of room
at the house for all three girls, so gradually Katie came to live at
Canon Drive.

When I think about how Natalie and I melded the kids

into one group, I realize that we did it together. No parental decisions were made independently. We decided things together, rewards and discipline alike. The key thing was that we loved each other—*everything* stemmed from that. We had found something that eludes many couples: true compatibility. We had a similar rhythm, and we both took a lot of pleasure in caprice. Acting had taught us that you have to take advantage of circumstances; if I wanted to drop everything and go to San Francisco for dinner, Natalie would enthusiastically go along, but we were just as happy to have a quiet dinner at home.

There were times when we would ask ourselves if it was okay to be as happy as we were. Was there something wrong with us? We both knew how chancy life was, and how difficult show business can be, and it seemed that we had come through every obstacle and landed on an island. And the other person on that island just happened to be the person we loved the most in the world.

I don't mean to suggest that there was never a cross word. I tend to accentuate the positive, while Natalie was a full-blooded Russian and at times could be moody. But she wouldn't allow herself to be overwhelmed by those moods. I found her to be a wonderful mother, with very good instincts about what the children needed.

Natalie was never a woman to dance around the kitchen, but she kept it all together. She could arrange things faultlessly. Along with all her other talents, she had a gift for assimilation and organization; she could run the house, tend the children, and also pay attention to her career when she felt like it.

All the kids were completely different, but the blessing was that they all loved one another. Katie has always been very self-possessed and self-sustaining. She always wanted to work. When she was a kid, she was a box girl at the market and later a clerk. She was a fine gymnast as a girl, loved tumbling and was very good at it, and has had a very successful career as a TV host.

Natasha was very sweet and insecure. It was difficult for her to be by herself. If Natalie and I had to go out, we'd have to sit with Natasha for a while and slowly edge our way out of the room. Even then, she always wanted to be with us and wanted to know where we were at all times.

Courtney quickly mastered everything she touched, but would get bored just as quickly. She's always been a wonderful artist and good at athletics, although academics were never her strong point. With my own history, I didn't exactly have the moral authority to read her the riot act. She picked up golf very easily, and I swear that the first time I took her out on a course after some time on a driving range, she parred the first hole. She was and is capricious in her brilliance.

The Canon Drive house was perfect for a family. There was a large garden in the back, and I grew a very nice selection of vegetables there. Other kids were always at the house, and we had a lot of garden parties in the afternoon. Courtney was swimming by the time she was two, so a lot of family time was spent in the pool. These were years of bounty and joy.

In my mind, that house is defined as a home for the children. Courtney would be roller-skating around the kitchen with a hamster on her shoulder, and the dogs and cats would be dodging her and running through the house. It was noisy, boisterous, and wonderful. And Natalie would walk through all this wonderful noise and clearly be delighted. She wanted a house that was fun—something she hadn't experienced as a child—and she got it.

In this, as with everything else, she was very down to earth and, unusually for a movie star, very skilled with people. If a friend was ill, Natalie would research the symptoms and find the best doctor. If we had a problem, she would outline the problem and her suggested solution, and more often than not, I agreed with her ideas.

Our primary consideration was always for the children. We took two vacations a year, one with the kids, one with just the two of us. And we made a commitment that we wouldn't both be working at the same time, that one of us would always be home with the kids. With very few exceptions, we kept to that rule.

At Thanksgiving I would put on a red scarf and we'd have an open house. The door would be open, the fireplace would be roaring, and everybody in our life was invited to stop by for some turkey and a drink—not just friends and agents and the like, but the servants, the delivery men, everybody who made our lives what they were. It was not a house where anybody stood on ceremony.

You can tell why I loved her. Why did she love me? I think it was because I made her laugh. Natalie had this great, boisterous guffaw, and I could always make her roll over with laughter. And she knew that I was there for her. A friend of ours once asked her how she managed to keep herself so together. "Because I have RJ behind me," she said. "I always know he's there."

Someone who was there for both of us was Paul Ziffren, who had always been Natalie's lawyer. Paul was an extremely dynamic personality, highly respected, a truly superb lawyer who was also the head of the Los Angeles Democratic Party. Paul and his wife, Mickey, had taken Natalie under their wing when she was single and introduced her to Los Angeles society, and they made sure to include her in the welcoming committee whenever any Russian artists came to town. I've always felt that the combination of intelligence and kindness contains the best of both worlds, and that described Paul. We quickly became very close friends, and he became my lawyer as well as Natalie's.

As if all this wasn't enough, Natalie brought Penny into my life. Penny was an Australian sheepdog; Cricket, Natalie's other dog, was a mixed breed. Along the way, there was also Fifi, the basset hound, who was particularly adored by the children.

But it was Penny who became a special love for me, as she was for Natalie. She had gotten Penny while we were apart, and she appeared in a couple of Natalie's movies. She was the most darling animal, and I just adored her. Unfortunately, she got old and developed problems. Finally, we took her to the vet for an examination and left her there. Later that day, we got a phone call telling us she had gone beyond the point of no return and he had put her down. We were both devastated—I don't believe in letting animals die by themselves, let alone one I loved as much as Penny. We had both wanted to be there with her when her time came.

The first time we were married, we had spent time at a lot of the established restaurants around town—Chasen's, Romanoff's, Patsy d'Amore's, Don the Beachcomber's. But the second time around La Scala became our place.

Jean Leon, who owned La Scala, had originally been the maître d' at Patsy's. One day he hailed a cab for Frank Sinatra, and Frank tipped him $200. That was how Jean was able to pay the hospital bill for his first child. Jean bought a place on the corner of Beverly and Little Santa Monica where several restaurants had failed. That didn't dissuade Jean; he had a vision of what it could become.

La Scala became the most successful restaurant in town, and without any publicity—Jean wouldn't allow it. Everybody loved Jean, especially me. When I came back to America from Europe and didn't have any money because of the custody battle, he carried me—he never charged me for anything. When you're on top, everyone's your pal, but it's when you're on your ass that you really find out who your friends are. Jean was my friend.

Jean eventually established his own vineyard in Spain and had his own wine: Chateau Leon. Whenever Natalie and I had a special occasion, we always went to La Scala. Jean loved to participate in the gifts I gave Natalie. Dropping a ring in some champagne was minor; Jean would put a bracelet or a necklace in a cake for me. Jean later opened another restaurant, in which Natalie and I were partners, but it didn't do as well as La Scala, not that anything did.

After many years, Jean sold the restaurant, bought a sailboat, and achieved his lifelong dream of sailing around the world. Tragically, Jean, who smoked heavily, developed cancer of the larynx. He didn't want people to see him that way, so he stepped back from business. Before he died, he lost the ability to speak, but we stayed in touch by faxing back and forth.

I decided it was time to move into producing, so I set up my own production company. My first effort was *Madame Sin,* a TV project with Bette Davis, whom I had idolized for years. We had originally met in the early '50s, when we were introduced by Claire Trevor, but Bette and I didn't become close friends for another ten years.

The 1960s were a bad time for Bette; she wasn't working much, but she gave an interview to the *New York Times* in which she cited me as a young leading man with humor and class. I called to thank her, and it turned out she was a big fan of *It Takes a Thief.* I asked her if she'd like to do an episode.

We wrote a show around a character named Bessie Grindell and provided Bette with a nice dressing room; the shoot went very well. While we were in production, Jack Warner threw a dinner for her, and it was preceded by a selection of clips from her great films at the studio, which gave the press agent John Springer the idea of putting her on the road with "A Night with Bette Davis." That show made her a good deal of money over the years and gave her something to do when she wasn't acting.

A couple of years went by, and I brought her the idea of *Madame Sin,* which was a pilot for a TV series in which Bette would play a sort of female Fu Manchu. Bette had never done a TV series, but there weren't a lot of good parts in the movies in that period for her, and Madame Sin was a good part. For my part, producing was about asserting control—over casting, music, camera, director. I wanted a say. I also wanted to see if I had the necessary sense of balance.

We shot the pilot in Scotland. I wasn't planning on being in the series itself, but I took a part in the pilot. The weather on location was difficult, and I went to Barry Diller, who was the head of ABC then, and told him I thought we were going to go over budget.

"How much?" he asked me.

"About $300,000," I told him.

He picked up the phone and had a check cut for the overage. We didn't actually go over by $300,000, and I was able to give him some of that money back. My point is that what Barry did wouldn't happen today. The decisiveness he showed is a thing of the past because everything is now done by committee; no one person could cut a check for $300,000 in overages today, nor would anyone be disposed to.

I found that Bette was great to work with. The only time she was troublesome in her work was if you didn't tell her the truth. If you tried to pull something on her, or if you weren't as attentive as she felt you should be, then she would get worked up, and Bette Davis worked up was not something any sane person wanted to provoke. She had immediate access to all emotions, but the line to her anger was particularly quick.

Otherwise, she was a consummate pro, knew her lines backward and forward, and knew her work as well as everybody else's. *Madame Sin* was a good movie and did well in the ratings, although it didn't get picked up for a series; the network was worried about protests from pressure groups because Orientals were the heavies.

*Madame Sin* was the beginning of our friendship. When we'd finished the picture, her daughter BD called me and said, "We're setting up an appearance for Mom on *This Is Your Life,* and I want to be sure she looks good. Could you help us set it up?"

The cover story we devised involved a photo sitting to promote *Madame Sin* at John Engstead's studio. I was going to be there with Frank Westmore, my makeup man and dear friend for thirty-five years, and Frank would be making her up for the photo session. Well, at the appointed moment, out stepped Ralph Edwards. "Hellooooo, how are you?" he said. "Well, this could be anybody's life. It could be yours, Frank Westmore, or it could be yours, Robert Wagner, or it could be yours, Bette Davis." I had this terrible sinking feeling that they had turned on me. But then Edwards said, "Bette Davis, *this is your life!*" and I was off the hook. Or so I thought.

After the surprise opening, we were supposed to get in our cars and go down to the studio, where the show proper was being taped. But as soon as we got in the car, Bette turned on me. "You son of a bitch! *You fucking son of a bitch!!*"

"Now, Bette. . . ."

"Oh, fuck you!" She was just furious about being tricked into it because she didn't like being tricked into anything.

The taping itself went fine; Olivia de Havilland was there, Bette's first editor was there, I was there. And then Ralph Edwards said, "And here's a person whose life you saved. Jay Robinson!"

And out came Jay Robinson, who had made a brief splash years before when he flounced around as Caligula in *The Robe* and *Demetrius and the Gladiators*. Jay Robinson made a little speech about how Bette had sent him a letter when he was in prison and by doing so saved his life. "I'd like to read that letter," he said. "It was the only thing that sustained me." And he pulled out the letter and read this very touching excerpt. Bette told Jay that he was the most wonderful actor she'd ever known and working with him was one of the highlights of her career and so forth. It ended with: "You will always be the closest thing in my life."

And the audience went, "Aaaahhhh," at Bette being so kind to a young actor in trouble. With the show over, we all piled into limos and headed over to the Bel-Air Hotel for the cocktail party that always followed a taping of *This Is Your Life*. As I got there, I come across Bette standing outside, smoking a cigarette as only she could, radiating rage to a distance of about twenty feet.

"Bette," I said, "what's wrong? The show went well, and that letter you sent to Jay Robinson was so touching, such a fine thing to do."

"I never wrote that letter!" she yelled. "I don't know who Jay Robinson is! *I never met him until tonight!*" Well, I looked around, and of course Jay Robinson hadn't come to the party, because he knew Bette would kill him. I began to laugh hysterically. That just got her angrier. "Oh, Robert," she said, "you laugh at idiotic things!"

That was the way our relationship went. She had something of a crush on me, and she was always getting angry, and I was always laughing at her and flirting with her and cajoling her out of her anger. When we went to Philadelphia to do the *Mike Douglas Show,* she locked herself in her room because she was under the impression that we were supposed to have had dinner the night before and she thought I'd stood her up. I told her, "Bette, if we were supposed to have dinner, we would have had dinner," and proceeded to jolly her out of it.

Another time I visited her in Westport, where she was living, and we went into town for lunch. We arrived at the restaurant about 1:45, after the crowd had left. We walked in past a group of men who'd obviously had a three-martini lunch, and one of them said, "Jesus Christ, Bette Davis—a face that would stop a clock!"

That wasn't the worst of it. The worst of it was that she heard him.

We sat down, and she was understandably upset. "What do you think?" she asked me. "Should I get my face done?" All the actresses of Bette's age—Ann Sothern, Lucille Ball, and so forth—utilized a system devised by a makeup man named Gene Hibbs that involved a system of rubber bands hidden by wigs that tightened their faces. It was a light, mechanical kind of face lift. At the end of the day, the wigs came off, the rubber bands were removed, and the faces would fall.

Obviously, this was very tender territory, but I decided to forge ahead. "I think it would be a great idea, Bette."

"You do?"

"Sure. And while they're doing the face lift, they can do your lips too."

Those glorious Bette Davis eyes widened, and she stared at me. "My lips? *What's wrong with my lips?* And what would people think?"

"Oh, Bette, who gives a shit what people think?"

After a great deal of back and forth, she eventually got the face lift, and we went out for dinner so she could show it to me.

"Well," she said, "what do you think?"

"I think it looks great," I told her.

"Great? You think *this* looks great? But what about *this*? And what about *that*. . . ." She was unhappy. And this naturally combative woman was off on another diatribe.

Like many people of any given generation, she grew land-locked by age and lost touch with what was going on around her. Late in her life I picked her up to take her to a party at Roddy McDowall's. Now, I didn't know this, but Frank Zappa's daughter Moon Zappa was an enormous Bette Davis fan. Moon found out I was taking Bette to a party and was in her car across the street watching for us. At the light, she pulled up alongside us and yelled out my name. I put the window down and yelled, "Hi, Moon. How are Dweezil and Ahmet?" She assured me they were great, I introduced her to Bette—which was the real reason for the whole exercise—the light changed, the car windows went up, and off we went.

Bette sat there staring at me. "What the fuck are you talking about? Moon and Dweezil and Ahmet? Who are these people? *Why do they know you?*"

Bette's life was her work. Her basic character was that of a tough, loving broad from New England. When she had a script to study, she became totally involved and totally animated. She had tried hard to make the domestic side of her life work, but it hadn't happened. The only truly trustworthy thing in Bette's life was her talent. She was a very good cook, loved houses, and also had a tremendous sense of humor. And from what I have been given to understand by several men who knew, she was an extraordinary lover who could take a man over the moon and back.

But Bette was extremely demanding, and I'm sure she would have been exhausting on a regular basis. She had one habit that drove me crazy: she would hang up the phone before you were finished talking to her. Let's say you would agree to pick her up at seven. She would say, "All right," and then without saying anything else she would hang up and you would find yourself saying good-bye to empty air. It was maddening, rude, and also funny—peremptory behavior she probably believed was the star's prerogative. I came to call this the Bette Davis Hang-Up, and she did it *all the time.*

When her daughter BD wrote *My Mother's Keeper,* a calculated, vicious book about her, it was without doubt the worst thing that happened to Bette in her entire life. It was a very primal betrayal—Bette had financially supported BD for her entire life—but Bette's devastation had nothing to do with money. Her daughter was the true love of Bette's life. Bette never once stinted on anything for BD, and to see all the love and hope she had lavished on her wasted, flushed down the toilet by the rage of an ungrateful, unsuccessful child destroyed Bette, as it would have anybody. She would allude to it every once in a while, but she was the sort of woman who carried her pain inside rather than present it for public consumption.

I stayed close to Bette, although she never exactly mellowed. After she came back from Maine, where she shot *The Whales of August* with Lillian Gish, all she could talk about was how difficult Gish was. "She can't hear!" she'd say. "Impossible, *impossible* woman!" Patience had never been Bette's strong suit, and now she had even less. "Speak up!" she'd yell at Lillian. "You're too old to be doing this. Why don't you just stop?" Lindsay Anderson, the director, thought Bette was deranged. As if Bette didn't want to be out there in front of a camera until she was one hundred too.

When Bette died in 1989, I helped arrange the memorial

service on stage 9 at Warner Bros., where she had made so many of her great pictures. There were enormous stills of her hung all around the stage, and as Roddy McDowall, James Woods, and Bob Osborne got up and spoke about Bette, a black, dark stage gradually became infused with love. By the time Angela Lansbury gave her extraordinary eulogy, we all knew that a remarkable, one-of-a-kind artist and human being was gone, but we were lucky—Bette had made the life of everybody on that stage better and richer, even if all they knew of her was what she embodied in her movies. At the end of the service, I turned out the ghost light on the stage. She was buried at Forest Lawn in Hollywood, which looks down at the Warner Bros. studio—just the way she wanted it.

I adored her—not in spite of her prickliness, but *because* of her prickliness. It was such a large part of what made her Bette Davis. She had a terrible need for love, as we all do, but she was wired in such a way that it was hard for her to ask for it. Actually, it was impossible. She could give love, but it was very hard for her to receive it, even though, outside of the opportunity to act, it was the only thing that really mattered to her. Bette's tragedy was that she never fully received the thing she needed the most.

# SEVENTEEN

# "I'VE ALWAYS HAD AFFECTION FOR A THEATRICAL ROGUE."

Arriving in London with Natalie and the girls, 1976. (STAFF/AFP/GETTY IMAGES)

After *Colditz*, the movies I made—*The Towering Inferno, Midway*—tended to make TV look better and better. Five years after *It Takes a Thief* went off the air, I went back to television. Natalie was now a full-time mother, and I was more than happy to become the provider. *Switch* was another caper show, about a partnership between a con man—me—and the ex-cop who sent him to jail—Eddie Albert. The two of us had a detective agency that specialized in conning con men. CBS was interested in the show because it bracketed two actors who had both been in previously successful shows—*Green Acres* for Eddie and *It Takes a Thief* for me.

Initially, CBS offered me the cop part, but I never wanted to play any character that could conceivably yell, "Freeze! Police!!" Every other show on television was a cop show, which makes a certain amount of sense because they're perfect for TV. There's a criminal, there's a good guy, there's a beginning, a middle, and an end. Anything that neatly schematic can be easily mass-produced.

But cop shows were too cut-and-dried for me, so I opted for the con man part, as well as a caper format, which requires more on the part of the writers and actors. *Switch* wasn't a critic's show, but the public liked it, and we ran for three years, from 1975 to 1978. It wasn't easy, because CBS changed our time slot six times in those three years.

Eddie Albert was an interesting man who possessed what could legitimately be termed a big set of balls. Before World War II, he was a contract actor at Warner Bros. when he had an affair with Jack Warner's wife, Ann. One time they were making love when Jack walked in and discovered them. As Jack told me,

"I didn't mind that so much; it was the fact that he didn't stop that bothered me." Well, that little episode got Eddie blacklisted for a while.

Then Eddie went into the service during the war and became a hero in the South Pacific. On November 21, 1943, when he was a lieutenant j.g. in the Navy, Eddie was stationed on the USS *Sheridan* when he commandeered four boats to rescue thirteen wounded Marines who were trapped on an exposed offshore reef at Betio Island in the Tarawa Atoll. He ordered three of the boats to hang back and return fire, while he took his boat in closer and loaded it up with guys who had been badly hit. Eddie had to make a couple of trips back to the *Sheridan* to get all the Marines to safety. He did all this under heavy fire.

Later, after the battle was mostly over, Eddie was in charge of body recovery when a last-stand Japanese sniper opened up on Eddie's party. He and some other soldiers opened fire on the sniper and killed him.

Tarawa was savage; nearly 1,000 Marines died, and 2,300 were wounded. Of the 20,000 Japanese soldiers who were holed up on the island, only 17 left the island alive. For saving the lives of all those stranded Marines, Eddie earned a Bronze Star, and I think he could easily have been awarded more than that.

After the war, the times were such that even war heroes such as Eddie could get into political trouble—he was very liberal, and his magnificent wife, Margo, was even more so. But William Wyler helped bail him out by casting him in both *Carrie* and *Roman Holiday,* two totally different kinds of movies. Typically, Eddie was excellent in both.

I originally met Eddie and Margo through Richard and Mary Sale, who were good friends of theirs. Eddie was a complete actor. He loved the theater, he loved to act, and he could play drama or comedy with equal facility. He was a fierce environmentalist long before it was fashionable. As a matter of fact, Eddie was crucial in preserving the pelican population; the use of DDT was weakening the shells of pelicans in their nests, and the pelican population was cratering. Eddie threw himself into the fight to ban DDT. As soon as the chemical was restricted, the pelican population began coming back. To this day, whenever I see a pelican fly by on the Coast Highway, I thank Eddie Albert, and so should everybody else.

In almost all respects, he was an admirable man.

But with his life experiences, Eddie wasn't fazed by things like stealing scenes, and he could be a bit devious and scratchy at times—about his character, his wardrobe, everything. Basically, he wanted to play both his part and mine, and sometimes he stole scenes for the hell of it. In his heart of hearts, he would have been very happy if *Switch* had been called *The Eddie Albert Show*. That said, I've always had affection for a theatrical rogue, and Eddie and I got along fine, mostly because if Eddie was going to steal scenes, so was I. Game on! For three years, we had a very pleasant competition.

Eddie was one of those veterans who didn't talk much about the terrible things he had seen in the war, but thirty years afterward, just about the time we were working together, he had lunch with an admiral who had also been through the battle at Tarawa. When he got back to his hotel, he began shaking and collapsed into a terrible crying jag that went on for an hour. He had carried post-traumatic stress around for decades.

*Switch* was created by Glen Larson, and we had a great cast and crew. Universal was going to drop Sharon Gless from its contract list, but I met her and liked her. She never even auditioned for the show; I just thought she was perfect and hired her. Plus, we had Charlie Callas around for comic relief, and he was sensational. The chemistry was good, and the only real problem we had was that we went on the air before we had enough scripts, so the entire first year it was run-and-gun production and there was no time to get better writing.

In television, the most important component besides concept and casting chemistry is preparation—once the locomotive leaves the station, it never really stops until it reaches the end of the line, or the end of the season. That was a problem in the beginning for *Switch*. Because it was a show about con men, the writers were too focused on angles and gimmicks, and I was constantly pushing them for more characterization.

While I was working, our family kept growing. Along with Courtney there was Willie Mae Worthen, who started out as a housekeeper and quickly became part of our inner circle. Willie Mae was always there for the children, and she's still there for them whenever they need her today, because she still lives with us.

One thing our remarriage gave us was a renewed appreciation of how much we loved the ocean. After Natalie and I divorced, I had spent very little time on the water, and neither had she. When she wanted to get out on the water, she'd charter a boat. We'd forgotten how important it was to our relationship, how the water nurtured and calmed us. Now that we had children, it was something we wanted as a continuing part of their lives as well.

It was during the run of *Switch* that Natalie and I bought our long-dreamt-of boat. She was sixty feet long and slept eight, and Natalie did the interior in early American. We called her the *Splendour*, after *Splendor in the Grass,* but with the English spelling to differentiate between then and now. There was also a motorized dinghy attached to the side that we called *Valiant,* in honor of the most embarrassing of my own movies.

From the beginning, the *Splendour* was less a yacht than a

houseboat. Although Natalie didn't particularly enjoy cooking at home, she enjoyed making *huevos rancheros* in the galley of the *Splendour*. It was a place for family and friends, and we were always loading it up with Tom Mankiewicz or Mart Crowley and some very special guest stars to cruise to Catalina or some of the other islands in the Santa Barbara chain. Some of the happiest days of our marriage took place on the *Splendour* because Natalie always enjoyed being on the water, although she was very nervous about being in it.

Elia Kazan came on the boat, and to my surprise I found that he loved to fish and was a terrific first mate. Perhaps I shouldn't have been surprised; on Gadge's farm in Connecticut, he enjoyed nothing more than climbing on his tractor and working the land. Gadge was very much of the earth and, as I discovered, of the water as well.

I think Gadge's great gifts as a director derived from his curiosity and openness. He would talk to anybody, ask them, "What do *you* think?" and mean it. He took time with people, and because he was Elia Kazan, his attention really meant something. Personally, Gadge was always nudging me to focus my career on comedy; he thought my instincts for comedy were excellent.

But so many people hated Gadge because he named names during the red scare period in the early '50s. I was with him in New York when people would walk up and literally spit at his feet. Then they would cross the street. And Gadge would just go on, as if what just happened hadn't happened. He must have had some bitterness about this—some of the people who were the most hostile wouldn't have had careers without him—but he never expressed it. He held it in.

Natalie and I were very attentive with each other. It came easily for us. She would write me notes on the anniversa-

*(Left) Hart to Hart:* Stefanie Powers, Lionel Stander, Freeway the dog, and yours truly. (HART TO HART COURTESY OF SONY PICTURES TELEVISION)

*(Below)* Natasha *(left)* and Courtney *(right)* dancing with Mom and Dad in Acapulco. (COURTESY OF THE AUTHOR)

*(Above)* Two friends of the family named Astaire and Niven, with Natalie and Courtney. (COURTESY OF THE AUTHOR)

*(Below)* Natalie's funeral was a painful day for all of us. (PHOTO BY PAUL HARRIS/GETTY IMAGES)

*(Above)* With Sir Lew Grade and the always ebullient, always hilarious, Roger Moore.
(COURTESY OF THE AUTHOR)

*(Below)* Meeting Pope John Paul II with my daughters Natasha and Courtney.
(L'OSSERVATORE ROMANO PHOTOGRAPHIC SERVICE)

(*Left*) With Elizabeth Taylor in James Kirkwood's *There Must Be a Pony*, which I produced for television. (THERE MUST BE A PONY COURTESY OF SONY PICTURES TELEVISION)

(*Below*) With Jimmy Stewart. (COURTESY OF THE AUTHOR)

*(Above)* At the ballet with Barbara and Cary Grant, Jill, and Greg and Veronique Peck. (COURTESY OF THE AUTHOR)

*(Left)* With Barbara Sinatra and my wife, Jill. (PHOTO BY ALEX BERLINER © BERLINER STUDIO/ BEIMAGES)

*(Below)* With Stanley Kramer, Susie Tracy, Frank Sinatra, and Sidney Poitier, applauding Kate Hepburn's entrance at the benefit for the Spencer Tracy Foundation in New York City. (PHOTOGRAPH BY MARCIA WEINSTEIN)

*(Left)* With Robert Stack, who was my close friend for more than fifty years, with never a harsh word between us. (PHOTOGRAPH BY STEVE KIEFER)

*(Right)* My makeup man and close friend, Lon Bentley. (PHOTO BY RODDY MCDOWALL, COURTESY OF THE AUTHOR)

*(Left)* With my friend and golfing buddy Mike Connors. (COURTESY OF THE AUTHOR)

*(Left)* With my grandson, Riley, in the Aspen, Colorado, snow. (COURTESY OF THE AUTHOR)

*(Below)* A very proud grandfather with his grandson. (COURTESY OF THE AUTHOR)

*(Left)* Fulfilling every golfer's lifelong dream—a foursome with close friends at St. Andrews in Scotland. From left are Marv Adelson, Steve DeMarco, Bud Yorkin, and yours truly. (COURTESY OF THE AUTHOR)

*(Above)* In Venice, with *(from left)* my friend Steven Goldberg, his wife, Elvia, and Jill. (COURTESY OF THE AUTHOR)

*(Above)* Jill, Courtney, and Katie celebrated with me when I was honored with a star on the Hollywood Walk of Fame in 2002. (PHOTO BY LEE CELANO/AFP/GETTY IMAGES)

*(Right)* My girls: Katie, Natasha, and Courtney. (COURTESY OF THE AUTHOR)

ries of our marriages or on my birthday. On my birthday in 1974, she wrote me, "This is always my happiest day, too—because of you. I love you." That same year, on December 28, the date of our first marriage, it was: "This was the happiest day of my life in 1957—but I didn't know you'd make me doubly happy in July of 1971."

On my birthday in 1975, we planted a fig tree in the garden, and she wrote me, "This fig may look bare now, but soon it will bear fruit—as we have. I love you with all my heart and I hope this tree grows as beautifully as my love for you does every single day." On Easter 1975, she wrote me, "Dearest, here's to smooth sailing for us from now on! I love you with all my heart and it belongs only to you." On Easter 1976, she wrote, "I love you more than love."

Without question, doing *Cat on a Hot Tin Roof* with Laurence Olivier and Natalie was my professional high point. To work with Olivier, to see how he approached acting, and to observe his competitiveness, his refusal to be defeated by illness, age, or any other actor, was a pure privilege.

I first met him through Spencer Tracy, who had been friends with Larry for years. When Olivier came to America to make William Wyler's *Carrie,* he worked with Spence on his accent to get the rhythm of midwestern speech. When Spence introduced us, I immediately took to Olivier, who was crazy about Natalie as an actress and as a woman.

My old friend Bill Storke created a series of specials called "Laurence Olivier's Tribute to the American Theater," and in the spring of 1976 we traveled to London and rehearsed for four weeks on *Cat on a Hot Tin Roof,* with Tennessee Williams in attendance. When Paul Newman and Elizabeth Taylor did the movie version with Richard Brooks, they couldn't mention homosexuality or cancer, without which the story doesn't make an awful lot of sense, but we went back to the original script.

It was a painstaking production; we had two weeks of costume tests before we started the month of rehearsals. Then we took nine days to tape it, working in complete scenes in front of four cameras. We were so prepared that we could have played that production on any stage in the world.

There were no private lessons with Olivier. He worked in hints. He told me to take my time, that I could sustain a moment. Maureen Stapleton was cast as Big Momma, but she would not fly. If it moved, she was nervous about getting on it. She was supposed to be in England with us to rehearse, but she had taken the *Queen Mary* and the ship had gotten held up by bad weather. She didn't make it to rehearsal until three days after we had started.

Now, I had memorized the entire play before we started rehearsing. I had borrowed an office at William Morris in Beverly Hills and hired an acting coach to work with me. I wanted to be set, I wanted to be confident, and I also wanted to be free to watch Olivier work and not have to worry about my lines. So I was off the book when we started to rehearse.

Larry was using his script. He would say to himself, "Let's see, I move here, then I go over there," and I would be standing there, without my script, cueing him. It was Maureen's first day at rehearsal, and she watched us working for a while, then took me aside during a break.

"What are you doing?" she asked.

"We're rehearsing, Maureen."

"Where's your script?"

"I learned the play. I don't need it."

"That doesn't matter. Take your script with you when you go out there."

"But Maureen, I don't need it, I . . ."

"Take it from a smart old Irish cunt, pick up your script. Don't be a smart ass."

I actually wasn't trying to be a smart ass, but Maureen was adamant, so I did what she told me to do. Looking back, she was right; her point was well taken.

Tennessee Williams was working with Larry on the third act—always the problem with that particular play. Tennessee and Larry trimmed it down and did some polishing. I had met Tennessee years before, when I was shooting some scenes for *The Frogmen* in Key West. He made it quite obvious that I was his type, and I had to gently disabuse him of that particular notion. Tennessee was always a very vulnerable man, but when we were working on *Cat* he was an open wound, noticeably frightened of the critics and what they might say. He was not in good shape, and he was particularly upset with a ridiculous English quarantine regulation that had kept his beloved bulldog from accompanying him to England. As partial compensation, his friend Maria St. Just was always nearby, hovering and holding his hand.

Olivier was always a text-oriented actor, but he had a way of transcending that. What was truly interesting was how fresh he kept his performance. He didn't lock in a performance at all; it varied from take to take. And like most of the people I have valued in my life, he was a very warm, emotional person, although I have no doubt he could be a killer if he thought it necessary.

There's a wonderful story about Larry and Kirk Douglas on *Spartacus*. Now, Kirk Douglas's ego is legendary even by the standards of the movie business. On Larry's first day on the film, Kirk came to Larry's dressing room on location to welcome him to the picture. But Kirk made the mistake of reminding Larry that, "in film, you don't have to do a lot."

Kirk was producing as well as starring in a very expensive

picture, so his concern was understandable, but he forgot that he was talking to Larry Olivier. It was waving a red flag in front of a very wily bull. Olivier was not only fully professional but had made nearly twenty-five movies by then, including great work for great directors: Willy Wyler, Michael Powell, and so forth, not to mention producing and directing some pretty good movies himself: *Henry V, Hamlet,* and *Richard III.*

Larry innocently said, "Why don't you do the scene for me, Kirk, so I can see your ideas?"

So Kirk gets up and does Olivier's scene as he thinks it should be done.

"Splendid, splendid, Kirk. Could you perhaps just do it one more time for me?"

Once again, Kirk does Larry's scene for him.

"Um, that was wonderful, Kirk. Might I ask you for just one more opportunity to study your movements?"

It was only after Kirk had done Olivier's scene for him four separate times that he realized he was being put on.

Olivier was the least indicative actor I've ever worked with. "Indicating" is actor's vocabulary for the original sin of forcing the audience to feel something. The goal is to make the audience cry, not yourself, and to do that you have to have the confidence that your emotion and your interior behavior and feelings can move somebody else. (This was Natalie's great gift.)

When Olivier was doing *Dracula* with Frank Langella, I asked him how it was going. "A bit too much with the cloak," he said.

That's indicating, and the peril of costume parts is that the actor can rely on the costumes and props instead of communicating the character's emotions to the audience. It's also the most difficult thing an actor can do. You get up in the morning, and you're thinking about the scene you have to do, and you keep thinking about it while you're being made up. You tell yourself to keep the scene in perspective with the whole of the film and not to push it. And then you go on the set, and sometimes the director will say, "Act!" And that's the thing you don't want to do.

You do not want to *act*. You want to *be*.

The reviews for *Cat on a Hot Tin Roof* weren't that good. Tennessee Williams's career was at a low ebb, and I think the idea of a couple of mainstream Hollywood actors coming to London and working with Olivier set people's teeth on edge. Too bad. It's a fine play and ours was a very good production. I remain proud of Natalie and myself for tackling it.

Larry and Natalie and I had such a splendid time together that he eventually brought his entire family to be with us on the *Splendour*. It's impossible to know what goes on in anybody else's marriage, but Larry's domestic situation was far from ideal.

In a biography that she authorized, Joan Plowright was very hard on Olivier for his ego and competitiveness. On the basis of the time they spent with us, I thought she was very hard on him—she was continually snappy and pettish. Larry was ailing—he was much older than she was, he had a debilitating skin disease, and he was still working hard to put money aside for his children. But she didn't seem to want to make any allowances for his situation.

Larry wasn't too tired to fight back, but he seemed to have made a private emotional calculation that it wasn't worth the trouble. It was obvious that the main reason they were still together was their children, whom he simply adored. He was determined that his son Richard would go to UCLA, as he eventually did. Larry and Joan did not have a love match by any means, and I thought that he deserved much more sympathy and consideration than he was getting.

Years later, after both Olivier and Natalie died, my dear friend Steven Goldberg gave me a beautiful German shepherd as a housewarming present for the house my wife, Jill, and I built in Aspen. The dog was two years old at the time, and we fell in love with each other immediately. For the next eleven years he was the blood of my heart, embodying joy as well as a nobility of spirit and form. I called him Larry.

# EIGHTEEN

# "NATALIE HID NOTHING."

With Larry Olivier on board the *Splendour*. (COURTESY OF THE AUTHOR)

S hortly after *Switch* went off the air, I was given the script for a television pilot that had been sitting on the shelf in Leonard Goldberg's office. It was written by Sidney Sheldon; it was called "Double Twist," and they wanted me to consider it for a series.

I read it, and I thought it was a lot like the Matt Helm movies that Dean Martin had been making a few years before. It was modern and, I thought, very tacky. The central character would push a button, a bed would come down out of a wall, a girl would fall on it—that sort of thing. I've never been interested in acting in shows I wouldn't want to watch, so I said I'd pass.

"What would it take to get you to reconsider?" they asked me.

I thought about it and said that I'd be interested in doing a show that would provide the audience with the same sort of feeling I always got watching the Thin Man movies with William Powell and Myrna Loy. What was special about those movies wasn't the plots, which nobody ever remembers, but the pure pleasure those two people got out of spending time with each other and the way they managed to communicate that pleasure to the audience.

For me, Nick and Nora Charles as played by William Powell and Myrna Loy constituted the ideal marriage: sure they loved each other, but every bit as important, they *liked* each other. They had fun, and their love for each other didn't preclude a little flirting with other people. It was actually one of the most realistic relationships offered by the movies of that period. That Powell and Loy weren't actually married, or even romantically involved, but were just amiable friends could have been the key to the relationship, not to mention part of the mystery of the movies.

At my suggestion, Leonard and Aaron gave the rewrite to Tom Mankiewicz. When Tom came out to see me in Hawaii, where I was shooting a miniseries called *Pearl*, he asked, "If you like what I write, can I direct the pilot?" Tom's rewrite was entitled *Hart to Hart*, and both the network and I liked it a great deal.

As it moved toward production, Aaron Spelling and Leonard wanted Natalie to play Jennifer Hart. Their thinking was the sales line: "Wagner and Wood in *Hart to Hart.*" Both Natalie and I thought it was a terrible idea, mainly because we had young children, and a one-hour show means long days, not to mention nights. A lot of the time you get up at six in the morning and quit at nine at night. We would both be working all the time, and the girls would be raised by third parties. Also, I had a hunch that it was best to keep our private life separate from our working lives. The proposal was a nonstarter.

When Natalie turned it down, Aaron and Leonard asked me to consider Lindsay Wagner, who they and the network were very high on. This time they were thinking of the sales line "Wagner and Wagner in *Hart to Hart.*" But I had my own idea for a costar. I had worked with Stefanie Powers on an episode of *It Takes a Thief* and I knew from our brief association on those shows that we had great chemistry together. Chemistry was the crucial element of the show, and chemistry can't be faked.

The network was leery; they pointed out that Stefanie had been on *The Girl from U.N.C.L.E.*, which had been a single-season flop years before, and that she had no track record with comedy. I got a lot of resistance, but Tom Mankiewicz agreed with me, and we just kept saying, "Stefanie Powers . . . Stefanie

Powers." Tom and I were both determined to have Stefanie in the show, and Aaron and Leonard finally agreed.

For the part of Max, I thought of casting Sugar Ray Robinson, which would have been a very interesting dynamic and would have opened up the possibility of Max's physicality saving Jonathan and Jennifer's bacon. But one day when Tom Mankiewicz was in the Fox commissary and ran into Lionel Stander, he called me up and said, "I've got Max right here!" I had worked with Lionel on an episode of *It Takes a Thief* and thought he was a terrific actor, so I wasn't hard to convince.

After we did the pilot for *Hart to Hart,* which featured Jill St. John and Roddy McDowall, Natalie and I went to Paris for a couple of weeks of pure vacation. While we were there, we ran into Mart Crowley, who wasn't doing much of anything. *Hart to Hart* had been quickly sold to ABC, and we were going to be shooting in a couple of months. The first scripts had arrived and weren't anything to brag about, so Natalie told Mart we needed him to come back to L.A. and rewrite the scripts. Natalie had always been Mart's good luck charm; she had paid for the first six months of therapy that led to Mart writing *The Boys in the Band.* Thankfully, Mart agreed to come back to America and go to work for me. With Mart and Tom Mankiewicz both working on the show, we had both a creative and a family nucleus.

*Hart to Hart* went on the air in August 1979, and Natalie made an unbilled guest appearance in the pilot. It was a scene in a movie studio, and in a delightful little in-joke, she was costumed to look like Vivien Leigh in *Gone with the Wind.* She even threw a line at Lionel Stander. Actually, she wasn't unbilled; she was listed in the credits as "Natasha Gurdin"—her real name.

From the beginning, the show jelled. After a couple of months on Saturday nights, ABC moved us to Tuesday nights, where we stayed for the rest of our five-year run. Stefanie proved to be a tremendous contributor to the show and a total pro—we meshed immediately. And then there was Lionel Stander.

During the un-American activities madness of the late '40s and early '50s, Lionel had distinguished himself by appearing in front of the House committee and basically telling them to go fuck themselves. Not only did he not inform on anybody, but he didn't equivocate, didn't take the Fifth Amendment, and didn't pretend not to remember anything. As far as Lionel was concerned, his politics were nobody's damn business, period. Then this immensely composed, self-sufficient man went to Europe and worked as a stockbroker on those occasions when acting jobs got scarce.

Twenty-five years later, he hadn't changed. He was a very tough-minded man and firm in his convictions, which remained proudly left-wing. He was very bright, loved to talk politics, and was the most amazing actor I ever worked with in that he never, ever missed a line. Well, he did blow a line one time. The scene had him exiting an airplane, and he stumbled over his line, and everybody was so shocked that we put this perfectly innocuous flub on the outtake reel.

*Hart to Hart* didn't succeed because of the plots. Television is all about characters you either have affection for or are fascinated by, and our show succeeded because of the relationship between Stefanie and myself and because it was a stealth *Lifestyles of the Rich and Famous* show. Jonathan and Jennifer Hart were rich and successful, never stopped adoring each other, and got to roam the world solving mysteries that baffled less enlightened souls like, for instance, the police. Who wouldn't want to live that life? It was straight wish fulfillment, and I am continuously pleased by the number of women who tell me that Jonathan and Jennifer Hart embodied their ideal of the perfect marriage.

Just about the time I started work on *Hart to Hart,* Natalie did a pretty good comedy with George Segal called *The Last Married Couple in America.* After Natalie finished her movie, we took off for Russia. NBC was televising the 1980 Moscow Olympics, and Bill Storke was producing a documentary about the Hermitage Museum in St. Petersburg, to be shown in conjunction with the network's coverage of the sporting events. Bill asked Natalie and Peter Ustinov to host the show. Natalie had always wanted to visit the land of her ancestors, and Bill would be there to shepherd us through, so she leaped at the chance. I thought it was a great idea as well, so we made the trip as a couple.

This was pre-*glasnost,* so the country and its greatest museum were far less accessible than they are now; there was a real sense of discovery in getting a close-up view of an unparalleled collection of art. Unfortunately, Russia itself proved to be a disappointment. We properly assumed our hotel room was bugged, so we either didn't speak or talked in a code we worked out. We also had trouble getting long-distance calls through to check on the girls, which raised our anxiety level. Moreover, it was obvious that the calls we did get through were tapped.

Finally, Natalie put a call through to the Minister of Culture in Moscow and told him that she was about to leave the country unless the wiretaps on our phone were lifted. End of problem.

Natalie was recognized occasionally on the streets, and the people were delighted that she spoke Russian like a native, although it seemed like the only films of hers that had been distributed in Russia were *Rebel Without a Cause* and *West Side Story.*

We both noticed that Russian women start out exotically beautiful, but something happens as they approach middle age—everything falls, including their spirits. They get dumpy. Natalie thought that on some level they gave up as they realized that their dreams wouldn't be realized. For Natalie, the biggest disappointment was the food; the service in the restaurants was terrible no matter how much I tipped them, and Natalie much preferred Mud's version of Russian dishes to the actual Russian dishes. After three weeks, we headed back to America. She was very glad she did the show, but she never had any interest in going back to Russia.

For my fiftieth birthday—if you're keeping score, the date was February 10, 1980—Natalie threw a surprise party for me at the Bistro in Beverly Hills. She had told me it was just going to be a small dinner with a few friends, but the few friends turned out to include dozens of the people I loved most: Mother Mitchum, Gene Kelly, Stefanie Powers, Suzanne Pleshette, Claire Trevor, Esther Williams, Fernando Lamas, and Henry Fonda. As if all that wasn't enough, she also gave me a silver-gray Mercedes-Benz. She had spent weeks organizing the party, and I was totally stunned. It was typical of the kind of grand, loving gesture that was her special province.

In November 1980, Natalie's father died. Nick had been an alcoholic for years and endured cardiac trouble for the last fifteen years of his life. It wasn't a surprise, but it was still a shock. You always think you're ready when a parent dies after a lingering illness, but you never are.

With Nick's death, Mud became more of a part of our lives, which created problems. In addition to being paranoid, Mud had a Machiavellian side left over from her days as a stage mother that she couldn't shut off, even when it was completely inappropriate. Despite her limited access to the children, she encouraged the girls to think about becoming child actresses, an idea neither Natalie nor I were in favor of, and she started intrigues in which she would play off one granddaughter against another, or—worse—against us.

It was maddening to have your parental authority undermined, not to mention counterproductive, and Natalie ended up by further restricting Mud's access to her granddaughters.

At the end of 1980, we had our usual New Year's Eve party. We'd given parties the first time we were married, of course, but the second time around the parties were easier and always wonderful times. The Canon Drive house was perfect for entertaining, both because of the house and because of the back garden. The parties were formal in the sense that they were black-tie affairs that recalled the old days of the balls and parties of the Hollywood I'd known as a young man. But they were informal in mood because only close friends were invited: Tom Mankiewicz, Mart Crowley, Howard Jeffrey, Guy McElwaine, George Segal, John and Linda Foreman, Greg and Veronique Peck, Gil Cates and his wife. Solid people.

In other words, there was no professional component to the parties, and no press photographs were ever taken. The guests would arrive, and then Natalie would come down the staircase, everybody would turn to her, and that's when the laughter began. There was always a sit-down dinner with live music, usually with my friend Jimmy Rowles, the great jazz pianist. Near midnight, we'd turn on the TV and watch the ball on Times Square come down. And after the New Year had come in, the party would continue for a long time.

For me, the key moment of the evening was always when Natalie and I toasted each other. That night, I told her, "I love you, my darling Natalie. You take my breath away."

After Natalie gave birth to Courtney on March 9, 1974, she was basically a homebody. My career was back on the upswing, so I was perfectly happy to spend most of my time working while Natalie spent her time with the kids. But after a while, she started to get restless, partially, she thought, because it seemed like the kids needed her less.

But that wasn't the real reason. Ultimately, acting was Natalie's identity. Beyond that, it was her security; if she wasn't interested in working, fine, but if she wanted to be working and wasn't, there was a sense of discontent. Although she was terribly proud of her girls, she had an underlying sense that acting was her real accomplishment—it was what she did best. Actually, she had great skills in both areas, but because actors discover their identity while they're still very young, it's not easily replaced with something else. As an actor myself, I understood.

When the restlessness hit, it became a question of what was going to come off the plate to make room for working. Her primary devotion was to Natasha, Katie, Courtney, and me. Altering that equation could build up guilt factors, especially if she wasn't as devoted to the project as she was to her family. In which case, the logical question was, "Then why do it?"

Natalie hid nothing; you always knew exactly where you stood with her. If she started to get frustrated or even lost her temper over things that ordinarily would not have bothered her, we both knew what was happening.

So Natalie picked up some projects. But after she decided to go back to work seriously, the offers were not overwhelming. Beginning in October 1977, she made a terrible movie called *Meteor*, directed by Ronald Neame, whom Natalie disliked. She felt he was a bullshit artist and was unconvinced. As for me, I had done a panel with him and got the impression that he was from the standard line of directors from time immemorial: actors should be treated like children. Aside from the fact that I thought he was insulting the actor on the panel with him, it gave me a window into the reasons Natalie had disliked working with him.

It became obvious that Natalie wasn't getting the kind of scripts she wanted. She looked spectacular, but she was a spectacular woman, not a spectacular girl. She was at that awkward age when the parts begin to dry up for leading ladies because there's always another batch of beautiful twentysomethings on the horizon, and they're easier to cast, not to mention cheaper.

It's possible that her iconic status worked against her as well, because there was a trend toward a different style of actress: Jill Clayburgh, Goldie Hawn, Mia Farrow, Diane Keaton, and Barbra Streisand were the hot actresses of the moment, and none of them were classic beauties. Sometimes they got parts they weren't really suited for, which makes the resulting pictures look somewhat strange today. Mia Farrow is great in *Rosemary's Baby,* but *The Great Gatsby* would obviously have been better served by somebody who was more conventionally beautiful. As always, there just aren't enough parts.

My own experience told me that good TV is preferable to bad movies, so Natalie began to think about directing her energies in that direction. In March 1978, I was in Hawaii doing *Pearl,* and the whole family was with me. While we were shooting, Natalie was offered a miniseries adaptation of *From Here to Eternity*—the part Deborah Kerr had played in Fred Zinnemann's movie. It was a good, rich part, and it was quality material, far better than anything she'd been offered lately in movies. She decided to make the move into TV.

The only area where TV really differs from movies is in the element of time. TV is quicker and cheaper than the movies. In some cases, that's good; the fast pace gives you less time to ponder, but it also keeps you from seizing up and getting self-conscious. The negative corollary is that corners can easily be cut.

Natalie had been acting since she was a little girl, and she was a total pro. She had a concept about her work that was terrific; she always figured out an arc for her characters and knew where the character was at all times in the production schedule, so adapting to the different pace wasn't intimidating for her. The only stipulation she made when she moved into television, with which I completely agreed, was to have a rehearsal period.

Ultimately, she was an actress who believed in the material. If the material and the director seemed right to her, she went for it, whether it was a movie, television, or the theater.

Natalie's costar in *From Here to Eternity* was William Devane. I hadn't been worried about her costars in the movies she'd made since we got back together—Michael Caine didn't play around, and neither did Sean Connery. But I think I probably had a permanent warning bell in my head after *Splendor in the Grass,* and there were times when I may have been expecting it to go off. Natalie didn't want me around when she was shooting a nude love scene in the ocean with Bill Devane. It made me nervous—needlessly so. She was first-rate in *From Here to Eternity* and won the Golden Globe for "Best Actress in a TV Series." I was over the moon with pride.

Another reward from that show was Elizabeth Applegate, who was hired as Natalie's personal assistant and remains by my side today. Liz has been involved in all of my professional and many of my personal activities ever since. She has sat with the kids while they did their homework, and she has sat with me through lawsuits. She helped me produce movies and TV shows and has been without question a great stabilizing force in my life.

NBC wanted to turn *From Here to Eternity* into a series and offered Natalie the chance to repeat her role. She turned it down and did *The Last Married Couple in America* with our friend George Segal.

In 1980 Natalie did a TV movie called *The Memory of Eva Ryker.* It was a dual part in which she played both mother and daughter. By this time, it was obvious that Natalie was determined to jump-start her career. She and Bill Storke optioned Nancy Milford's biography of Zelda Fitzgerald and started work on setting up a movie version. She would have been wonderful in the part, although it occurred to me that, like Vivien Leigh in *Streetcar,* a total immersion in such a damaged character could very well have negative consequences for the actress playing her. (Playing Blanche Dubois had exacerbated Vivien Leigh's manic tendencies.) Nevertheless, I thought the girls were big enough, and the part of Zelda was so great that it was worth the risk.

At the same time, Elizabeth Taylor was touring the country in a revival of *The Little Foxes,* and that gave Natalie the idea to make her stage debut. She had flourished during the intensive rehearsal period for *Cat on a Hot Tin Roof,* and it had removed a lot of her fear of the stage. Robert Fryer was a friend who was also a movie producer and on the board of the Ahmanson Theater in Los Angeles. Robert sent her a copy of Guy Bolton's play *Anastasia,* the basis for the 1956 movie in which Ingrid Bergman made her comeback as Anna Anderson, a homeless refugee with amnesia who gradually comes to believe (falsely) that she is the lost daughter of the Romanov dynasty. *Anastasia* was, I think, a canny suggestion dramatically, and it appealed to Natalie because of its romantic nature and her Russian heritage.

Natalie had seen Viveca Lindfors play the part in New York, and all it took was a commitment from Natalie for Robert Fryer to agree to do the show at the Ahmanson Theater in Los Angeles. The opening was scheduled for February 1982, and Natalie was determined to excel on a fast track. Arvin Brown agreed to direct, and Larry Olivier got Wendy Hiller to play the Grand Duchess—the part Helen Hayes had played in the movie.

While Bob Fryer was working on setting up *Zelda,* Natalie and I spent the last two weeks of May 1981 in France. It was a great, joyous trip. We left the kids in California and took our time driving down to the south of France, stopping at small places along the way. It was very low-key sightseeing, the sort of trip during which you rediscover how many things you have in common and how much you love each other. I surprised her one night in a restaurant when I gave her a ring. We concluded the trip by staying with David Niven at Cap Ferrat.

While we were in France, John Foreman called and offered her a part in a picture he was making at MGM called *Brainstorm,* opposite Christopher Walken. It was an interesting idea technically—the story concerned itself with a device that enabled personal experiences to be transferred from one person to another. Those sensory experiences were to be shot in 70mm, so that they would have a size and texture that was far more enveloping than the surrounding "real-life" footage. The director was Douglas Trumbull, who had done the special effects for *2001* and *Close Encounters of the Third Kind* and directed *Silent Running.* Natalie's part, as written, was ordinary, but the picture sounded like it could be cutting-edge, if only because of the technology and the fact that it was science fiction. It seemed like a good idea.

When we got back to Los Angeles, Fryer told us that he'd had trouble setting up *Zelda.* The story was completely downbeat— Zelda ended up in a mental institution and was killed in a fire some years after Scott Fitzgerald died. Natalie wasn't commercially strong enough at that point to get the movie set up on her name alone. Natalie agreed to do *Brainstorm* in the hope that *Zelda* would follow in due time. She started location shooting around Raleigh, North Carolina, at the end of September.

In mid-October, I took a long weekend from *Hart to Hart* and flew to Raleigh to visit Natalie. During those couple of days, the little bell in my head went off. Chris Walken was a very exciting actor and a very exciting guy who delighted in taking great risks. The bell wasn't exactly clanging, but I was aware that I didn't have her full attention. She was more involved with the movie than she was with her family, and the thought occurred to me that Natalie was being emotionally unfaithful. I chose not to confront her with my feelings. I flew back to my series, and Natalie continued production on *Brainstorm*.

A few weeks after my visit to Raleigh, I was doing *Hart to Hart* in Hawaii and Natalie was still working on *Brainstorm*. It was the first time we'd been separated since we'd remarried more than nine years before, but she was full of plans, and we were doing well.

The mood on my show was shattered on November 16 when William Holden was found dead in his apartment in Santa Monica. He had gotten drunk, fallen, and hit his head on a table. Not realizing how badly he had been cut, he had lain down on the bed and bled to death. He had been dead for four days before he was found. It was a terrible, ignominious death for a fine man and underrated actor who had been unable to shake his addiction to alcohol.

Bill Holden and Stefanie Powers had been separated for some time when he died, and I think the separation was permanent. Stefanie simply couldn't live with Bill's drinking anymore. That said, they would always have been friends, and she was completely devastated, as was everybody who knew Bill. He had given Stefanie a great deal, introducing her to Africa and other aspects of life that she had never experienced. She would always have been there for him, and it was typical of Stefanie that she took up his causes after he died. The William Holden

Wildlife Foundation is only part of what Stefanie has done to perpetuate the things that mattered to Bill.

Bill's death marked the beginning of the most shattering period of my life. There's a temptation to see tragedy as inevitable, to look back with hindsight and say, "*That's* where it went wrong. *That* was the moment when the dominoes began to fall."

But I don't think I really believe that. All I know is that, as I've said, life can change—irrevocably change—in a minute.

No, that's not right. Life can change in a moment.

# NINETEEN

# "EVERYTHING WENT AWAY FROM ME."

Natalie, 1960. (PHOTOGRAPH BY ERNST HAAS/ERNST HAAS/GETTY IMAGES)

Throughout our marriage, Catalina Island had been a large part of our lives. As I've mentioned, I had spent a lot of time there as a kid playing baseball with John Ford and his crew. When Natalie and I got together, she joined me in my devotion to the island. For the Thanksgiving weekend of 1981, we decided to take the *Splendour* out to Catalina. We invited Chris Walken, Delphine Mann, and another couple to be our guests, but the couple and Delphine had to cancel.

On Friday morning, November 27, we picked Walken up at Marina Del Rey, where our boat was docked, and made the twenty-two-mile voyage to Catalina. We anchored *Splendour* offshore from Avalon in the afternoon. A couple of hours later, we took the *Valiant* to the island, where we did some shopping. Then we went to a place we liked called the El Galleon and had margaritas and beer chasers. I found Chris Walken to be an interesting, pleasant man, and there was certainly nothing remarkable in the atmosphere.

Around nine o'clock we headed back to the boat, but Natalie was worried about the water, which had developed a swell. As always, Natalie was comfortable on the boat itself, but she didn't like being in the water, or the possibility of being in the water, because she was a bad swimmer. She finally agreed to go back to Catalina on the dinghy, and we had some more drinks over dinner.

By this time we had had slightly too much to drink, and things were getting combative. When I suggested moving the *Splendour* closer to shore to avoid having to ride out the swells, Natalie gave me an argument, and I gave her an argument right back. She got angry and told Dennis Davern, who took care of the *Splendour* for us, to take her to Avalon in the dinghy. She spent the night at the Pavilion Lodge. Chris just shrugged and went below to his cabin. I secured the boat and went to sleep myself.

The next morning Natalie came back to the boat and everything was fine. She cooked breakfast for Walken and me on the *Splendour,* and I again suggested moving the boat to calmer waters. This time she had no problem with it. By 1:00 P.M., we were anchored offshore at the Isthmus Cove, on the northern end of the island, which is far more isolated than the southern end.

A little while after that, everybody took a nap. When I woke up, I found a note from Natalie saying that she and Chris had taken the dinghy and gone to the island. They went to Doug's Harbor Reef for about two hours. I wasn't angry, but I was agitated. I called the shore boat and joined them. It would be fair to say that I was upset, but not so much that I let on. We stayed at Doug's for dinner, finally leaving for the *Splendour* around ten o'clock.

Again, we had had quite a bit of wine with dinner, but I would categorize our condition as tipsy; certainly, nobody was anywhere near drunk. We got back to the salon of the *Splendour* and had some more drinks. And it was at that point that I got pissed off.

Chris began talking about his "total pursuit of a career," which he admitted was more important to him than his personal life. He clearly thought that Natalie should live like that too, which rather neatly overlooked the fact that she was the mother of three small children. He also said it was obvious that I didn't share his point of view, which was an understatement.

I finally had had enough. "Why the fuck don't you stay out of her career?" I said. "She's got enough people telling her what to do without you." Walken and I got into an argument. At one point I picked up a wine bottle, slammed it on the table, and broke it into pieces. Natalie was already belowdecks at that point. She had gotten up during our argument—she didn't rush out, she just got up—and went down the three steps from the salon of the boat to the master cabin to go to the bathroom. The last time I saw my wife she was fixing her hair at a little vanity in the bathroom while I was arguing with Chris Walken. I saw her shut the door. She was going to bed.

By the nature of the disagreement, it was a circular argument, and the fact that neither of us was feeling any pain made it harder to break the circle. About fifteen minutes after Natalie closed the door, Chris and I moved from the salon up the three steps that led out onto the deck. If I had to categorize the emotional temperature, I would say that things were threatening to get physical, but the fact is that they never did.

After some minutes on the deck, the fresh air helped us calm down, and we came back into the salon and sat there for a while, but not long. At this point, everything was fine between us. Then Chris went to bed. I sat up for a while with Dennis Davern. And then it was time to go to bed.

I went below, and Natalie wasn't there. Strange. I went back up on deck and looked around for her and noticed the dinghy was gone. Stranger. I remember wondering if she'd taken the dinghy because of the argument, and then I thought, *No way,* because she was terrified of dark water, and besides that, the dinghy fired up very loudly, and we would have heard it, whether we were in the salon or on deck.

On the other hand, if she wasn't on the *Splendour,* where else could she be except on the dinghy? I found Dennis Davern and said, "I think Natalie took off on the dinghy." At that point, I thought she had gone back to Doug's Harbor Reef, the restaurant where we had had dinner.

I radioed for the shore boat and went back to the restaurant. Christopher and Dennis stayed on the *Splendour*. When I got to the island, the restaurant was closed. Natalie wasn't anywhere around the dock area, nor was the dinghy.

By this time, it was about 1:30 A.M. on the morning of November 29, and I was scared and confused. Dennis radioed for help on the Harbor Channel, which is monitored by the Bay Watch, a sort of private coast patrol. Then I called the Coast Guard. The Coast Guard came out to the boat, and they went through the *Splendour* from top to bottom, from the bilge on up. They checked everything. Then they started search and rescue, which is very difficult at night, crisscrossing the ocean surface with searchlights from Coast Guard helicopters. Hour after hour—nothing.

So we sat there through the night, in the salon, waiting to hear what happened. Chris Walken was there, Dennis Davern was there. Once in a while one of us would go to the bathroom, but there wasn't much conversation because the only possible subject was Natalie and nobody knew anything.

I kept running the possibilities through my mind, and there weren't many. She could have taken the dinghy to a cove someplace and the engine could have gone dead. But why hadn't any of us heard the engine start? As for the other possibility, I knew what it was, but I didn't allow myself to contemplate it. Aft, there was one step down to the dinghy, the only way on or off the boat when you were at sea. This step, which we called the swim step, was near the water line and could be very slippery.

In the morning, about 5:30 A.M., they found the *Valiant* in an isolated cove beyond Blue Cavern Point. The key was in the off position, the gear was in neutral, and the oars were fastened to the side. They radioed and told us that they had the dinghy, but Natalie wasn't on it. We had just run out of options, but I didn't allow myself to actually contemplate what that meant—it was too unthinkable.

Two hours later, they found my wife. Natalie was wearing a down-filled red parka Windbreaker, and that helped them spot her. The harbor master, Doug Bombard, was the one who got her out of the water, and he was the one who came onto the *Splendour* and looked at me.

I remember that the morning was sunny. I remember that I was standing on the aft deck when Doug pulled up and got out of his boat.

"Where is she?" I asked him.

Doug looked at me. "She's dead, RJ."

My knees went out; everything went away from me. Soon afterward, a helicopter came and took us to the mainland.

So many of the best times of my life had been spent in and around Catalina Island. It was always one of my favorite places on earth.

From the day Natalie died to this, I have never gone back.

# TWENTY

# "WHAT HAPPENED TO US, BABY?"

Exuding icy malevolence as Number Two in *Austin Powers*. (© NEW LINE
CINEMA. A TIME WARNER COMPANY. ALL RIGHTS RESERVED.)

I never saw Natalie dead, not at the morgue, not at the funeral home. I wanted to remember her alive.

The *Splendour* was impounded, pending an investigation. The autopsy revealed that Natalie had an alcohol level of .14, slightly above the .10 level of intoxication for California. The coroner estimated it as the equivalent of seven or eight glasses of wine, which sounds about right. She also had taken a seasickness drug and some Darvon, but no sleeping pills.

There was a heavy bruise on her right arm, a small one on her left wrist, small ones on her legs, her left knee, and right ankle, and an abrasion on her left cheek.

I've had several decades to think about what happened. My conclusion, as well as that of the people who were there and of Frank Westmore, who wasn't there but who knew the boat and Natalie, is this: while Walken and I were on the deck hashing out our argument, Natalie was in the master cabin and heard the dinghy banging against the side. She got up to retie it. She slipped on the swim step on the stern, hit the step on the way down, and was either stunned or knocked unconscious and rolled into the water. The loose dinghy floated away.

Some people said she was trying to get in the dinghy and drive away from the argument Chris and I were having, but she had gotten in and out of that dinghy a thousand times. She knew that getting in and out of the *Valiant* was very tricky in rough water because the swim step was slippery when it was wet. Even if the water was calm, one person usually held the line to keep the dinghy close to the *Splendour* while the other person hopped in. To do it in rough water in the dark was more than tricky; it was dangerous. Besides that, the state of the controls when they found the dinghy proved that she had never actually gotten into the boat.

Likewise, if she had hold of the dinghy's tether line, or if she was conscious while she was in the water, she would certainly have screamed or yelled and we would have heard her. My theory fits the few facts we have.

But it's all conjecture. Nobody knows. There are only two possibilities: either she was trying to get away from the argument, or she was trying to tie the dinghy. But the bottom line is that nobody knows exactly what happened.

Natalie's body was taken straight to the morgue. I called Mart Crowley and told him that Natalie was dead and asked him to pick me up at the Santa Monica airport. When I got off the helicopter from Catalina, I went directly to psychiatrist Arthur Malin, who told me how to break the news to the children.

"Don't ever minimize it," he said. "Don't try to make it accessible. This is a terrible thing that has happened, it has happened to all of you, and you will have to deal with it together."

I went to the house, where our core group of friends had already gathered: Roddy McDowall, my son Josh, Linda Foreman, Guy McElwaine, Tom Mankiewicz, Paula Prentiss, Judy Scott-Fox, Liz Applegate, Delphine Mann, and Bill Broder. Dr. Paul Rudnick, my general physician, was there, as was Arthur Malin, who offered to give me something to calm me down, but I didn't think that was a good idea; I needed to be completely there for our kids.

Natasha, Katie, and Courtney came down the stairs. "I've got something terrible to tell you," I began, "but I want you to know that we're going to be all right, and we're going to stay together." And then I told them their mother had died. Unfortunately, they had already heard about it on television. We cried and held each other. Our lawyer, Paul Ziffren, came and wouldn't leave. "Promise me one thing," Paul said. "I will not leave this house until you promise me this. Whatever is written, whatever is said, do not answer any questions from the media. Do not respond to anything. None of that is important. All that is important is you and your family. Promise me this."

I promised, and I'm glad I did; Paul had just given me very sound advice. For the rest of it, that day and that night I held the children while they cried, and Josh held me while I cried.

Throughout that long, terrible night off Catalina and the next few days, Chris Walken was there. He was at the house as people started coming by, and he stayed through the funeral. He went back to New York afterward. When all the shit came down and people made outrageous claims to the scandal sheets, he never said a word, never made a statement that added fuel to the fire.

I hold no grudge against him; he was a gentleman who behaved honorably in an impossible situation.

I was in a zombie state. It was as if there were a dark film over my eyes; I looked but I didn't see. I was there for the kids, but otherwise I was going through the motions. The police came a couple of times and asked a lot of questions, which I answered as best I could. There were a lot of people hanging around to make sure that I wasn't going to go off the deep end, which I would never have done. I may not have known much at that point, but I would never have committed suicide; I knew I had to take care of my kids. They needed their father; their father needed them.

Late on December 1, I came downstairs for a while. Mart Crowley was there, Josh Donen, a few others. The doorbell rang, and Elizabeth Taylor came in. She had just finished a performance of *The Little Foxes* at the Ahmanson. We held each other. "Oh, baby, baby," she said. "What happened to us, baby?"

Fred Astaire was there, and Gene Kelly came every day.

Gene understood loss—his beloved wife, Jeanne Coyne, had died of cancer. He was a solid force, an unshakable wall of support; he would hold me and say, "We'll get through this." David Niven was making a film in Europe, but he was on the phone to me every day, talking me through it.

Cumulatively, these friends and my children saved my life.

The funeral itself remains a blur. Natalie's death was an enormous story all over the world, and when a tragedy like this occurs and there are no facts, or the facts are inconveniently bland, the vacuum is filled with inaccuracies or suppositions. The least offensive was that Natalie's death made her the latest victim of a jinx on all who had made *Rebel Without a Cause*. The press had completely staked out 603 Canon Drive. We were besieged. When we left for the funeral, publicist Warren Cowan said the kids and I could go out the back way, but I said, "We're not going out the back door to their mother's funeral. We're going out the front door."

So we went to the cemetery, where we were surrounded by loving and caring friends. There was balalaika music, and all the people Natalie loved were there: Frank Sinatra, Elizabeth Taylor, Fred Astaire, Rock Hudson, Greg Peck, Gene Kelly, and Elia Kazan. Larry Olivier wanted to come, but his doctors wouldn't let him. Richard Gregson flew in and offered his unconditional support. Hope Lange, Roddy McDowall, and Tommy Thompson delivered the eulogies. Natalie's pallbearers were Howard Jeffrey, Mart Crowley, Josh and Peter Donen, John Foreman, Guy McElwaine, Tom Mankiewicz, and Paul Ziffren. We had the service, and then we walked out and buried Natalie.

I had chosen Westwood Cemetery because it was close to the house and the kids. They could go and visit whenever they wanted. I was trying to make it as right as I could for the children. I distinctly remember buying a double plot, but the cemetery contended that I didn't, and they lost the records. Years later, they offered to exhume Natalie and move her to another spot where we could be buried together, but I didn't want to do that. I just let it go.

After the funeral, we all went back to the house for a wake. President Reagan and Nancy called, and Queen Elizabeth sent a telegram: "On behalf of the Crown and the Commonwealth of Great Britain, I send heartfelt condolences to the family and friends of Mrs. Wagner. The tragic loss of great persons is felt the world over. However, loving memories of Mrs. Wagner will live with us always." Princess Margaret and Pierre Trudeau also sent telegrams.

It was at this point that I went to bed and stayed there. It may have been for seven days, it may have been for eight. I was catatonic and don't really remember. I didn't shower and I didn't shave. I don't know if I was in some form of catastrophic mourning; I don't know if I was in the midst of a contained nervous breakdown. I only know that I was obsessively, continually trying to understand what had happened—to figure out if there was anything I could have done that I didn't do. It all went round and round in my head, and for those seven or eight days I couldn't face anything that constituted the world. We had had everything, and our lives had been on an upswing ever since we remarried. To lose Natalie to an incongruous accident fueled by too much alcohol seemed more than tragic—it felt impossible.

Grief mixed with shock is such a difficult state to be in; it's hard to even describe it. On the one hand, I was numb and felt like I was in some sort of dream state—I couldn't believe Natalie was gone, but I knew it was true. And despite the shock, which makes you feel like you're muffled in cotton, my nerve ends were screaming. I was in emotional pain so intense it was physical.

Did I blame myself? If I had been there, I could have done something. But I wasn't there. I didn't see her. The door was closed; I thought she was belowdecks. I didn't hear *anything*. But ultimately, a man is responsible for his loved one, and she was my loved one.

Yes, I blamed myself. Natalie would have felt the same way had it happened to me. Why wasn't I there? Why wasn't I watching? I would have done anything in the world to make her life better or protect her. *Anything*. I would have given my life for hers, because that's the way we were.

She was my love. She was the woman who had defined my emotional life, both by her presence and her absence, and now she was gone and this time there was no getting her back.

Finally, Willie Mae, the children's nurse, came in and said, "Mr. W., you have got to get up! You have to get these kids to school! You have got to go back to work!" That was the moment that finally penetrated the fog. I got out of bed, got into the shower, and made myself presentable. And then Natasha and Courtney and I went for a walk in the garden, and I told them that it was going to be all right. They had lost their mother; they had to know that they weren't going to lose their father as well. That was the beginning of my return to the land of the living, and for that I have to thank Willie Mae. We all have saviors in our lives, and she was one of them.

And there was another thing. A doctor gave me a line from Eugene O'Neill: "Man is born broken. He lives by mending. The grace of God is glue." For me, my children and the people who threw themselves into holding us together were the glue.

It was a strange, disorienting time, filled with strange, disorienting events. In the following weeks, women—famous women—began showing up at my house uninvited. It was soon after Natalie died, and women I had known for years were suddenly bringing food by the house and effecting concern, which

I didn't believe for a minute—they weren't exactly dressing like they were in mourning. It was such a disconcerting display, and it added a level of discomfort I didn't really need in my life at that point, this idea that I would be in the market days after my wife died. It was so disrespectful of our relationship and of my love for her.

Nine days after Natalie died, I went back to work on *Hart to Hart*. I had lost ten pounds and most of my emotional equilibrium. Stefanie Powers was in only marginally better shape than I was, but she shepherded me through it. She never let me out of her sight, and if I blew my lines or got upset, she smoothed everything over. On December 12, the police concluded that Natalie's death was a tragic accident, and the case was closed.

Before that happened, Thomas Noguchi, the Los Angeles celebrity coroner made various speculations, just as he had with Bill Holden, and as he would when he re-opened the investigation into the death of Marilyn Monroe. Noguchi seemed to enjoy his celebrity status and his speculations put him right in the spotlight. Frank Sinatra was furious—he adored Natalie and knew the truth of what happened. He would never have been so loyal if there was even a shadow of doubt.

It was after the final determination of Natalie's cause of death that David Niven came to my—our—rescue. He insisted we get out of Los Angeles for Christmas and come to Europe. I took the kids, Willie Mae, and Delphine Mann, Courtney's godmother, to Gstaad, where David waited for us for four hours in a blizzard. When we finally got there, he held me in his arms, and then he drove us to a chalet he had rented.

No man could have had a better friend. He had been where I was; he had lost Primmie in a similarly stupid accident, and he had raised their two boys in spite of Hjordis, not with her.

Through the next several weeks, he was with me every day.

*Every day.* He never left me alone. He would take me for long walks and talk to me about what I was going through and what he had gone through. He gave me the benefit of the wisdom he had gained from being in the same situation. He told me that this was going to be an incremental process; it was not something you got over, he told me. It was something you learned to live with.

"Don't make any hard-and-fast decisions," he said. "Let your feelings go where they want, and don't let anybody else intrude or tell you what's appropriate or inappropriate." David's wise counsel, and getting away from Hollywood, gave me some distance and enabled me to begin to get my bearings. Those weeks with David were the beginning of the long process by which I put my life back together.

Looking back, I can see that it took years until the haze lifted. What I came to realize, gradually, incrementally, was that Natalie had a tragic death, but she didn't have a tragic life. She lived more in her forty-three years than most people—felt more, experienced more, did more, gave more. She was loved, fulfilled, and worshiped; she caught her rainbows. The way a life ends doesn't define that life; the way a life is lived does.

Even though Natalie has been dead for more than twenty-five years, there are still unexpectedly painful moments, like a loose floorboard that snaps up and hits you in the face. Life does have to go on, and with the children I couldn't be so overcome by it that I couldn't keep their spirits up. And they were so very helpful to me, because they were getting hit by the same floorboards I was. Katie, the oldest, stepped up and took something of a maternal position with her sisters, which helped. The fact that we all held on to each other and kept going—Natalie would have wanted that. And the way the children have handled themselves in their lives, their strength, fills me with such pride. Natalie raised our children well.

On the way back from Gstaad, we took a New Year's stop-over in Wales, where Richard Gregson was living with his wife. Then it was back to Los Angeles and work. The *Hart to Hart* crew was so respectful and caring, and it felt good to be back, to feel the warmth of the lights on my face.

Over the years, I would have epic legal battles with Aaron Spelling and Leonard Goldberg, almost always over my profit entitlement which they ended up paying me.

But.

In the worst days of my life, when I needed Aaron and Leonard, *really* needed them, they were there for me. Anything I needed was customized for me; if the production schedule had to be rearranged, then it was rearranged. If that cost them money, they didn't utter a word of criticism. They were solicitous, they called, they bent whatever needed bending to enable me to function, and I will always be indebted to them for that.

Likewise, Stefanie was continually marvelous; she knew only too well what I was going through. Bill Holden's death was devastating for her, and I'm sure there was much attendant guilt. There was a sense in which Stefanie and I were united by far more than working on a TV show; we were united in a shared grief.

The fallout went on for months . . . years. The Ahmanson Theater chose not to try to recast the production of *Anastasia* and canceled it. As for the incomplete *Brainstorm,* MGM tried to use Natalie's death as an excuse to make an insurance claim and scrap the picture. The studio lost the case, and after some rewriting to give Natalie's scenes to another character, the film was finally released in late 1983. Unlike the last films of other great stars, which often serve as a sort of summing up of their gifts and their meaning, *Brainstorm* was completely unworthy of Natalie. It wasn't successful, and it didn't deserve to be. If it hadn't been Natalie's last picture, nobody would remember it at all.

Natalie's will didn't leave her sister Lana any money, just her clothes. A few days after I went back to work on *Hart to Hart*, Lana called the house and said she wanted her inheritance. Liz, Natalie's secretary, explained that the will hadn't been probated yet, but Lana kept calling and demanding her property, which included some fur coats that were particularly valuable. I wanted Natasha and Courtney to have those, so I told Liz to have the coats appraised and I would send Lana the money. The coats were appraised at $11,000, so I sent Lana a check for that amount and told her she could have everything else.

Damned if Lana didn't take me literally. She pulled up in a truck and proceeded to strip Natalie's walk-in closet down to the walls. She even took the underwear. The clothes ended up on sale in a store on Ventura Boulevard that dealt in second-hand clothing. Lana then promptly rushed to write a ridiculous book about her sister that was published a year after Natalie died. Her writing career went about as well as her acting career.

At least she was consistent.

Once some order was restored to our lives, my first priority was to keep my girls together. Courtney was very young and completely shattered, as only a young girl who has lost her mother can be. One of the problems that Courtney has carried with her through the years is that she didn't know her mother that well. When something tragic happens, people go out of their way not to bring it up to the people involved because they know how painful it is. So Courtney didn't talk with me or with anybody else very much about her mother; she buried a lot of those feelings, as did Natasha.

Natalie had custody of Natasha after her divorce from Richard Gregson, and the girls had become totally devoted to each other. Although Richard would certainly have been within his rights to ask for Natasha, I asked him if I could keep her with me so I could raise her and Courtney together. "The last thing those girls need," I told him, "is to be separated from each other." Thankfully, Richard agreed absolutely, so we raised the girls together, and very amicably. He could have Natasha for visits anytime he wanted, but her main residence was with me. Because of Richard's decency, there were no more losses piled on top of what had already happened.

I've always believed that there's a lot to be said for going back to the land, so soon after Natalie died I bought eighty acres from Richard Widmark in Hidden Valley. Dick held on to a large property next door, so we were gentleman ranchers together. With the help of a great old cowboy named Tom Ulmer, we raised cutting horses and grew hay. It was a working ranch, and I was out there on the weekends riding and running the tractor. We had five mares that produced five foals a year and fifty head of cattle that produced another fifty head—not enough to make any money, but enough to compel hard work and force me to work amid the natural cycle of life. I had had enough death, so I made up my mind that none of my animals would go out the door to the slaughterhouse; we sold them strictly as breeding stock.

I had every intention of holding on to the ranch, but one day a guy showed up unannounced and offered to buy it at any price I cared to name. I named a price, he nodded, and the deal was done. I took some of the money and turned around and bought another ranch, this one encompassing 184 acres. In retrospect, I believe the Hidden Valley ranch was a crucial component of my healing.

On Sunday, July 11, 1982, nine days before Natalie's birthday, my mother wrote me a letter:

> *Dear RJ,*
>
> *You are very much in my thoughts and prayers as I know this is a sad time for you with Natalie's birthday and an anniversary just ahead—but although it's hard to do—you must tuck these days away and only have happy memories—these you will always have—yours alone.*
>
> *Have no regrets, RJ, as there was no one who loved their wife, children and home more than you did—and you were always so in tune together and you were so good to Natalie, so do not have any unhappy moments.*
>
> *Natalie had a very full life for her age—much more than many actresses ever achieve at a much older age. She had a happy home life—beautiful children and a husband who adored her—so what more is there in life?*
>
> *I feel very sad that she was taken at such a young time in her life, but there are things one has no control over—[so] remember only all the happy times you had together.*
>
> *I love you dearly, RJ, always and always will until the end of time.*
>
> *Love,*
> *C.*

Thank God for *Hart to Hart*. The show kept going, although it always gets harder the longer a show runs. The writers get bored and want to move on to something else because the characters are set. Besides that, relationships are the toughest things to write for television—or, for that matter, for any media. The nature of our show meant that we couldn't spice things up by inventing domestic squabbles or kitchen-sink drama. But it was a wonderful company; Tom Mankiewicz and Mart Crowley ran the show and did a wonderful job, and the entire cast and crew were a pleasure to work with. The fact that we were a success meant that we were always able to get good actors, which keeps the regulars on their toes.

After our fifth season, our ratings were still good, and we had eight scripts ready for our sixth season. We were going to take the Harts to France, then shoot a couple more episodes in other European spots. And then a new regime at ABC canceled us because they wanted to make room for their own programming.

We were all totally shocked; Aaron and Leonard came out to the house while we tried to figure out a way to keep things going. The problem was that the network canceled us very late, and the other networks had already set their schedules. Today a show that was as successful as ours would be easily moved over to cable or one of the other networks, but in 1984 those alternative venues didn't exist.

Once again, I was an actor at liberty.

I had always promised Natalie that if anything happened to her, I would take care of her mother, which I did. At first, Mud handled my fan mail and would come by the house to see her granddaughters. I bought the condo that Natalie had been renting for her and gave Mud $2,000 a month for her expenses. But it was gradually growing apparent that she was getting a touch forgetful and could no longer live alone.

Lana moved in with Mud and brought her boyfriend with her. Lana and her boyfriend were in the big bedroom, and Mud was in the small bedroom, and in between were about ten cats. (Lana has always been an animal collector.) The neighbors finally demanded that we do something about the smell. The drapes were shredded from the cats, there were droppings everywhere, and rolls of toilet paper littered the floors. Basically, they were living like derelicts.

We moved Mud into her own apartment at Barrington Plaza, and we cleaned the old place up. For a time, Katie lived there. Then I got a call that Mud had set fire to her apartment. When we asked her what had happened, she said that she had been looking for her jewels under the bed with a lighted candle.

It was clear that Mud required constant supervision and needed to go to the Motion Picture Home, which, since it began in the 1920s, has provided a wonderful, nurturing refuge for elderly people from all branches of the industry. I called up Edie Wasserman to arrange it. Natalie and I had raised a great deal of money for the Home over the years, and I've continued to do so. Arranging residency for Mud would have been very easy.

But Lana didn't want her mother to go to the Home, largely, I believe, because if Mud lived with her, she could live off Mud's Social Security and my monthly check. Olga, Natalie's older sister, is a wonderful woman and was very much on my side in this entire unfortunate business. Olga and I tried to pry Mud away and get her into the Home, but without Lana's permission Mud couldn't be admitted. It wasn't long before Mud's carelessness accelerated into dementia, and she had to be moved to a hospital. She died in January 1998, a month before she would have turned eighty-six.

A few years before I received a letter from Lana asking for help. As I sat there thinking, I remembered how her husband at the time sold the pictures of mine and Natalie's second wedding to the tabloids. I remembered all the misleading stories about Natalie she gave to the tabloids. I remembered how she ran up her mother's credit cards. I remembered the way she ransacked Natalie's clothes. And I remembered the last time I had given her money. She had come to me for help with her house and the water bill and so forth. I had given her a check for $25,000. A month later she was back for more.

I remembered all this, and I said no. To paraphrase Walter Huston in *Dodsworth*, "Family has to stop somewhere short of suicide."

Then Lana appealed to the kids, and Natasha gave her some money. "It will never be enough," I told her.

We stored all the paraphernalia from the *Splendour* in a facility in the valley. There was a great deal of memorabilia—wonderful photographs that we'd had framed and mounted, all the silver and china and clocks and barometers from the boat. In 1994 the Northridge earthquake hit, and a bridge collapsed onto the storage facility. There was nothing left. A bulldozer came in and loaded the shards onto a truck. Everything was carted away to a landfill.

Gone, all gone.

# TWENTY-ONE

# "A GIFT FOR LIFE."

The first time I met Jill St. John, on a soundstage at Fox in 1959.

Like me, Jill St. John is a Hollywood kid. Her dad ran a very successful bar and restaurant in Westwood, and Betty Lou Oppenheim, her mother, created the Screen Smart Set, a program through which people donated clothes and furniture to the Motion Picture Home in return for a tax deduction. The Home raised more than $8 million because of Betty Lou's idea.

Natalie and Jill knew each other, but not well. Nat and Jill were kids in daily ballet class together, both with ferocious stage mothers. (Stefanie Powers was in the same class!) Jill's mother got her into radio by the time she was six, and she was making movies when she was a teenager. When we were married the first time, Natalie and I would say hi to Jill and Lance Reventlow, her husband, and as my career at Fox slowed down, hers was heating up. Jill was a leading lady to some major stars: Sinatra, Dean Martin, and, of course, Sean Connery in *Diamonds Are Forever.* We had worked together in *How I Spent My Summer Vacation,* and *Banning,* not to mention the pilot for *Hart to Hart,* and the association had been pleasant but purely professional, despite the imaginings of my wife, Marion.

Jill and I first went out for dinner with Tom Mankiewicz and my daughter Kate about six months after Natalie died. A few days later, I called Jill and asked her out. She got flustered and said she'd call me right back. Then she immediately called Tom Mankiewicz.

"RJ asked me out," she said. "Should I go?"

"Well, if you don't, someone else will," he replied.

You can't argue with logic like that, so Jill and I started seeing each other.

I don't particularly like being alone. I'm one of those men who likes being in a relationship—it centers me. As we spent time together, I realized that Jill brought many things to the table. There was a sense of kismet in what happened between us. Whenever we'd run into each other in the past, one or both of us was in love with somebody else, so neither of us ever particularly contemplated the other's potential. But now we seemed to be finding each other at a time when we were both alone. Besides that, we were at similar stages of our lives. I'm ten years older, but we're both old enough to have loved and lost, so we valued each other all the more.

I found that Jill was remarkably empathetic; she understood what I was going through, perhaps better than I did. She had lost Lance Reventlow, with whom she was always close even after they divorced, in a plane crash. She had known and liked Natalie. We knew a lot of the same people, we were from the same era, we understood the same music.

From the beginning, we were comfortable with each other, and that is something that only gets better with time. From the beginning, both my mother and my sister also thought the world of her, which served as a confirmation of my own instincts.

While Jill and I were slowly discovering each other, the uproar over Natalie's death continued. The promise I had made to Paul Ziffren—to not acknowledge anything that was written or broadcast about Natalie's death—was immensely valuable. Of course, I was aware of what was being said, but I tried to ignore it.

There was only one thing that truly enraged me: the stories that I had somehow conspired to kill Natalie. That was the last straw, and I wasn't going to take it quietly. Finally, Jill called Henry Kissinger, whom she's known for years, and Henry called me. He explained that, legally speaking, I had little recourse. He talked about the things that had been written about him, some of which were nearly as crazy as the things that were being said about me. The sense of the conversation was "this too shall pass," and it helped me get past my reflexive outrage.

Jill never pressed me for any kind of definition in our relationship. She was there, with her hand under my arm. She let me vent and be what I needed to be. She didn't try to put lights on the Christmas tree, she was just there for me and the kids, with no expectation of return. She loved me, or she wouldn't have stayed, because at this point I was lugging enough baggage to fill a 747 to Heathrow. I was a heartbroken man who was drinking too much and just trying to get through the night, every night. I had three kids who were also reeling. I wasn't exactly a catch.

Although we started going out about six months after Natalie died, it probably took two or three years before I could look at her and really see her. I do not believe I would be alive today without her. There's a reason my pet name for her is "Magic." Jill is very bright, very caring, and has what I can only call a gift for life. She is, for example, a wonderful gardener. She *tends* things. She's also a superb Cordon Bleu–trained chef. Soon things started happening for us together.

It was Jill who helped me find the house the kids and I moved into. The belief had been growing in me for some time that the Canon Drive house was too permeated with Natalie for the girls and me to ever be able to make a fresh start. I started looking for an alternative.

Cliff May was a developer and architect who had basically invented the California ranch house, with the sliding glass door leading out to the backyard. Because of my father's interest in California real estate, which he passed on to me, I was aware of the community of houses Cliff had built near Will Rogers State

Park. Cliff had started building the houses in 1936 or so, and the house Cliff built for himself was the one I bought.

It's a long ranch house on two and a half acres. The living area is in the center of the house, and the seven bedrooms and the office spike off from the center. There was room for the kids as well as Willie Mae, and there was plenty of room to build a perfect cottage for my mother. And there was a stable for horses—the most therapeutic of all animals. The house is just minutes from Hollywood, but it feels rural; around the corner, there's a neighborhood riding ring for working with the horses. It's not pretentious, but it is comfortable. From the beginning, it felt like home, and for more than twenty-five years that's what it was.

The house had been featured in *Architectural Digest* in 1946, when Cliff May was still living in it, and those photographs show nothing but forest around the house. The magazine categorized it as a "Modern Ranch House" in "Riviera Ranch, West Los Angeles," which is fair enough, although now it's just Brentwood. But ranch houses didn't have some of the beautiful rounded adobe features of the entry, or the rural feel that the land gave the house.

Unfortunately, the house had been altered over the years, and some of its charm and beauty had been lost, but Cliff was still alive when we bought it, and I asked him to restore it. Cliff was a fascinating man, very romantic, in love with Mexico and women, some of whom he married. I'm glad I got to know him.

In late 1982, the girls and I moved in . . . slowly. It was another wrenching experience. Natalie had decorated the Canon Drive house so very carefully, so very beautifully. I couldn't bear to just pull up stakes all at once, so we moved out gradually. We would drive over to the new house, perhaps paint a room and move in a few pieces of furniture. I told the girls that they could take any furniture they wanted from the old house for their new rooms; if there wasn't room in the new house and they still wanted it, I told them I would keep things in storage until they had houses of their own and could reclaim the pieces that carried such memories of their mother.

And if the Brentwood house wasn't enough, Jill opened up Aspen for me. Jill had lived in Aspen since the mid-1960s, when it was a slightly down-at-the-mouth silver mining town in the process of becoming a world-class ski resort and you could pick up lots for $750. The people who lived in Aspen were highly educated, although most of them didn't have a lot of money. But they loved the arts and they loved the mountains, and long after everybody became quite wealthy because of the skyrocketing value of their land, they continued to be devoted to the extraordinary environment and atmosphere.

I fell in love with the town at the same time I was falling in love with Jill. Finally, in 1995, we bought property there, and three years after that we completed the house we'd planned and built together.

The house that had been on the seven and a half acres was small, almost Bauhaus in style, and it had nothing to do with its surroundings. We built a different structure, higher, more open, with a lot of windows that brought the house into the world of the mountains that lie beyond our veranda. The house has bare timbers and is surrounded by trembling aspen trees and spruce. You can't see any other houses from ours, so there's a feeling of splendid isolation in the view, and the atmosphere is serenely western. Surrounded by the trees, Jill's collection of Russell Chatham paintings, and the twelve-foot Tiffany window, I am at home.

I think that Jill and I found each other at the right time. There have been none of the tensions that arose in my other marriages, and I think that's because when you find someone at our stage of life, you're much less likely to do anything to derail trust. Jill is a man's woman, and I'm lucky she chose me to be her man. And whenever we have to go somewhere, she's packed and ready before I am, and with fewer bags. Unfortunately.

Our favorite times together have been on fishing trips or the various times we've gone to Europe. There have been driving trips through France and four or five trips to Paris, where we love walking around the Ile St. Louis or the gardens of the Rodin Museum—my favorite place in France. These times together contain nothing fancy, nothing pretentious. The hotels are out of the Michelin Guide, the food is bread, cheese, and wine, and it all fills my soul.

My friendship with David Niven never weakened. We spent many happy days on his sailboat, the *Foxy,* around Cap Ferrat. We'd fish for sea bass and dive for sea urchins, which he ate as if they were popcorn. For liquid refreshment, David hung bottles of white wine over the side of his boat so that the Mediterranean would keep them cold. He also had a taste for *loup de mers* and would tell me, "We have to catch them here before they go across the border and become bronzino." The secret to David's personality was that he loved life as much as he loved to work; the secret to the love that people had for David was not just that he was quick, clever, and witty; it was that he had a gift for friendship like few people I've known.

David's house at Cap Ferrat was called Lo Scoglietto, and it was near a little medieval village called St. Paul de Vence. Niv adored his house, and he adored the sunshine and the flowers that grow in such profusion around Cap Ferrat. He was so sentimental about living things that he would walk around his pool fishing out bees and wasps so they wouldn't drown. He ordered his life around summers at Cap Ferrat, and he flatly refused to take any film that would interfere with his lifestyle.

His personality never changed, not even after he was struck by amyotrophic lateral sclerosis—Lou Gehrig's disease. Despite his weakened physical condition, he retained the wonderful joie de vivre that always came through in his acting. Jill would say that even after he could no longer speak intelligibly, he could still make her laugh, because his eyes were still alive with his personality and she could tell what he was trying to say.

On one level, I don't think he ever got over Primmie's death. By the time David was diagnosed with ALS, Hjordis was a total alcoholic, and not a quiet one. They had adopted two girls, Kristina and Fiona, in order, I assume, to try to give the marriage more of a foundation, but it never seemed to me that Hjordis had any feelings for David at all. Why he stayed with her, I've never understood. I thought a divorce was in the offing at one time, around 1977, but then one of the girls had a very serious auto accident, and he felt that he couldn't leave his family. The woman he had been seeing was English, about thirty-five, and loved to sit at his knee and listen to the uproarious stories David could tell so well. She adored him, and to see David with her, as opposed to Hjordis, was to see a flower open to the sun.

Even marinated in alcohol, Hjordis retained much of her beauty, but she had a bleak, dark, driven personality, and his invariable response was to do everything he could to placate her, to no avail. When he was diagnosed with ALS, I told her, "Hjordis, you have to be here for David now; he needs you."

Her response was a simple declaration: "I never loved him anyway."

My reaction was a combination of shock, anger, and despair. As long as I knew them, Hjordis never gave any indication that she did love him, although if ever a man was deserving of love, it was David. It's possible that he stayed with her because a divorce would have been very expensive, but his attitude toward her didn't seem based on finances. It was more like he was doing penance. But for what?

While the disease had its way with David, Hjordis was elsewhere—drinking, having affairs. In the spring of 1982, we went to France to shoot *The Curse of the Pink Panther,* which Blake Edwards put together as a last hurrah for the series. Niv played his old part, I played my old part. It was just a couple of days of shooting, but we all wanted to do it for David. After he did his last scene, he said, "I'm afraid you've just seen the last of an actor who had quite a career." Tears came to my eyes.

Unfortunately, the ALS had slurred Niv's voice. Before a take, he would work at enunciating the dialogue clearly, sounding it out syllable by syllable, but when the camera was rolling a word like "gorilla" would come out "golilla." Blake felt he had to dub David's voice with Rich Little, who didn't sound anything like David, which made the situation that much worse. Niv was terribly distressed; it's one thing to acknowledge a disease privately, but to have its effects paraded before the whole world is something else entirely.

Niv had always intended that *The Curse of the Pink Panther* would be his last movie, but the fact that Rich Little's dubbing job became a matter of public knowledge meant that it was no longer David's choice.

Toward the end, David knew he was dying, even though he had always been determined to beat the illness. Sometimes he would talk about death and how different his life would have been if Primmie had lived. He would like to be reincarnated, he said, as a cat.

As if the agony of his illness wasn't bad enough, the last couple of weeks of David's life were disturbed by a paparazzo who used a long lens to get a picture of David in his garden looking mortally ill. The pictures were published all over the world by the jackal press, and I'm glad to be able to report that a group of us made sure that it would be a long time before that son of a bitch was able to take any more pictures.

David died on July 29, 1983, with only his nurse present. David Jr. and Jamie had been completely attentive to their father, but he died unexpectedly and nobody was there. Just a couple of days before, a drunken Hjordis had taunted David to the effect that he was no longer a man. The doctor called to tell me that David was gone, and I called Roger Moore. Roger was close by, in the south of France, and drove to David's house immediately. He was the first on the scene, and Roger, his daughter, and a few others organized David's funeral. About a day after David died, Hjordis finally showed up, half-pissed. They took a rug and threw it over the windshield so the photographers couldn't get any shots of her drunk. They managed to get her inside David's villa, and Roger was already there.

"I knew you'd be here for the publicity" was the first thing out of her drunken mouth. I would not have been able to contain myself—I would have knocked her on her ass. But Roger has impeccable self-control and just walked away. I was in London when David died, but I couldn't bear to see Hjordis and pretend I had any sympathy or affection for her. I waited until after the funeral and then went to the cemetery and left flowers at David's grave, as I have continued to do whenever I'm in Europe.

It's a mark of David's personality that the porters and baggage handlers at Heathrow airport sent a giant wreath to his funeral. He had always treated them generously, and they felt it was the least they could do.

After David died, most of his friends simply shut Hjordis out. One of the few people who was close to David who was also fond of Hjordis was Grace Kelly. I heard later that Hjordis quit drinking and filled up her time by socializing. David's will made it possible for her to continue living in the house; when she died, the house was sold and the estate split the money up.

David's sister was a very talented artist and did a remarkable bust of her brother for the immediate family. David's daughter and sons Jamie and David each have a copy, Roger Moore has one, and I have the other. It's among my most treasured possessions—as was my friendship with David.

This was a time when the generation of actors I had idolized as a child were growing old and frail. The last time I saw Jimmy Cagney was around 1983, at a restaurant in Beverly Hills. He came shuffling in, a shrunken little man who had obviously had a stroke and was barely recognizable as James Cagney, the titanic talent who had been very kind to a green kid thirty-odd years before.

I went over to him. "RJ!" he said brightly. And then, realizing how he appeared to people at this stage in his life, he sort of waved a hand at himself and said, very quietly, "These things happen." His simplicity, his acceptance of the frailties of his age, made tears well up in my eyes. It still does.

When my father died, my mother sold the house, packed up all the china and cookware, and gave it to my sister. She never did another domestic chore for the rest of her life. She was out from under—she was free. She didn't want to live in a house, she didn't want any responsibility for taking care of anything. She wanted to live in a nice hotel, so we got her into the Bel-Air Hotel, where she and my dad had always been connected. Joe Drown, the owner, knew her and knew me, and my lawyer and I arranged a deal whereby her rent rose with the cost-of-living index.

She lived at the Bel-Air for more than twenty-three years.

When she would walk into the hotel bar, Bud, the piano player, would swing into "Hello, Dolly," and she would have a glass of champagne and talk to the waiters, who always made sure to make a fuss over her. She was just a fabulous character. She kept her great sense of humor, even after her eyesight began to fade, and when she and Jill's mother, Betty, got together, it was hilarious—two women obsessively devoted to their adult children.

After a certain point, it became obvious that she wouldn't be able to stay at the Bel-Air, which is not, after all, a geriatric care facility. She developed macular degeneration and then fell and broke her hip. Kathy Constantino was working at the hotel and helping my mother out with things like writing checks and letters. Cliff May built my mother a very comfortable house on our property in Brentwood, a kind of southwestern-style cottage with a fireplace and an extra bedroom for Kathy, who came to work for me and helped take care of my mom.

She lived with us very happily, even as she grew increasingly frail. By November 1993, she was ninety-five years old. I had told the staff that if anything happened, I didn't want extreme measures taken. But when I was at our ranch one day, she collapsed. The fire department was called and climbed all over her trying to resuscitate her.

They got her heart beating and took her to the hospital. The doctor asked me what I wanted to do. I told him that we should just see how it went. A little while after that, she just stopped breathing. My mother's beautiful blue eyes were still open. I looked right at her, and for the first time in my life she couldn't see me. My friend Sister Marie Madeline came in the room, put her hands on my mother's eyes, and shut them. At that precise moment, I felt something rush past me. I believe it was my mother's soul.

# TWENTY-TWO

# "YOU HAVE TO HAVE *IT*."

Jill and me on our wedding day, May 26, 1990. (PHOTOGRAPH BY ALEX BERLINER © BERLINER STUDIO/BEIMAGES)

I had gone from playing a charming rogue in *It Takes a Thief* to playing a charming rogue in *Switch* to playing a charming non-rogue in *Hart to Hart*. My public image was—and probably remains—a cross between Alexander Mundy and Jonathan Hart.

I realize that there are actors who bridle at being typecast; they find it limiting, or even insulting that the public fails to recognize their versatility. But about the time I was doing *Switch* I had a crucial realization. I was in Palm Springs, standing in a supermarket checkout line. A woman in back of me said, "Oh, how are you?"

"I'm just fine, thank you."

"I'd like to invite you to come over to my house for dinner tonight."

"Oh, I'm sorry, I have plans. But thank you so much for the invitation."

"But I'm really a very good cook, and my husband's a nice man. You'll like him."

Well, I managed to beg off, but I realized that something remarkable had just happened. This very nice woman wanted to invite me to her house. It struck me then, and it strikes me now, that this is lightning in a bottle. The public sees me as a member of their family. They love me and want me, not just in their living room, but in their kitchen or dining room. I was and am delighted. More than that: I'm honored.

When I was a kid watching movies in Westwood, I was in the dark, looking up at the screen at people who seemed more than human—larger, grander than life. I wasn't talking to anyone—hell, I was barely eating my popcorn, because I was totally involved in that glowing silver frame on the wall. You didn't actually imagine that you'd ever see Clark Gable in the flesh—that's why I was so stunned that day at the Bel-Air Country Club. The proper response to actually seeing Gable or Cary Grant was gaping awe.

But when viewing habits changed, when more people started watching actors in their living room than in theaters—in other words, with the lights on and with occasional conversation—it signaled a sea change. As an actor, you were in people's living rooms, and that meant you could be a part of their lives in a way that the great movie stars of my youth weren't—*if* the people in that living room accepted you.

I don't think it's an accident that great stars like Jimmy Stewart, Henry Fonda, and Bing Crosby all failed on television. They were somehow too big for the medium, and in trying to scale down their personalities to be more domestic, more approachable, they lost what made them interesting in the first place. Jimmy Stewart's volatility, the possibility of rage, was gone; likewise Fonda's remoteness, which always translated as integrity. Great actors, great stars, wrong medium.

The change has continued, and not just at the movies. Now in a theater people are talking and cell phones are ringing. It's one of the reasons movies are so loud—so they can be heard over the din of the audience. When I used to go on an airplane, I wore a jacket and a tie. Now people get on board in tank tops and flip-flops. For a half century, I worked in front of cameras loaded with film; now I work in front of cameras loaded with digital tape. It's all changed, and some of it's an improvement and some of it isn't.

But one thing never changes: then and now, in movies or television, millions of people arrange their lives so that they can watch actors who mean something to them. For those of us lucky enough to be singled out, there can be no greater compliment.

*art to Hart* went off the air in 1984, and a year later I was back with ABC on a show called *Lime Street*. My part was not dissimilar to Jonathan Hart; this time I was a horse breeder who also investigated insurance fraud. I had two children and a father, played by Lew Ayres. I had admired Lew ever since I observed the quiet grace with which he endured being black-balled at the Bel-Air Country Club for being a conscientious objector.

Lew was pushing eighty when we did *Lime Street,* but the wonderful thing about good actors is that the varying ways in which they prepare themselves for work fall away when the director says, "Action." Acting is acting. Men like Lew Ayres or Melvyn Douglas weren't method actors, but no method actor would think Lew or Melvyn had anything to apologize for.

For an actor, there are two key questions: Do they believe me? Can I move them? Nothing else really matters.

Lew was always looking for the reality of a scene—the emotional truth. I loved working with him. He was a very good, kind human being. For years he had devoted himself to a study of comparative religions and the different ways people worship God, but near the end of his life he switched to something a little more quantifiable: meteorology.

One of my daughters on the show was played by Samantha Smith, the little girl from Maine who had become famous when she wrote to Yuri Andropov, the leader of the Soviet Union, urging peace. Andropov had then invited her to Russia for a lot of Kodak moments.

*Lime Street* was a good idea, and I loved Samantha Smith,

although I can't take credit for her presence in the show—casting her was the idea of Linda Bloodworth-Thomason and her husband Harry, who were producing the show and who had brought in sufficient budgets to allow for European location shooting. I kissed Samantha good-bye on Piccadilly and flew to Gstaad for some location shooting. Samantha and her father were flying home to Maine, then were due to quickly turn around and come to Switzerland to join the shoot.

When I got off the plane in Geneva on August 25, 1985, they took me to a private room, where Ray Austin was on the phone from Gstaad. It was Ray who told me that Samantha and her father had been killed in a plane crash. This lovely, gifted child was thirteen years old.

It was as if the breath left my body. My own kids and Samantha had played all the time. She had a career and, more importantly, a life ahead of her that would have been wonderful. I had just said good-bye to her the day before. I had given her a bracelet that became one of her treasured possessions; she never took it off, and she had been wearing it when she was killed. It was another stunning death in my life.

By the time I recovered my equilibrium and got to a phone, Columbia, the studio that was producing the series, was already making noises about recasting her part. I said flatly that I wasn't going to be party to that. I went to the wire services and told them I was closing production down, and that was the end of *Lime Street*. Harry Thomason and I flew to Maine for Samantha's funeral. Her mother was wearing the bracelet I had given Samantha.

The first episode of *Lime Street* ran on September 21, the last on October 26.

Columbia continued to behave very badly. Samantha's tickets had been bought from American Express, and the studio didn't want to acknowledge that she was being relocated for the show. They should have just shut up and made a settlement, but they fought it by saying that she wasn't on the company payroll at the time, even though she was flying to Maine to pack up and go back to Europe for studio work.

This went on for a couple of weeks, and one day as I was driving to the studio for a conference, I noticed that I was gripping the wheel so tightly that my knuckles were white. Finally, I told the studio that if this matter went to court, I would testify for Samantha's mother and I would make sure to bring as many of the press as I could get into the courtroom.

With the exception of Natalie's death, Samantha's death and its aftermath was the most emotionally upsetting thing I've ever gone through, and it drained a lot of the affection I always had for the business.

*Lime Street* would be the last TV show I starred in, and that wasn't by accident. I've continued to appear in TV movies and individual shows, and a few series ideas have come up that never came to fruition, but those were all ensemble projects, not shows in which I would pull the train. Samantha's death and what came after were the events that finally convinced me that it was time to begin a judicious retreat from the business that had defined my life.

Also contributing to my disaffection was my terrible disappointment in the Thomasons. They wanted to run the show their way, and their way was the way it had to be. I had heard incredible stories out of the set of *Designing Women,* and most of them turned out to be true.

We had been shooting in Amsterdam, and Ray Austin, a great and loyal friend who had directed a lot of *Hart to Hart*, and I had gone over the rushes on tape, making notes. When I got back to California, I found the box of tapes and notes sitting unopened in Harry and Linda's offices. It struck me that they could make no space for anybody's ideas but their own. As it turned out, *Designing*

*Women* was their lightning in a bottle; as far as I know none of their other projects succeeded on that level.

I am indebted to them for one thing, though. They introduced me to Bill Clinton. A few years before he was elected president, he came over to the house for three hours, and we talked about everything under the sun. I have seen a lot of people in Hollywood who have lofty ideas about their own charisma and fancy they can work a room. Occasionally, I've imagined I had some skills in that regard myself. But I have never seen anybody who's the charming equal of Bill Clinton.

After *Lime Street*, I remained in high demand and threw myself into producing a lot of TV projects. Throughout the years that followed Natalie's death, work did what I hoped it would. Everything in my life had stopped, and I had to rebuild myself piece by piece. Throwing yourself into work does many things, but mainly it embeds you in a different reality, one that's more manageable than the one you're avoiding. A couple of the TV movies—a form I like a lot more than series—were very good, and the run of projects culminated in six two-hour *Hart to Hart* TV movies.

It was a great deal of fun to be reunited with Stefanie Powers and Lionel Stander, although the changes in the business created some resistance to hiring Lionel. The studio thought he was too old. "What if he dies?" some executive asked me. "If he dies, we'll write it into the shows," I said. I pointed out that Lionel was a large part of the show's chemistry and that, aside from being disloyal—and I don't believe disloyalty should ever be tolerated—it wouldn't have been *Hart to Hart* without him.

I concluded the conversation by saying, "If you're not interested in having Lionel in the show, there will not be a show. I will not make *Hart to Hart* without him." That ended the conversation, but it was not a conversation I should have had to have.

Among the stand-alone projects, I was particularly pleased with *There Must Be a Pony,* which had been a very good novel by James Kirkwood Jr. It was a roman à clef about his mother, silent film star Lila Lee, and her affair with the director James Cruze—one of those negatively symbiotic relationships in which each party increased the speed at which they were heading for the bottom. Jimmy Kirkwood was a delightful man—flamboyant, funny, and self-deprecating. He cowrote *A Chorus Line,* the best musical I've ever seen, and I've seen them all.

I asked Mart Crowley to write the script, and it was his excellent work that helped me sign Elizabeth Taylor as my costar. I was already with Jill when we made *There Must Be a Pony,* and I was concerned that Elizabeth might be interested in re-kindling our relationship, but nothing happened.

I hired Joseph Sargent to direct the picture, and before we got started we talked over everything thoroughly and rehearsed the staging and the attitudes. As soon as we started shooting, Joe changed everything. He seemed to become an impulsive egomaniac, and I wondered why we bothered rehearsing for two weeks if he was throwing everything we had agreed on out the window.

If it had been a feature, I would have fired him, but on a television film that's very hard to do because the schedule is so short. My main worry was that Joe wasn't leaving Elizabeth alone; he had completely altered what he wanted from her, and I thought the way we had planned her performance in the first place was wonderful.

I knew that if he lied to her, she would kill him and, by extension, the entire film. She would kill him with time—take an hour and a half to make up one eye, that sort of thing. The problem was that I had personally guaranteed the production— the insurance company didn't want any part of Elizabeth be- cause of her long history of health problems. Any overshooting was on my tab, and if Elizabeth decided Joe had to be shown who the real diva was, I was in danger of a financial blood-bath.

Well, Elizabeth showed up every single day and was totally professional, even though her director wasn't. She was perfect in her lines, perfect in her attitude, perfect in her performance. We went over schedule by one day, because of a problem at Hollywood Park that was unavoidable, but it was a smooth production and a fine film—in my view in spite of Joe Sargent, not because of him.

The experience of working with her confirmed my feeling that Elizabeth Taylor is one of the best screen actresses ever, a fact that has been overlooked because of her beauty and because her private life has clouded the public's perceptions of her ability as an actress.

It was at this time that I had another insight into the simmering rage of the red scare period. I was proud of *There Must Be a Pony* and had a screening at Warner Bros., after which we had a party at my house. I had unthinkingly invited two people who meant a lot to me: my old director Eddie Dmytryk and Lionel Stander. Eddie had been one of the original Hollywood Ten and had gone to jail for his beliefs, after which he recanted and named names. Lionel, of course, had stood firm. They both came to the house, and each refused to acknowledge the other's existence. For the whole of the evening, they stayed far, far apart, all because of shameful events of forty years before, when good people were asked questions they never should have been asked and saw their lives torn apart.

I had asked Howard Jeffrey to produce *There Must Be a Pony*. Howard was always there for Natalie, and he was always there for me after she died. I trusted Howard absolutely; I made him executor of my will and gave him the responsibility of raising my girls if anything happened to me. But the day came when Howard came to me and told me he was terribly ill with AIDS. It was typical of Howard that he was less worried about himself than he was about us. "What can I tell the children?" he asked me.

In the lives of the people who loved Howard, there will never be anybody to replace him.

My next project was a TV film with Audrey Hepburn—her only movie for television. I had met Audrey shortly after she came to Hollywood and was always mad about her. The project we worked on, *Love Among Thieves,* was a lighthearted charmer about an elegant lady—Audrey—and a raffish, cigar-chomping guy—me.

The network had offered the man's part to Tom Selleck but he couldn't do it, and when Audrey told them she wanted me, I jumped at it. Audrey was sensational to work with: professional, relaxed, engaging, endearing—the most helpful, loving person you could imagine. She had finally jettisoned her second husband, a psychiatrist who wasn't any better for her than Mel Ferrer, her first husband, had been. Somewhere in there she had had a major affair with Ben Gazzara, and I understand that when she left, it brought him to his knees, which I could certainly understand. When we made *Love Among Thieves,* she was with Rob Wolders, with whom she stayed for the rest of her life. Rob gave Audrey something she had always needed and had never gotten—security. He wasn't with her for the glory and perks that came to the consort of Audrey Hepburn. He was there because he loved her, and he was at all times attentive, loving, and caring. Simply, he made her very happy, which is what she had always deserved.

It was a good picture and a good group of people—Jerry Orbach and Samantha Eggar were also in the cast. But I don't believe that any of Audrey's pictures were as important or as meaningful as Audrey. Audrey's essence as a human being shone through her acting and lifted her movies up by yards, not inches or feet. I have never known any woman other than Jill whose personality was so reflected in everything she did.

Audrey's spirit was embodied in her garden, her furniture, her paintings, her jewelry, her dogs, her linens. She absorbed everything she experienced and saw in her life, took it into her subconscious, her soul, and then somehow contrived to radiate it outward onto everything she touched. If I were to show you four or five pictures of different houses and gardens, you could easily pick out the one that was Audrey's place in Switzerland— it reflected security, serenity, and, through the beautiful flowers on which Audrey lavished so much attention, astonishing beauty.

*There Must Be a Pony* and *Love Among Thieves* were both rewarding experiences, but a couple of the TV projects weren't as good as they could have been. *Indiscreet* had been a good picture with Cary Grant and Ingrid Bergman, and I wanted to do a remake with Candice Bergen. But the network said they wouldn't make the picture with her. "She doesn't have any humor, and she's an ice queen," they told me. So a year later, *Murphy Brown* went on the air and proved that she was never an ice queen and had a spectacular sense of humor. Unfortunately, I had to do *Indiscreet* with Lesley-Anne Down, who I found opinionated and irritating.

The capstone to this phase of my life came when Jill and I were married under the two-hundred-year-old sycamore trees in the back garden of the Brentwood house on May 26, 1990. Roddy McDowall brought his video camera and shot what seemed to be endless hours of the ceremony and the toasts of the guests, intercutting them with shots of the house and the ranch. To the best of my knowledge, the only people who sat through the tapes in their entirety were my mother, Jill's mother, and Willie Mae. They watched the tapes incessantly, saying over and over, "Oh, look at that! Isn't he/she adorable?" My son Peter Donen, as well as my daughters Katie and Natasha, would also be married under those trees.

The years since have been the most serene of my life.

I always had a sneaking affection for Aaron Spelling. He was a bug-eyed, asthmatic Jewish kid who grew up in Texas and got the shit beaten out of him by the other kids damn near every day. Not only was he a Jew in Texas, he was a *little* Jew in Texas. He grew up, went to Hollywood, was mentored by Dick Powell, and became a billionaire. A great story.

But Aaron and his partner Leonard Goldberg and I had epic battles over the years. A lot of them were over the profits due me and Natalie over *Charlie's Angels,* and a lot of them ended up in court. I'm proud to say I won nearly all of them.

This went on for *decades*! In the spring of 1980, Los Angeles County District Attorney John Van De Kamp began an investigation into Spelling/Goldberg and it focussed on whether profits (that should have come to Natalie and I) from *Charlie's Angels* had been reallocated to the accounts of *Starsky and Hutch. Charlie's Angels* was then in its fourth year, and we hadn't received any money from it at all at that point, which is not unusual—most TV shows run a deficit until they go into syndication, which is where the real money is.

I couldn't say anything about the investigation publicly, for the very good reason that Aaron and Leonard were also our partners in *Hart to Hart.* As it worked out, Van De Kamp did not take matters further, but he did advise all the profit participants on their shows to hire independent auditors to make sure they got what was coming to them.

All this was classic creative bookkeeping and, sad to say, classic Hollywood. Years later we had a fight over the profits from *Hart to Hart*. There were other profit participants besides me—Stefanie had been hired as an actress on straight salary, but I thought she deserved more and gave her a piece of my piece of the show. Tom Mankiewicz was also a profit participant. My problem was that I was sick of having to fight for what was contractually mine, so in a moment of anger I had called Leonard a crook. We were sitting there in a lawyer's office trying to work things out. The lawyer outlined the situation, then Leonard said, in a hurt tone, "I'm not a crook, and I don't want anybody calling me a crook."

We then went around the room so everybody could lay out their position. The statements told you a lot about each individual's character.

Tom said, "I think you owe me money."

Stefanie said, "There's a great deal of poverty in the world, and so many want for so much. We're all fortunate to have as much as we do, and I just hope we can all work it out."

I chimed in with, "Leonard, you're a fucking crook."

We worked it out. Aaron finally said, "Let's pay the money and get on with our lives." But having to fight for what is rightfully yours is not fun, even though it's all too often a necessary part of Hollywood.

Years ago, I was having a drink with William Holden and Cliff Robertson after a day of shooting *The Mountain* at Paramount. Out of nowhere, Cliff said, "Jesus, Bill, what does it take? What does it take to have a career like yours?"

Bill Holden thought about it for a few seconds and then said, "Well, you have to have *it*."

"*It?*"

"*It.* You know, *Sunset Boulevard.*"

He meant that you have to have that one signature part in that one signature picture, the picture that defines your screen personality and your career. That never quite happened for me in the movies, although I certainly had signature parts in television.

I had a couple of near-misses. *Butch Cassidy and the Sundance Kid* was dangled in front of me for a while, but then it went away. Robert Evans wanted me and actually cast me in *Rosemary's Baby,* as Mia Farrow's husband, but Universal queered the deal by refusing to hold off production on *It Takes a Thief.* John Cassavetes got the part.

Paul Newman and Robert Redford were sensational in *Butch Cassidy,* so I can't say I would have done any better, although I have to confess to a tight little feeling of continuing disappointment when I think about playing that part. Losing that one hurt. Without false modesty, I think I would have been considerably better in *Rosemary's Baby* than Cassavetes. One look at Cassavetes and you know he's a minion of Satan, but I could have brought something else to the plate, something more deceptive. And I would have looked more believable with Mia Farrow as well.

When I lost *Rosemary's Baby,* I was upset, but I wasn't suicidal. I tried everything to make it work, and nothing could be done to make it work. Let it go. I was disappointed, but there are moments like that in the life of every actor. Also, if you're going to be an actor, and if you want to have a long career, you have to make a crucial mental adjustment, and that comes down to: "It's not me. It's them." I can do only so much to get a part, whether it's Butch Cassidy or

Jonathan Hart. They either want you or they don't, and once you realize that, it's helpful because it takes some of the burden off you.

If I lost a gig, it wasn't the end of the world. I could always stand in a river with a fishing rod or play golf. My life now is not show business; it was when I was young, but the deeper I got into it, the more time I spent with people like David Niven, Claire Trevor, and Sterling Hayden, the more I realized how important it is to have something else in your life, something that can fuel your acting.

Otherwise, this is what happens: You get a pool, and you need a pool man; you get the larger house, you need the staff to cover it. And gradually you find that you have to start taking jobs that you might not really want in order to cover your overhead. Abe Lastfogel put it best when he told me, "Once you get a pool, they got you." I can think of hundreds of people I've known in the movie business who got what they thought they wanted, only to find out they didn't want it after all, but it was too late to get off the merry-go-round. Not good.

Ultimately, I think it was David Niven who made me realize that a life has to encompass more than show business; David *shaped* his life, and acting was just one part of it. He liked to sail, he liked to fish, and he enjoyed people tremendously. The next part, the next movie, was not at the top of his list of priorities. And my children have been very important in providing a different horizon for my life. There are no negatives to children. There are disappointments and concerns—terrible concerns, as any parent will recognize when I say that if the phone rings after 10:00 P.M., I levitate out of the chair to a height of at least three feet. But my children are more than my loves—they're my pride and sustenance.

Jill was also a major contributor to this realization. She knew that the importance of show business is transitory and that life involves more than whether or not photographers go crazy when you show up at a restaurant. She was less concerned about her career than I was, and she had a way of drawing me back a bit to enjoy the fruits of the life I had built over the previous thirty-five years. You can luxuriate in a garden and watch the different way the light hits the mountains as the afternoon wears on, or you can get on another airplane and make another movie.

The latter will fill your bank account, but the former will fill your soul.


Claire Trevor died in 2000. Before she passed away, she designated a group of people who had meant a great deal to her and left each of us a gift of money in her will—what she called "a hug and a kiss" that she was unable to deliver in person. Since Claire was partially responsible for my appreciation of art, I used some of the money to buy two sculptures from nature: a bear, which I have in my bedroom, and a pair of owls. With what was left over, the next time I was in Paris I went to a caviar bar that she had introduced me to, ordered some fine caviar and a bottle of champagne, and drank a toast to a great, great lady.


By 1990, I was open to other things besides television, so Stefanie Powers and I began touring with A. R. Gurney's play *Love Letters*. I hadn't been on the stage since *Mister Roberts* a quarter-century earlier, but the more I thought about *Love Letters,* the more I had to do it. For one thing, it was a part I identified with—I was raised in camps and boarding schools. I knew Andrew Makepeace Ladd III, and I knew his WASP background. And I could also relate to his constant pursuit of one woman, and his ultimate loss of her. It's such a well-written play, and it's so very sad.

Stefanie and I did the play in a rolling series of one-nighters for about five years, five or six consecutive shows in a week, then three weeks off. In 1990 we took the play to London and did it for six weeks at the Wyndham Theatre in the West End. The reviews were terrible, but I knew they would be because I know how critics think. Two American TV stars who sit down on a bare stage and read letters? In the land of Shakespeare? Not bloody likely. But I honestly didn't care; I was playing the West End in front of sold-out houses, something I never thought I'd do.

After five years, Stefanie became a little worried about becoming a permanent double act. She invoked Laurel and Hardy, and I still can't quite figure that out, perhaps because I've always loved Laurel and Hardy. So Stefanie stepped out, and I asked Jill to step in. She initially refused, because she didn't want to be compared to Stefanie and because she hadn't been on the stage since she was a child.

"How many actresses have done this part?" I asked her. "Dozens! The part's never been identified with any single actress." She thought about it, then said yes. Jill and I did the play together for nine years, from 1995 to 2004.

On balance, I think Jill's performance was more real than Stefanie's. Stefanie is more theatrical; when Stefanie is in England, she becomes English, complete with accent. She has an incredible ear and picks things up automatically, and because of that, her emotions can be in a constant state of flux.

Whether I was doing it with Stefanie or Jill, it was very hard work. Not the play—that was a constant joy—but the traveling. Because it was mostly one-nighters, I realized after a time that I wasn't being paid to act, I was being paid to travel.

If at all possible, we'd use a hub system that Jill developed. If we were playing towns in Illinois, we'd stay at the Four Seasons in Chicago—Jill picks hotels by how good their room-service eggs Benedict are. Every afternoon we'd drive to the airport and head for someplace like Springfield or Joliet, and we'd come back that same night. That way, we could spend five or six nights in the same hotel, although there were lots of times when that wasn't possible and we'd be at an airport twice a day.

Other than the travel, it was a totally positive experience. One of the high points was the month we played in Chicago to great reviews. We were *the* hot ticket. I told Jill, "This doesn't happen often. Enjoy it."

I loved that play. To be able to sit down and say words, without the crutches of music or scenery, just words, and have those words move thousands of people every night so that they were stunned and in tears and standing up and applauding—there can be no greater reward for an actor.

I remember when we opened at the Wilbur Theater in Boston, the director gave us a note: "Don't play it. Just read the letters and let it happen." And that's exactly what we did, bringing our own emotional coloring as actors and through that discovering the layers of the characters, and the layers of ourselves. I never looked at Jill onstage, and she only looked at me once, at the very end. We had some extraordinary nights. We found new values in that play every night. *Every night!*

We took the images of different people out onstage with us. In Jill's case, it was the young Barbara Hutton. Barbara had been Jill's mother-in-law when she was married to Lance Reventlow. Barbara was one of those people who didn't like to be alone—a woman whose life just didn't work out. Jill never particularly liked her, but she admired her wit and intelligence and felt sorry for her. Occasionally, Barbara told Jill stories about her terrible childhood, and in Jill's mental image of her character, she was similar to the "poor little rich girl" that Barbara Hutton had been.

We covered America two or three times over, played Europe, played Atlantic City twice, Vegas three times. We played casinos, we played basketball stadiums, we even played synagogues. We played everything but a men's room. When we played in Texas, words like "fuck" and "snatch" lifted some people in the audience right out of their chairs, out of the theater, and into their cars. Alabama had the same response. When we played the synagogues, Jill took those words out of the script. "I'm not saying 'snatch' in a synagogue," she told me. Other than that, we never changed a word of Gurney's script.

Paul Newman and Joanne Woodward and I had some discussions about doing *Love Letters* with a revolving cast. One night it would be Paul and Jill, another night it would be me and Joanne, and just to keep things really interesting, every third night Paul and I would do it. Just kidding. The revolving cast never happened, but I still think it was a good idea.

After Stefanie Powers and I had done six *Hart to Hart* TV movies, I was offered $10 million to produce three more. It seemed like a good idea to me, and Lionel Stander and the rest of the team were up for it, but Stefanie opted out in favor of doing a road company of the musical *Applause*. I was furious at her decision, regarding it as a betrayal—not just of me but of all the cast and crew who had worked with us for years and certainly could have used the work. But Stefanie had come to believe that *Hart to Hart* had typecast her and the show was somehow holding her back. There was some halfhearted conversation about recasting her part, or even writing her out of the shows, but I pointed out that if we did that, it wouldn't be *Hart to Hart* anymore. I felt I had to be loyal to the audience's expectations. I walked away.

*Applause* closed quickly, and I suppose we could have re-constituted the *Hart to Hart* TV movies, but I had lost interest in working with Stefanie. Last year, her agent called to ask if I would be interested in doing a reunion *Hart to Hart* project. "Who the hell wants to see people our age cuddling in bed?" I asked him. I love Angela Lansbury, but I'm not about to give her a run for her money as the oldest detective in television history.

Mostly, I've continued to work as much as I want. A movie or two a year, a couple of TV shows a year. Lately, the biggest hits I've been associated with have been Mike Myers's *Austin Powers* movies. I met Mike when I hosted *Saturday Night Live* in December 1989. At that point, Mike and his wife, Robin, were living in a tiny apartment in New York, and she cooked for them on a hot plate. I had a great time on the show, and I did a couple of skits that Mike wrote, in particular a hilarious bit playing a gay nurse—Nurse Stivers.

Years went by, and in 1997 Mike sent me a script he'd written about a secret agent from the Swinging Sixties who was cryogenically frozen and became the ultimate fish out of water in the modern era. I was to be the jealous second-in-command to Dr. Evil, Mike's take on James Bond's nemesis Blofeld.

*Austin Powers* looked good on paper, and it looked better on film. Everything you saw in the film was in the script—my eye patch, everything. Mike is extremely shy but fantastic to work with—he knows exactly what he wants. Those pictures are definitely Mike Myers productions—Jay Roach is the credited director, but Mike calls the shots and does the editing. The success of the film, and the notice people took of me, confirmed Gadge Kazan's suggestion that my instincts for comedy were excellent and I should do more in that line.

The odd thing about the *Austin Powers* pictures is that they sometimes look like we're improvising, but we're not. Everything's written. I did feel that on *Austin Powers in Goldmember*, the last of the trilogy, the script was better than the film. There were some terrific scenes that ended up getting cut, including one of all of us in drag singing, "What's it all about, Alfieeeeeee . . . ," and there was another sequence with me and a herd of llamas that was quite funny.

Mike's brand of comedy certainly pays dividends for a modern audience, although my favorite kind of comedy comes out of reality. The people I grew up laughing at, like Buster Keaton and Laurel and Hardy, usually started with a very realistic premise. That tradition was carried on by Blake Edwards, who I think was the best comedy director of his generation.

With all the quantum changes in show business—the transition to multinational conglomerate owners and the growth in foreign audiences, which affects the way a lot of movies are made—one thing hasn't really changed since I drove onto the Fox lot in 1949: it's a brutal business.

Just like sports, show business is for front-runners: they either boo you or applaud you, and it changes day to day. It's particularly hard for actors. Logistically, a writer needs nothing more than a legal pad in order to write, but an actor needs a stage or a camera. Basically, someone has to hire him, and that changes the dynamic because it becomes money-intensive; it's less of a talent issue and more of a sales issue. Add to that the fact that very few films are made because people have a passion to make that film. Mostly, films exist because corporations think they will be profitable, which results in a very different kind of movie.

In any case, I've been an actor for nearly sixty years, and nobody with that kind of career has any cause to complain. I've been very fortunate, and I think it's largely because I was determined to be a working actor, emphasis on working. I just kept going to the plate and swinging. It didn't matter whether the reviews were great or terrible, whether the films and shows were successful or unsuccessful. *I kept showing up.* Some actors go into a depressive shell when something doesn't work, as if a critical or commercial failure is somehow a reflection on them and their ability. I've never believed that.

When I was a kid and just starting out, I read my reviews, but I came to realize that if you believe the good reviews, you have to believe the bad ones. Rather than focusing on what other people thought of me, I chose to concentrate on the work, the job, and my commitment to that work. I was at the studio, I was on time, and I knew my lines. As Spencer Tracy told me more than a half-century ago, don't worry about anything but the scene. I extrapolated that to the big picture. From focusing on the scene, I focused on the job, then I focused on the next job.

Beyond anything else, I loved the business, and I loved working. And I don't think people understand how important behavioral choices—not being an asshole, showing up on time, knowing your lines—are to sustaining a career. It's easy to go from job to job when you're hot, but it's when things cool down that you can spot the jerks, because nobody will hire them.

I'm amazed that I've sustained a career for this length of time, because my contemporaries are either dead or haven't worked in twenty years. The young actors with me at Fox were Cameron Mitchell and Jeffrey Hunter. Chuck Heston was at Paramount. Farley Granger was at Goldwyn, and John Erickson, who got the part in *Teresa* and got hammered for his trouble, was at MGM.

But the ironic reality is that no matter how devoted you are to your craft, it won't necessarily have anything to do with whether or not lightning strikes. That's actually a matter of the right part. Bill Holden, for instance, was not fully respectful of acting, but he got two films with Billy Wilder, and they changed his career and his life. Bill was a bit like Errol Flynn: he was ambivalent about his career choice but followed the path of least resistance and had a lot of doubts about himself as a result.

All my life, when I think about acting, I think about Spencer Tracy. *Spence knew his work.* He would say, "You've *got* to know the lines. If you know the lines, you can do anything you want to do." Actors are really the least rehearsed of performers. The performers who really rehearse are musicians; they have those notes *down,* and that's why they can go anywhere they want.

I remember sitting with the cellist Lynn Harrell. He was fretting about a problem he was having with a section of a piece. "I'm just not playing it the right way," he said. The conductor offered some suggestions, and then Lynn said, "I know! I'll think of Picasso." These guys have played the music so many times that the problem of getting a fresh sound is in the forefront of their minds. The same thing happens with actors, except very few actors know their lines the way musicians know their notes.

I try to maintain a positive outlook about all the changes in the business and in the world, but I don't like entitlement: kids who are pissed off if they don't get into Harvard, Yale, or Princeton; actors who think they have to get where they're going by the time they're twenty-five because they're afraid it won't be there by the time they're thirty-five. Recently I was talking to a young actor, and he mentioned a director he said was great because "he didn't get in my way."

This is insane. Acting is a give-and-take between the director and the actors. You have to have someone say the lines to you in order to prompt your lines. If that other actor is good, he will make you better, and if the director is good, you will be better still. But there are actors today who don't care about that reciprocal arrangement. Their attitude is, "Fuck 'em, bring in somebody else." These kinds of people are more concerned about their status than they are about the quality of the job they're doing.

I've worked with guys who do push-ups or run around the block before a scene to work themselves into the proper state, but I tend to think that acting is analogous to music. When you hear a musician blowing a great sound, you don't think about everything he's gone through to be able to create those notes. You're just interested in the result. The audience isn't interested in what the actor goes through; they're only interested in being transported, in being moved, and that's what I find most thrilling—moving somebody.

After nearly sixty years, at this point it's supposed to be Miller Time: hit the marks, say the words, go home. But I'm still nervous, and I still want to be as good as I can possibly be. The problem is not unlike Lynn Harrell's: you want it to be there, but you want it to have a different value without pushing it.

I think my ability to sustain a long career has been at least partially a result of my ability to sustain long relationships, sometimes through succeeding generations. I've mentioned how much I valued Paul Ziffren, my lawyer. He was so innovative, so brilliant. It was Paul who set up the deal for *Charlie's Angels,* and Paul who set up my profit participation in *Hart to Hart.* When Paul died, I simply moved my representation over to his younger brother Leo, who has fought my battles with all of the consideration, purposefulness, and accomplishment that his brother brought to my career. When Jill and I got married, it was Leo who gave her away. And Paul's son John, who began his career in show business as a production assistant on *Hart to Hart,* is now a successful producer.

Fifteen years ago, after I'd fallen out with my agent, my daughter Natasha suggested I consider a man named Chuck Binder. Fifteen years later, on nothing more than a handshake, I'm still with Chuck, who has always had an overall view of my career and what I can do. I think Chuck is a large part of the reason I'm still working when most actors my age are sitting around twiddling their thumbs.

And then there are the friendships that have lasted longer than most people have been alive. Friendships are particularly difficult to sustain in a competitive, migratory business like show business. I'm thinking of people like the late Guy McElwaine, and Steven Goldberg, the man who gave me Larry, my German shepherd—actually imported from Germany by Steven. My friendship with Steven began as a straight business deal when he hired me to represent his company, but we began playing golf together, and more than fifteen years later we're still doing it. We're bound together by our love of dogs and golf and by similar senses of humor—the trifecta! I'm lucky to have him in my life. More than that—I'm grateful to have him in my life.

# TWENTY-THREE

# "THE WORLD MOVES ON."

The extraordinary women to whom I dedicated this book: my wife, Jill, and, from the left, my daughters, Katie, Courtney, and Natasha.
(© SAM JONES/CORBIS)

ny long life is pummeled as you lose the people you love, and because I've always been comfortable with an older generation, I've lost more than most. The last time I saw Noel Coward was in London at a party Swifty Lazar gave for him. Noel was very shaky, and Roger Moore and I helped move him around. At one point Roger and I were sitting at Noel's feet, and he leaned down and told me, "I think this is my last party, dear boy. Don't think there will be any more." A little while after that, he went back to Jamaica to die.

I was living in the desert in the mid-1970s when Darryl Zanuck came back from Europe. His health was breaking down, and mentally he wasn't what he had been. Virginia, his wife, had been waiting for this moment for twenty years, since Darryl left for Europe. She had always been Mrs. Darryl Zanuck, and she would always be Mrs. Darryl Zanuck. She took him back, and no man could have been more tenderly cared for in his last years. When I would go to see him, he knew who I was, but not a lot more.

In some senses, it was a sad and disconcerting end, but God, look at the bigger picture. Darryl created a great movie studio out of his own blood, sweat, and tears, and he made dozens of great movies that audiences are still analyzing, still being moved by. Darryl's life *mattered*.

In addition, Darryl's son Richard became one of the finest producers of his generation, which nobody could have foreseen when he was just the kid I used to play with at Darryl's house in Malibu. People outside the business don't know how difficult it is to follow an act like Darryl's, but Dick Zanuck is the only mogul's son to have a career comparable to his father. He's a great producer (*Jaws, Driving Miss Daisy, Sweeney Todd,* and dozens of others), a standup guy, and, when Darryl was alive, he was also a wonderful son.

Gene Kelly and I were never lucky enough to work together, but we played a great deal of tennis over the years, and we enjoyed many skiing vacations with our kids in Sun Valley. Gene was a wonderful man with great joie de vivre, terribly active and athletic, and one of the most competitive personalities I've ever encountered. But Gene had some bad luck in the later stages of his life. He had a very nurturing marriage to Jeanne Coyne, a dancer, a glorious lady who had had the misfortune to be married to Stanley Donen at one time. Gene and Jeanne had two children, to whom they were completely devoted.

But Jeanne died in 1973. Gene's career was winding down, the kids grew up and moved away into their own lives, and he was lonely. He married a much younger woman who many of the family and friends did not warm to. Then Gene's health broke, and he lost his eyesight and the use of his legs. To see a man like Gene Kelly confined to a wheelchair before his death in 1996 was one of the most prominent examples of nature's cruelty.

The deaths of these great friends might have been expected; they had run their race. But the death of my son Peter Donen in 2003 was stunning. Peter was still a young man, only fifty years old. He had become overweight and hadn't had a checkup for a couple of years, and his loner personality worked against him.

Peter had become one of the finest creators of special effects who ever lived. You can see his work in movies like *The Bourne Identity.* Peter's work was so seamless that critics commented on how nice it was to see a movie without computer images, even though *The Bourne Identity* was full of Peter's computer images. Peter was almost a genius, and his great gift was that his special-effects shots couldn't be identified as special effects. I loved Peter, as

I do his brother Josh. Peter wanted me to adopt him, but I told him it was impossible because his father would never allow it.

In retrospect, I should have done it anyway.

My ex-wife, Marion, and I remain good friends, bound by our mutual love for our daughter.

There aren't that many people left from the period when I broke into the business. Tony Curtis and I were friends for a long time, but we had a serious breach over the way he treated Janet Leigh. Janet was a considerable person, and I didn't think Tony was treating her well. I got angry and told a *Los Angeles Times* columnist named Joyce Haber that Tony was an asshole and she could quote me. Which, with a few emendations, she did. Tony blew up and challenged me to a fight, and I said, "Anytime you want to go outside I will kick your fucking ass." I was very hot under the collar, and I was also in good condition.

But that was a long time ago, and we've patched things up; we even worked together on an episode of *Hope and Faith*. Tony is perennially buoyant, always full of piss and vinegar, and I love that about him. I'll call Tony up and ask, "Is this Ali Baba?" and he'll automatically respond, "Prince Valiant?"

Once upon a time, we were young together. Whenever we get together, we still are.

People ask me why I haven't retired, and sometimes it feels like I have. The truth is, I don't want to drop dead on a sound stage; I want to drop dead in a river, with a fishing rod in my hand, or in my house in Aspen. There was a period of about ten years when I worked practically every day. My career is important to me, but I've learned from therapists like Arthur Malin, Gerald Aronson, and Cheryl O'Neal—as well as my friend and personal physician, Paul Rudnick—that you can only take out of yourself what you put in. It's ever so important to have life experiences.

That said, I like to work. To appear on a cracking good show like *Boston Legal* or *Two and a Half Men* and not have to pull the train is a treat. But the day when I carry a show is over. That said, I'd love to be in an ensemble cast. My professional goal is the same as it was when I was twenty-five: do good work and keep doing it.

In other words, I don't believe in retirement. I never wanted to sock my money away for a rainy day and spend my eightieth birthday reading the paper. I don't think building a life around cruises and golf is a healthy mind-set, although I know that a lot of people love it. I think retirement is a hype that has nothing to do with life as it needs to be lived. It's a collusion between industries that barely existed fifty years ago—life insurance companies and cruise companies—that need to manufacture endeavors in order to sustain themselves. I've never bought into it.

Jill has continued to be very influential as a sounding board for my career—guiding and suggesting, never commanding. She's only put her foot down once. I was asked to do *Dancing with the Stars,* and I was leaning toward doing it. And she stepped up and said, "I've never said anything to you about whether or not to do something. But you shouldn't do this." She didn't think it was the right thing, and I think she was absolutely right. Beyond that, at those times when I've been really down and on the bottom, Jill has *always* been there. You can't ask for more from any human being. Plus, there is the fact that she's loving and caring, a wonderful wife, 100 percent for me.

As I said, our experience with *Love Letters* was entirely positive, but I sweated over it; most nights I would stay up and think about the next performance, because I was doing it for a different person in my mind every night. I knew where the high points were, and I didn't want it to become rote, which is the great danger in the theater.

Because of the success we had with *Love Letters,* I've had lots of offers to do theater, but I don't want to work that hard. When my agent calls me with a part, the questions I ask are basic: "What is it? Where is it? How much? For how long?"

I have finally learned that when you work, you work, and when you play, you play. Jill and I have designed our lives so that we can be away together on vacations. It's a continuation of the rule Natalie and I made when we remarried: the first thing is the family.

I don't really understand those people who say they wouldn't change anything about their lives. Hell, I would change a lot of things. Among other things, I lost a woman I loved with all my heart, not once but twice, and that is a truth I will never completely come to terms with. But I have learned through grueling experience that there is no such thing as "what if. . . ." There is only "what is."

For the rest of it, I would have taken more time in certain ways. I'm not proud of everything I've done. There's no way to get through life without hurting people, whether because of ignorance, or because you think it's necessary for your own survival, or because you're just too full of yourself. Those are the moments I regret.

As for Warren Beatty, we run into each other occasionally around town. And when we do, he always puts his arm around me, and I do the same with him. In a sense, we were brought together by the loss of Natalie. Her death was so much bigger than any animus I might have had.

The world of movies and TV has changed, but I'm not going to pontificate about how things were better in my day. Well, maybe just a little. Some things were indeed better then, but some things are better now. Certainly, there's more independence for young actors now—nobody is trying to marry people off because of inconvenient pregnancies. But that increased independence also means that it's everybody for himself—there's no studio watching out for young actors, trying to build a career step by step. The only people with a vested interest in young talent are managers and agents, and there aren't many who possess a developmental skill set. That's why many careers are more erratic, not to mention shorter, than they were fifty or sixty years ago. There's more independence, which equals freedom, but there's also much greater risk. For everything you get, you have to give something up.

I'm sure the people who were my age now in, say, 1960 thought things were going to hell too. I will say that money has changed things, and not for the better. In the world at large, everything is a corporate commodity. A football game isn't just a football game; it has to be sponsored by a corporation—Toyota, or AT&T, or Capital One, or, for God's sake, Tostitos.

In terms of show business, the economics are entirely different as well. A few years ago, I proposed a revival of *It Takes a Thief.* I would have the Fred Astaire part; I would be running a place in Las Vegas called Mundy's. Catherine Deneuve would come to see me and tell me that we had had a child years before who was trapped in the Middle East. I would have to go in and get her, and we'd be off into a variation on the original show. It was a good idea, and I think it could have worked, but Universal was practically out of the TV business, because it's no longer profitable unless you have a big, big hit. Since nobody ever knows what's going to be a big hit, they had simply edged over to the sidelines.

It used to be that you made a show for a network, they got three runs of each episode, and then the studio owned the show for the rest of the world, for the rest of time. The rule of thumb was that you broke even with the networks and made a profit in syndication. But to make a series today costs $2 million an hour. Twenty-four shows cost $48 million, and there's no way to recoup that much money unless the show is a success and runs five years' worth of negative for syndication. It's not a business Universal is particularly interested in. So I suggested doing six two-hour movies, which didn't go down. And they wouldn't let me take the property and do it someplace else, and now they want to do a theatrical version of the property. They might offer me a part, but I doubt I'll take it.

But let's face it: the world moves on. Last Christmas I picked up my daughter Courtney to take her to a Christmas party at Natasha's house. She was on her cell phone to the airlines to check on her airline ticket, then called about a car she had to pick up. Then she needed to stop at an ATM to get some cash. I sat there in the car thinking about my daughter getting money out of a wall and how, right around the corner from the ATM, I had built hot rods as a teenager. It was one of those moments when you realize how much change one life can encompass.

There's a general perception that show business is far more pervasive than it used to be. Actually, American show business has ruled the world for most of the last one hundred years—Japanese people in the 1930s went to see Charlie Chaplin movies in droves. What has changed is the immersion in show business of people who are not themselves part of it.

Years ago, there was a man named Milton Sperling who produced *Marjorie Morningstar* for Natalie. Milton decided to take his family to see the most magical place on earth: Venice. He painstakingly prepared his son for the experience he was about to have, and being a producer, he also prepared the experience. He positioned a man with a starter's pistol way back in

St. Mark's Square. He was to fire the gun when he saw Sperling wave a red handkerchief, so the pigeons would swoop up in a magical swirl at just the right moment.

Sperling brought his boy blindfolded around the corner of the Doge's Palace and placed him right beside one of the columns at the entrance to the square. Then he waved his red handkerchief, the starter's pistol was fired, Sperling uncovered his boy's face, and the pigeons swooped up.

"What do you see, son?" Milton asked proudly.

"I see . . . *Dore Schary*!"

A confused Milton Sperling followed his son's line of vision and saw a smiling Dore Schary passing in front of the boy, blocking out the carefully prepared vista of St. Mark's Square.

That's one of my favorite stories because, besides being true, it's an accurate metaphor. For those of us in it, American show business has always had a way of blotting out the real world. That's because American show business is cleaner, smoother, and easier to process than the real world, which, unfortunately, is where we actually live. But I've learned to have one foot in both camps, and I like to think I'm able to appreciate both the gamesmanship of the movies and a stream full of trout in the Rockies.

If somebody had told me sixty years ago what my life was going to be like and had enumerated the terrible pain I had waiting for me, I would have gone ahead anyway. Because, along with that pain, I've experienced great joy, and I'd like to think that I've given some as well.

In many respects, I remain pretty much as I was. That little boy who basked at being the center of the photographer's attention at the preview of *The Biscuit Eater* became a man who needed attention and could get disappointed if he didn't get it. In other words, I had the essential personality of the actor— wanting, *needing* a reaction—before I became an actor. Another character flaw is a plethora of optimism, which can mean I sometimes lack objectivity. In my own defense, I should say that I've become more realistic as I've grown older.

I look around me and see so many wonderful actors. Johnny Depp is probably the best one working these days—the face of a leading man and the soul of a character actor, which is probably the ideal combination. And I think that Brad Pitt is, for some reason, very underrated. He's very simple, very basic, and you never catch him acting.

Recently I went out to the Motion Picture Home to visit Helena Sorrell, my first dramatic coach. She's 104 years old and still pretty sharp. She was in the Audrey Hepburn Room in the hospital, and it was lovely—the sun was coming in, and it was Edie Wasserman's birthday. Every year, on Edie's birthday, she goes out to the Motion Picture Home, and everybody there gets wonderful food catered by Alex's, which has all the recipes from Chasen's—the chili, the hobo steak, and everything else.

"Do you like it here, Helena?" I asked her.

"No," she said, "I don't."

Helena gave so much to so many people, myself among them, and she ended up alone. So many people end up alone, and for what must be the millionth time, I realized how lucky I've been.

No, not just lucky. *Blessed.* I have a wonderful family and true friends. I never walked away from my own life, like so many people in show business do, and I've worked hard, but as I sit looking out over the valley in Aspen, I feel gratitude for my life and think, *Am I the luckiest man on earth?*

As much as I loved the house in Brentwood, I simply didn't need seven bedrooms and a cottage anymore, so in 2007 we sold it for an astonishing price. I'm not going to pretend it was easy; Jill and I had been married in the garden, as had Natasha, Katie, and Peter Donen. We had a hundred parties there over the years, and when I looked out over the expanse of lawn and trees, I could see my mother, Jill's mother, Roddy McDowall, Howard Jeffrey, Peter Donen, Bill Storke, Watson Webb, and dozens of other dear friends who had brightened our lives in that house.

But it was time.

Now Jill and I spend most of our time in Aspen, although we retain a condo in Los Angeles.

My children are all well and happy in their lives, and recently Katie and her husband, Leif Lewis, gave me a spectacular gift: my first grandchild, a boy named Riley John—yet another RJ! I've maintained my health and seen and done a lot.

Show business has been my college and my doctoral program. I've met queens and kings, seen America and the world. Years ago, Jimmy Stewart got me involved in the Jimmy Stewart Relay Marathon for the Child Care Center at St. John's Hospital. When Jimmy died, his will made me a founder for the hospital, and my continuing work for them and the John Tracy Clinic has been one of the most rewarding experiences of my life.

For my family, the goal was to go to college, but I rolled the dice and opted to go to work; I like to think that I've grabbed hold of life and shaken it. If some of it blew into my eyes, well, that's called being alive.

When my time comes, I will be buried in Aspen, in an old cemetery that was originally laid out in the nineteenth century. A lot of children are buried there, and it's in the middle of a glade of aspen and birch trees—very wild and overgrown. As soon as someone is laid to rest, the land is allowed to return to its natural state. The cemetery looks out over the valley, and deer and elk walk through it all the time. Sometimes you'll notice a large patch of grass crunched down, and you realize that a bear has been sleeping there after dining on the berries that grow wild in the middle of the cemetery. It's absolutely pure and totally peaceful.

I have four plots in the cemetery, and Jill and my beloved shepherd Larry will be buried with me. And any of the kids who want to be with us. Things change in children's lives, and I'll be fine with whatever they decide. It will be a peaceful place for them to come and pay their respects. They won't have to bring flowers—just some seed, so that the birds and flowers will arrive every spring and enable me to once again be surrounded by life.

I hope that the site enables them to appreciate their father, and, beyond that, reminds them of the beautiful confirmation of life itself.

# ACKNOWLEDGMENTS

Some of the following people have gone ahead, some are still here, but all of them have earned my devotion many times over. You have my thanks and my love, and anyone I may have inadvertently overlooked has my apologies.

Brian Estabrook; Merv Adelson; Bud and Cynthia Yorkin; Mike and Mary Lou Connors; David and Gloria Wolper; John Ma; Robb Baxter; Frank and Gloria Westmore; Dick and Margaret Michaels Fleming; Bob and Sandy Papazian; Blake and Julie Edwards; Paul Rudnick; Tom Mankiewicz; Alan Nierob; Arthur Malin; Ron Shelton; Jim and Judy Hirsh; Mart Crowley; Howard Jeffrey; Sister Marie Madeline; Roddy McDowell; George Hamilton; Lon and Manu Bentley; Grant and Brook Tinker; Leo Ziffren; Arthur and Regina Loew Jr.; Tom Todderof; Guy McElwaine; Don Johnson; George Segal; Lionel and Stephana Stander; Watson Webb; Paul Ziffren; Bill Storke; Richard Widmark; Dionisio Munoz; Greg Barnett; Stymie; Harold and Sandra Guskin; Joe Barrato; Tony and Sue Morris; Bill Smith; Steve and Elaine Wynn; Quincy Jones; Tom Ulmer; Peggy Griffin; B. J. Jiras; Ted Bell; Ernie and Marlene Vossler; Gil Cates; David Marlow; Jaclyn Smith; Randy Ringger; Ed Marrins; Bob and Nancy Magoon; Jack and Marisia Silverman; David Niven Jr.; Delphine Mann; Perry and Abby Leff; Veronique and Greg Peck; Jamie Niven; Barbara Sinatra; Jason and Amanda Bateman; Bob Bennett; Ray and Wendy Austin ; Jim and Pat Mahoney; Larry Auerbach; Linda Marshall; Bill and Terry Hickey; Little Joe Torrenueva; Sue Block; Fred Gibbons; Jimmy Borges; Dotty Gagliano; Dick Butera; Joe Pantoliano; Wendell and Nell Niles; Dick Clayton; Leslie and Evie Bricusse; Alan Folsom; Sydney Chaplin; Bernie Yumans; Irving Brecher; Pat Newcomb; Nancy Sinatra Sr.; Russ and Karen Goldsmith; Jill Donahue; Nikki Haskell; Jerry Ohrbach; Lazslo George; Michelle and Giuseppe Torroni; Robert Osborne; Helen and Gene Offut; Tony and Cristina Thomopoulos; Agnes Gund; Steven and Elvia Goldberg; Chuck and Lori Binder; Woody Stuart; Russell Chatham; Patricia Moore; Howard Curtis; Larry Manetti; Elizabeth Pepke; Marcy and Leo Edelstein; Jeff Pogliano; Fabian and Fritz Benedict; Woody Stuart; Bernard Lochner ; Jack Frey; Harvey Eisenberg; Lew Ayres; Elia Kazan; Mort and Linda Janklow; Alex March; Geri Bauer;

Sid and Jane Harmon; Bill and Peggy Ruser; Jimmy Stewart; Bill Wilson; Steve and Edie Lawrence; Dick Powell; Bob Greene; Jimmy Cagney; Walter and Fieldsie Lang; Kelly Ripa; Mike Myers; Jane Russell; John Linden; Roy Palms; Elizabeth Applegate; Clark Gable; Angela Thornton; Dick and Dolly Martin; John Ziffren; Irene Ma; Gloria DeHaven; Jim Bailey; Roy Stork; Cheryl O'Neal; Jerry and Ann Moss; Fred Astaire; Lew Spence; Tom Selleck; Ray Smalls; Dick Zanuck; Conrad Stoddinger; Cubby and Dana Broccoli; Bob Conrad; Dorothy Lamour; Rosemary Stack; Dan Dailey; Holland Taylor; Alan and Cindra Ladd Jr.; Ella Fitzgerald; Peggy Lee; Bill Shatner; Chita Rivera; Rory Calhoun; Ken and Pauline Annakin; Tom Poston & Suzanne Pleshette; Stefanie Powers; Tony Curtis; Billy and Audrey Wilder; Florence Henderson; Jennifer Stander; Margareta Sierra; Kate Hepburn; Charlie Barron; Andy Williams; Gloria Puentes; Suzy Tracy; Willie Mae Worthen; Jane Withers; Dick Williams; Elizabeth Taylor; Burt Lancaster; Gene, Dorothea, and Barbara Rodney; Jane and Dick Moore; Laurence Olivier; Barbara Lawrence; Sandy Koufax; Sonja Fitzpatrick; Gloria Swanson; Howard Keel; Roland Kibbee; Debbie Reynolds; Stewart Stern; Peter Lawford; Lennie Gershe; Ron Macanally; Marisa Ma; Judy Garland; Lew and Edie Wasserman; Rosalind Russell; Tommy LaSorda; Martha Luttrell; Eric Calderon; Maureen Stapleton; Jonathan Ma; Susan Zanuck; Ruben and Maria Agular; David Walsh; Senta Berger; Faith Ford; Steve DeMarco; Roger Moore; George Folsey; Kevin Costner; Lawrence Rudolph; Sam Pryor; George Kirvey; Paul Kleinbaum; Mortimer and Caroline Adler; David Capel; Malachi Throne; Ronnie Rondell; Howard Curtis; Sylvia Sidney; Mary and Dick Sale; Larry Stein; Barbara Rush; Leonard Pennario; Terri Garr; Sharon Gless; Anne and Terry Jastrow; June Allyson; Newton Brantley; J. Stanley Anderson; Melinda Markey; Gloria Lloyd; Carol Lee Ladd; Cary Grant; Claudette Colbert; Nancy Nelson; Louise Fletcher; Glen Larson; Nick Adams; Robert Ward; Abie Bain; Dick Crockett; Susan Schlundt; Susan Saint James; Angie Dickinson; Kirk and Anne Douglas; Charlie Callas; Bob Webb; Dr. Zeus; Bill Brant; John Derek; Debbie Reynolds; Paul and Joanne Newman; Jim Garner; Noel Clarbut; Jeff Hunter; Terry Moore; Flo Allen; Scott Dolginow; Nancy Nelson; Sidney and Caroline Kimmel; Abe Lastfogel; Joe Schoenfeld; Bob Jacks; Sophia Loren; Uncle Joe and Aunt Adair; Jean Leon; Melanie Griffith and Antonio Banderas; Judy Vossler; Stanley Wilson; Judy Shepherd; Vittorio de Sica; Darrylin Zanuck; Jane Smith; Samantha Smith; Sydney Guilaroff.

And my literary collaborator, Scott Eyman, who gracefully drew me back to places both dark and light. I'm glad we made the trip together, my friend.